HEINEMANN GNVQ

INTERMEDIATE

Information and Communication Technology

Molly Wischhusen • Janet Snell
Andrew Scales

D1380151

Edexcel
Success through qualifications

Heinemann Educational Publishers
Halley Court, Jordan Hill, Oxford OX2 8EJ
a division of Reed Educational & Professional Publishing Ltd

OXFORD   MELBOURNE   AUCKLAND
JOHANNESBURG   BLANTYRE   GABORONE
IBADAN   PORTSMOUTH (NH) USA   CHICAGO

© Molly Wischhusen, Andrew Scales, Janet Snell 2000

First Published 1996
Second edition published 2000

03 02 01 00
8 7 6 5 4 3 2 1

A catalogue record for this book is available from the British Library
on request

ISBN 0 435 45598 2

Typeset by 🡒 Tek-Art, Croydon, Surrey
Printed in Great Britain by Bath Press Ltd, Bath

Tel: 01865 888058 www.heinemann.co.uk

Contents

Acknowledgements

Once again I wish to say thanks to all my colleagues for their invaluable advice, in particular to Jenny Johnson for her bright ideas, to Loretta Godsafe, who proofread the work so carefully, making many really constructive comments, and to Steve Potter for the salary model.

My very sincere appreciation also goes to Margaret Berriman for her cheerful encouragement and many prompt e-mail replies to numerous 'help' calls, and to Alex Gray for his patience in the final editing. I would particularly like to say what a pleasure it is to work with Andrew and Janet.

Lastly, thank you to my wonderful children, Mairion, Alun and Jackie, who have continually encouraged and supported me, and my now three grandchildren, Hannah, Michael and Megan, who didn't delay me too much. However, it's impossible to exaggerate the contribution of my husband, Peter, who gives me total support, allowing me to 'keep bashing on'.

Molly Wischhusen BA

I would like to express my gratitude to Margaret Berriman, Molly Wischhusen and Andrew Scales for inviting me to join them in re-writing and updating the GNVQ Intermediate IT book and for the advice, encouragement and help I have received from them and Alex Gray.

I too am indebted to my colleagues for their help, especially Loretta Godsafe who, during a very difficult period, found the time to read my work – thank you Loretta.

Finally, my sincere thanks to my family and friends for their constant support and interest, in particular to my parents and my father-in-law, and especially Diana and Anita, my daughters. My greatest thanks, however, are reserved for my husband, Bob, for his confidence in me and his enduring patience.

Janet Snell BA

I'd like to express my gratitude to Margaret Berriman for giving me the opportunity to participate in writing this book and for her invaluable advice and suggestions. I am also indebted to my two marvellous co-authors, Molly and Janet, for their constant hard work, good humour and great ideas. It was our use of ICT that made it possible to write this book in Britain and North America at the same time.

It is with particular pleasure that I thank my parents, Geoff and Betty Scales, for their encouragment in this and in all other things. Finally, I should like to thank my lovely wife Anongluk and my son Geoffrey for their endless enthusiasm and confidence in me.

Andrew Scales

The authors and publishers are grateful to the following for permission to reproduce photographs and other material:

Croydon College, Royal Society for Prevention of Accidents, Royal Society for Prevention of Cruelty to Children, First-E – The Internet Bank, The Daily Telegraph, IT Training, Europress – Interior Designer 3, Epsom Motor Group

Introduction

Welcome to your GNVQ Intermediate programme of study, which is equivalent to approximately 4 GCSEs at grade C or above. This book has been written to help you achieve your GNVQ Diploma in Information and Communication Technology (ICT), a course directed towards the acquisition and improvement of skills which are related to the business and computing world. If you are prepared to work hard and are really interested in ICT, you will find the course an excellent introduction to a subject which is increasingly central to every type of business. It may be a stepping stone to higher level courses or set you on the path for a career in many industries.

To be successful you must complete the three compulsory units plus at least three optional units.

The compulsory units are:

1 Presenting Information

2 Handling Information

3 Hardware and Software

Depending on which awarding body your school/college is registered with, **the optional units are:**

Edexcel Foundation	OCR	AQA
4 Design Project 5 Information Resources 6 Graphics 7 Multimedia 8 Networks and Communication 9 Modelling Numerical Information 10 Database Techniques and Applications 11 Programming 12 Computer Aided Design	4 Design Project 5 Communicating with Multimedia 6 Graphics and Desktop Publishing 7 Numerical Modelling using Spreadsheets 8 Databases 9 Monitoring and Control Systems 10 Networks and Communications 11 Programming 12 Impact of ICT on Society	4 Design Project 5 Communicating with Multimedia 6 Graphics and Desktop Publishing 7 Numerical Modelling using Spreadsheets 8 Databases 9 Monitoring and Control Systems 10 Data Communications and Networks 11 Programming 12 Impact of ICT on Society
Units 1 and 5 are externally assessed.	Units 3, 6 and 9 are externally assessed.	Units 3, 6 and 9 are externally assessed.

In addition to your programme of study you will have the opportunity to achieve key skills. The key skills remain an integral part of the GNVQ and much of the evidence required will occur naturally through the vocational assessments.

The key skills are:

1 Application of Number

2 Communication

3 Information Technology

4 Problem Solving

5 Working with Others

6 Improve Own Learning

A separate certificate of achievement in these areas will be issued to successful candidates.

What is meant by a unit?

A unit is similar to a subject or a topic, and each unit sets out clearly what the unit is about and what you have to learn. The topics given under 'What you need to learn' are then explained in more detail. You will find that there are close links between the three compulsory units; some of the optional units build on the knowledge already acquired.

What do you have to do to succeed?

You have to provide **evidence** which proves that you have covered and understand the various topics in the units. Each unit specification includes a section entitled 'Assessment evidence' which states clearly what you need to do to pass that unit. Your tutor will be able to explain the requirements for a pass, merit or distinction. It is important to pay *close attention* to what is required.

You will also need to keep the internally set assessments together in a carefully indexed portfolio. The assessments will often be a report, but don't panic, there are all kinds of reports such as:

- a printout from a database or spreadsheet

- templates for memos, e-mail, fax, letters or invoices

- a company logo

- a leaflet/news sheet designed using a word processor or desktop publishing package

- a slide show using a presentation package

- a diagram or chart produced using a drawing package.

These assessments will allow you to generate the **evidence** which is saved in your **portfolio**.

Assessment and grading

There will be a combination of internal and external assessment, but one-third of the overall assessment (i.e. at least two units) will be externally set and marked by the awarding body. Your work will be graded pass, merit or distinction. Complete units are assessed by means of the type of evidence required for that unit as indicated in the section 'Assessment evidence' referred to earlier. You will notice that this section of each unit also indicates what you have to do to achieve a pass, merit or distinction. A final grade of pass, merit or distinction will be awarded for the whole qualification depending on the grades for each unit.

Please do **READ** the Student Guide very carefully. It explains:

- how this book has been designed to help you

- how you can collect evidence for your portfolio

- how you can achieve a merit or distinction

- what is meant by the key skills and personal skills.

Your tutor will give you any other details you need, such as:

- the name of your awarding body, which will be either Edexcel, OCR or AQA

- which option units you will study

- how your evidence should be recorded and stored.

You will very probably find all this information overwhelming and confusing at first, but do remember you don't have to do everything at once, and your tutors will be guiding you through the units and completion of the portfolio. At the beginning, concentrate on those areas which you do understand, and in particular make sure you keep up-to-date with any assessments which have been set. Gradually you will find that you do understand more and more about how the GNVQ programme works, until eventually everything fits into place.

We do hope you will enjoy your GNVQ programme, that you will find the book helpful and interesting and we wish you every success.

The optional units

In addition to the three mandatory units you must also complete a further three optional units to achieve your GNVQ Intermediate award. If you look on page vii of the Introduction you will see that each of the awarding bodies offer a different selection of optional units.

No matter which awarding body you are registered with, one optional unit **must** be externally assessed and the remaining units will be assesed through the work in your portfolio.

This textbook gives you detailed guidance for Edexcel who have nominated Unit 5 for external assessment.

Unfortunately we were not able to include all units in this textbook and we have elected to give you detailed information on:

* Unit 4   Design Project
* Unit 5   Information Resources
* Unit 6   Graphics
* Unit 10 Database Techniques and Applications

Your tutor will help you decide which optional units you will study. You might combine Unit 4 – the Design Project – with another unit or your tutor might want you to work on units we have not included in this book.

Whichever units you do study, we would suggest you look through Unit 4, the Design Project, since it contains ideas that will be useful for all the optional units.

We wish you good luck with the rest of your course.

Molly Wischhusen
Andrew Scales
Janet Snell

Student guide

The layout of this book

The three main sections of this book correspond to the three compulsory units.

Within each chapter you will find:

- **the main text** – which explains all the topics you need to learn

- **activities** – which will help your understanding and which may provide evidence for your portfolio (**NOTE:** the answers to some of the activities in the main text are to be found in the Tutor Resource File.)

- **'Did you know?'** – small, interesting snippets of information which are relevant to the particular section, but are not necessarily essential.

If you work through each chapter, completing the activities, you should gain the understanding required to pass the programme.

Collecting evidence

The most important opportunities for collecting evidence will be the evidence assessments available through the Tutor Resource File (TRF). As this is an ICT course, almost all your evidence will be produced on the computer and consist of various types of printouts, such as:

- a word processed report

- a spreadsheet printout showing the data

- a spreadsheet printout showing the formulae (the latter is very important, as the tutor cannot tell whether you just worked out the answers on the calculator and entered them into the spreadsheet unless you print the formulae)

- a database report – form design, printout of records, printout of searches

- a graphics printout – a news sheet, leaflet, diagram, scale drawing, advertisement.

Quite often it is necessary to **produce printouts at certain stages** to show the development of the assessment. For example, you might be asked to create a *template*, which is a master document, rather like a blank form. In this case you would need a copy of the *blank template*, and then further copies of *completed examples*. It is very easy to spoil an excellent piece of work simply by not reading carefully each part of the assessment. Most of us are impatient at reading instructions, but try to avoid the temptation to read the first sentence and think you know what is going to follow. Sometimes you will be right, but often you will miss something significant.

When you first read an assessment, highlight important points. When you have finished the assessment, *read it through again checking the tasks against the work you have produced and the criteria given for the grading*. This cannot be stressed enough and should ensure that you do not hand in uncompleted work.

Grading

In order to pass the programme, you must provide all the assessment evidence for each unit. You will notice that there are requirements specific to a task, e.g. '. . . sort on multiple keys', but other requirements are more general, e.g.

- checking your work for accuracy

- showing you can work independently

- evaluating your work to make suggestions for improvement.

After completing the assessment, it is very natural to want to give it in and forget about it. However, evaluation may be an essential requirement to achieve the higher grades. Before handing it in you should look at the work and evaluate how it could be improved. The following suggestions may help.

- Did you gather enough information/evidence?

- Do you feel satisfied with the report and its presentation?

- Could you have achieved the assessment in a better way – e.g. oral/visual – used more images/made a presentation instead of producing a written report?

- What particular improvements might be possible – e.g. a long paragraph of text could have been listed in bullet points, as in this section, or perhaps a diagram could be included to make the text easier to follow.

The portfolio

This is the file in which you store all completed assessments, and it is *essential* that it is quite *separate* from your everyday file where you keep notes and any current work. This internally set evidence is likely to be two-thirds of all your work and is clearly very important. Portfolios which are well organised, clearly referenced and neatly filed generally do contain the work the index says they contain. On opening such a file the external moderator will naturally be impressed, whereas a disorganised, messy portfolio may well contain all the necessary evidence, but if the external moderator cannot *find it,* he or she cannot confirm that the evidence *actually* exists.

Key skills

Most of the opportunities to acquire evidence for the key skills will occur naturally through the assessments. However, don't assume because you complete an assessment, you will *automatically* achieve the key skills indicated. For example, Application of Number 2.2 – Carry Out Calculations – requires notes on how you checked your methods and results. You might have carried out calculations in a spreadsheet, but if you have not included these notes, you cannot achieve this section of Application of Number.

Improve Own Learning and Working with Others require you to take responsibility for yourself, your learning and self-improvement, as well as working as part of a team, making a valid and worthwhile contribution to the team effort.

Your tutor will monitor your progress in these areas during tutorials, and will discuss with you your strengths and weaknesses. Your ability to prepare and monitor action plans, revising them as necessary, but ensuring that you keep deadlines, will provide useful evidence towards the personal skills.

Evidence for Problem Solving could include demonstrating how you resolve difficulties which arise, and finding alternative solutions when the original plan does not work.

GNVQ programmes do expect you to take a great deal of responsibility for yourself. You will need to:

- manage your own time

- decide which tasks to complete and when

- keep track of your work (most students have some work returned indicating certain aspects not yet achieved – *don't* file it under the bed and forget all about it! Finish it *now!*)

- record completed work in the portfolio index

- store it neatly in the file

- revise for external assessments.

GNVQ programmes are very definitely achievable. Although the requirements may *sound* formidable at this stage, as already stated, they do not all have to be done at once or immediately. If you follow the advice **you will succeed**, and you will finish the course with a portfolio of which you can be justly proud. If you wish, you can then progress to an Advanced programme and possibly continue into higher education and university. If you prefer, you can seek employment either when you complete your Intermediate programme or, if you go on to the Advanced, on completion of that. You will have acquired very marketable skills, useful in the world of business.

Preparatory Unit Standard ways of working

The prepatory unit applies to all the other units, so it would be a good idea to read this unit first. You will not remember all that it contains first time around, so come to it from time to time to refresh your memory.

This unit is about understanding the need for good practice and standard ways of working in ICT, both in your studies and in your future work. After studying the unit you should be able to:

- appreciate and begin to develop good practice as you work through each unit in this book

- understand and develop good practice in your use of ICT.

It is important to remember that the techniques you learn in this unit must be applied to all your GNVQ ICT work.

Most organisations have guidelines and rules that help people to work efficiently and to avoid problems. Your college, for example, probably has a rule against consuming food and drink in computer labs, so as to avoid problems that affect the equipment. A general name for these guidelines is Standard Ways of Working. These are especially important for people working in information communication technology to avoid the sort of problems that occur.

Here are some typical problems that can occur in ICT environments:

- Data files may be lost, corrupted by a virus or damaged in other ways. For example, someone may download files from the Web that contain viruses. If the computer that has the downloaded virus is part of a LAN (local area network) – and they usually are – the virus can infect the ICT system of the whole organisation.

- Computers may be damaged so that data stored in them cannot be recovered. This can happen if sectors of hard drives are damaged. Files on those sectors can sometimes be retrieved, but only by a slow, very expensive process.

- Unauthorised people may gain access to confidential information. This is a serious problem that you must constantly guard against. It is very easy in the work environment to get distracted by the phone or get called away from your desk by a colleague, and forget to close a confidential file. If this happens, the file is there to be read by anyone passing.

? Did you know?

In December 1999, a Russian hacker gained access to the computer systems of a North American credit card organisation. He emailed the company asking for $500 in return for the credit card numbers he had stolen. The company refused to pay, and within an hour the hacker published the credit card numbers on the Web. The cost to the company ran into hundreds of thousands of dollars.

- Having an ICT system, and especially the Web, makes it very easy for someone to copy any kind of data and present it as his or her own. This is called plagiarism. Because it breaches copyright law (see page 10), it is a serious offence.

- The high standards of presenting information that can be achieved by technology have made people less tolerant of inaccurate or poorly written information. In the case of a web-site it is a basic requirement that the design makes it easy and clear for users to find what they want to know. Word processors have also improved the standard of presentation, for example through sophisticated spell checkers that help you to avoid spelling mistakes.

- In some ways technology has made it harder to judge the quality of information. A document beautifully laid out using technology but containing inaccurate information may be believed because it looks right. It gives the impression that whoever produced it knows what he or she is talking about. Advertisers are keenly aware of this: a professionally presented product will sell much better than a poorly presented product, even if the quality is significantly lower.

- Poorly laid-out workplaces may cause physical stress or be hazardous to IT operators. If you sit in front of a computer for any length of time, you will need a chair that can be adjusted to your shape and posture. Sitting on an ordinary chair will soon give you backache. The wires and cables that connect the different parts of computers together must be tidied away so that you don't catch your feet on them.

Here are the four most important Standard Ways of Working that will help you avoid or overcome these kinds of problem:

1   Managing your work

2   Keeping information secure

3   Ensuring that the information you produce is accurate and readable

4   Following safety at work procedures.

You will need to learn about these in order to achieve good practice in ICT.

Managing your work

One of your most important qualities as a student or employee (including, and especially, the boss) is the ability to manage your work. You have probably noticed that some students progress quickly and successfully even though they don't seem to do more work than anyone else. This is because they are good at managing their work. In the workplace, people who become good at managing their own work often step up to supervise or manage other people's work too. Good basic ICT work management skills include the ability to meet deadlines, to file information in a logical way so that it is easily retrieved, to work with reference logs, and to evaluate your own work. Applying these skills to your GNVQ work will directly increase your success in this course.

Deadlines

'When will it be ready?' 'Oh, any time now, I'll get to it as soon as I can.' In an efficient and professional working environment this is not an acceptable answer. Giving a date and time – a deadline – by when the work will be done is like a milestone. This is why your tutor sets a date for the completion of assessments – and everyone knows what they have to do. It helps you to plan your work day and week, and in the same way it helps your classmates, colleagues or customers plan theirs. For example, a secretary may be having problems with a monitor. If you can say that it will be fixed by 3pm tomorrow afternoon, the secretary can plan to work on something different, knowing he or she can start his or her computer work again at the deadline you have given.

Unlike at college, workplace supervisors don't always set deadlines for you. If they don't, then it's a good idea to set your own. This is called planning your work day or work week. Most people have trouble setting deadlines because they underestimate how long a task will take. A rule of thumb is to decide how quickly you could get a job done, then double it. Your tasks and the deadlines you or others set give your day a structure. They tell you where in your list of tasks you should be by when, which allows you to work at a comfortable pace and enjoy a sense of accomplishment as you pass each milestone and hand in each assessment, rather than rushing to get everything done at once – which never works.

Filenames, directory and folder structure

A filename is the set of letters, numbers or symbols that you assign to a file to distinguish it from all other files in a directory. Some programs, such as MS-DOS or the older Windows versions (up to 3.11), restrict you to eight characters. Macintosh computers accept filenames up to 31 characters. Win95 and later versions also accept filenames up to 32 characters, including spaces, so it's easy to give your files clearly identifiable names that remind you of the contents.

Have you ever lost or mislaid a file then tried searching through the different directories? On a typical stand-alone computer there are hundreds, even thousands, of files. If you happen to remember the exact filename, you can use the Find File function (see Figure 1) to search through the whole system, or at least the folder(s) where you think the file may have been saved.

Figure 1 The Find File dialogue box

However, good work management would avoid the problem in the first place by using sensible filenames which help remind you of the contents. This is the key to saving and then finding files. If you save that letter to your girlfriend or boyfriend as Mary1.doc, Mary2.doc or Sanjay1.doc, Sanjay2.doc, by the time you get to Mary23.doc or Sanjay23.doc you won't have a clue which is which. So why not save it with a name that gives you some idea of the contents? For example, Mary's party.doc, Sanjay's holiday.doc. Do the same when you create new folders or directories. When you choose a name, think about how easy it would be for someone else to find that file and to know roughly what it contains. The more obvious the name is, the better.

When you save a file, don't forget to check that you have the correct extension. Program files and data files have sets of characters added to a filename that are called extensions. Extensions further define the type or purpose of the file. In Windows, for example, filenames are followed by a stop (.) and then an extension of up to three letters. The extension tells the computer which program to open the file with. For example, an MSWord document will be followed by .doc. This tells the computer to open your document using Word rather than a graphics or spreadsheet program, for example. Here is a list of some of the most common extensions:

.tmp	temporary file
.htm	Netscape hypertext document
.txt	text document
.doc	Microsoft Word document
.bmp	bitmap graphic
.exe	executable program (a program that will load and run an application)
.xls	Microsoft spreadsheet
.mdb	Microsoft database
.msg	mail message.

 ## ACTIVITY

Next time you are using a computer, open Windows Explorer. On the right side of the screen you will see lists headed Name, Size, Type, Modified. Compare the file extension with the Type. Often you will see that the extension is a three-letter version of the type. Flick through a few different folders and see what other types you can add to the list above.

ICT reference logs

While you are studying or in your job, it is a good idea to keep a reference log. You will begin to practise this skill in Unit 1.

Technicians and staff on help desks often do this, especially when they are learning about new equipment or systems. Then, if they come across a similar situation they can refer back to see what action they took, and what the answers were. If they find the same fault recurring, they know there may be an underlying reason which needs to be identified.

Sometimes the problem can be as simple as a loose connection. At other times faults can be more complicated or unusual. For example, monitor screens sometimes turn a yellow or pinkish colour – not their usual plain white. The problem may be a loose connection between the monitor wire and the back of the

LOG BOOK		
Date	**Problem**	**Solution**
August 2000	cursor sticks and won't go smoothly	clean mouse ball

Figure 3 Reference log

computer. The solution is to replace the wire. A reference log reminds you what you tried, what worked, what didn't, and what you couldn't do because of a fault in the system.

Your log should have three columns (see Fig 3) – one showing the date, the next briefly describing the problem and the third explaining the solution. You may decide it's best to limit the time you spend trying to fix any problems to, say 10 minutes. If it takes you longer than that it may be easier to call a technician.

Keeping information secure

Studying and working with ICT means dealing with highly valuable equipment and data. This requires the skills to use security techniques that protect ICT systems from accidental or intentional damage. This damage includes viruses, theft of hardware and software, the loss of data, breach of confidentiality, and breach of copyright.

In a many ways protecting data is more important than protecting hardware because it is easier, if expensive, to replace the hardware. It can be very difficult, or even impossible, to replace data.

The techniques to avoid or limit this loss or damage are:

Did you know?

A very useful work standard that will help in your studies and your job is to include references in your documents' footer zone. The first reference should specify the filename and path. Then you will always be able to trace the electronic version of any hard copies. The second reference should specify the date and time a document was produced. Then when you're working on an assignment with other classmates or colleagues, you'll always know which hard copy is the latest and most up-to-date version. You wouldn't want to work with a draft that had already been updated and so contained information that was no longer accurate.

Figure 2 Document footer zone

- virus checking
- anti-theft procedures
- regular saving, backups and retaining source documents
- non-disclosure of confidential information such as passwords
- maintaining copyright
- following the Data Protection Act.

Virus checking

A computer virus is a program, developed by someone either for general mischief or to attack a particular organisation. The virus copies itself without the user intending it to, or even being aware of it happening until problems occur. Sometimes, in an attempt to defy virus detection, the program will mutate (change) slightly each time it is copied. Problems can include clearing screens, deleting data and, in the worst case scenario, making the whole system unusable.

Viruses can affect both floppy and hard disks and are usually transferred from one computer to another via Internet downloads or floppy disks. If disks are used only on one system then the risk of 'catching' a virus is much less. The more often disks are used in different computers, for example a home computer and a college network, the greater the risk of 'catching' a virus.

In fact some colleges and other organisations do not allow floppy disks to be taken from work to home or vice versa, for this very reason. If the disk is to be loaded into a computer just to show or demonstrate the contents, then write-protecting the disk will prevent any viruses on that computer being transferred onto the disk. It is a good idea to write-protect disks containing the software programs before putting them into the disk drive, to ensure that they are not accidentally

infected. You may need to re-load the program at a future date and it would be very annoying to find the disks damaged.

Computer viruses have become an ever more serious problem, but anti-virus software, such as 'McAfee Antivirus', or 'Dr Solomon's Antivirus Toolkit', or 'Norton Antivirus', is available. This software scans files, detects and removes any known viruses. You may find anti-virus software installed on your college network, which automatically checks every disk as it is accessed, and prevents loading of files from an 'infected' disk. Sometimes the check is not automatic, and the best precaution is to check every disk before use. It is annoying to find one of your disks has a virus, but if you do find out, at least you can stop using it and thereby prevent the virus being passed on.

ACTIVITY

Find out which anti-virus software is being used on your college network.

Did you know?

Computer 'viruses' are far more of a threat to security of data than industrial espionage, dishonest employees, fire, theft or simple errors.

Anti-theft procedures

The risk of theft depends on the environment of the system. In public places basic anti-theft procedures include building hardware into casing, bolting it to desks and locking up equipment. Make sure you are informed about the organisational security procedures wherever you are, and follow them carefully.

Both data discs and software are usually kept in disaster proof safes. Less valuable data or

Figure 4 Various methods of protecting data

software may be kept in locked filing cabinets. Some organisations bolt filing cabinets and computer hardware to the floor to avoid theft.

Regular saving, backups and retaining source documents

There are always people with stories about how they lost hours or even days of work because of a system failure. However, if you save and back work up regularly, you will never lose more than a few minutes' worth.

Data is sometimes lost before it's saved, perhaps by accidentally overloading a system's memory and freezing it. When that happens, it is too late to save whatever you are doing. All you can do is reboot the system. This is a great shame (but not an excuse) if you are doing your homework. If a network fails, for example because of a voltage overload or spike, everyone loses unsaved work. So the message is simple – save regularly.

Saving also refers to retaining source documents. When valuable data, or any data

Figure 5 Where to find AutoRecovery-saved documents

that is not easily replaced, is transferred onto disk, the source documents must be retained in a filing cabinet or safe. Whenever you digitise any information for someone else, always return the hard copy when you have finished.

One of the most important ways of keeping information secure is to have backup copies. Making these copies – backing up procedures – is usually carried out at the end of every day. To avoid the damage done by viruses or other system-wide disasters, it is not enough to back up files into a different directory in the same computer. Files should be regularly backed up onto other storage mediums such as floppy disks or your college network. The college like any other organisation will do further backups, usually onto tape drives.

Data stored on the hard disk of the computer can be backed up on:

- floppy disks – generally used for small computers (PCs or laptops)

- a tape streamer, which is a magnetic tape and generally used as an off-line backing store for large computers and networks.

The advantages of storing backup copies on disk are:

- the files can be accessed directly and quickly, whereas a magnetic tape has to be read starting from the beginning until you reach the file you want – just like a tape for music

- tapes are light and compact, easy to store for long periods, easy to carry, and far cheaper than disks.

Tape is therefore an ideal medium for storing large volumes of data in a college or business context, especially when the use of the tape is anticipated only if the original disks are lost or damaged. For most organisations, speed and ease of access are not prime considerations; cost and ease of storage are more important.

? Did you know?

One of the main reasons that Microsoft lost the lawsuit accusing them of being a monopoly was because most of their internal discussions were carried out by e-mail. The special prosecutor gave lawyers access to Microsoft's backup tapes and so they were able to go through every last piece of correspondence and reveal the full truth.

Non-disclosure of confidential information

People or companies may wish to keep information confidential so that others do not know about it. In such cases you must learn

to keep the information secure and not pass it on to others. Access to medical or criminal records, for example, is controlled by privacy laws. People rely on network administrators to protect the confidentiality of information or messages in their e-mail accounts.

Information can be priceless. Although you may not be dealing with priceless or highly sensitive information at college or when you start out in your career, any information is potentially valuable to an organisation's competitors. Unauthorised access to a company's systems, such as its databases, is only possible if people do not follow security and confidentiality procedures properly.

Different computer systems allow different confidentiality procedures. Among the most common are passwords and time-restricted access. Passwords may be changed daily or weekly and be available at different access levels. Time-restricted access systems limit the time that you have to find the information you want – if you do not know the procedures, you are unlikely to retrieve the information you want within the given period.

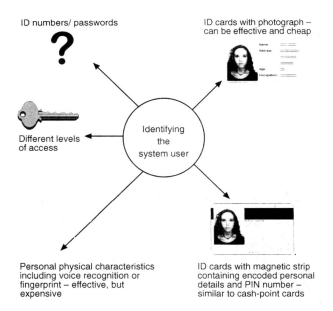

ID numbers/ passwords

ID cards with photograph – can be effective and cheap

Different levels of access

Identifying the system user

Personal physical characteristics including voice recognition or fingerprint – effective, but expensive

ID cards with magnetic strip containing encoded personal details and PIN number – similar to cash-point cards

Figure 6 Ways of identifying the user

If you use a network system in your college, you will almost certainly use a unique ID number to gain access to the system, followed by a password which is either given to you or that you choose. When selecting a password, it is crucial to choose a word which:

- is easy to remember – but not your boy/girl friend's name – in a few weeks you might have had several new ones (!) and forget which is the right one

- is not obvious – e.g. your own name or birthday.

This password should be kept confidential and in a business context should also be changed frequently, to make it more difficult for the password to be discovered. You will notice that when you enter the password, the characters are not displayed on screen, but appear in a coded form, frequently as a series of asterisks (see Figure 7). This is known as encryption and is designed to prevent someone casually observing your password as it is shown on the screen.

In addition to passwords to access the system, modern software programs also allow the use of passwords when saving files. Figure 8 is a screen dump showing part of the options dialogue box from the 'Save As' facility in Word for Windows version 6.0.

A password entered in the Protection Password box prevents anyone opening the file unless he or she knows the password. A password entered in the Write Preservation Password box allows access to read the file,

Figure 7 Password encryption

Figure 8 Part of a dialogue box which enables passwords to limit access to the file (from Word for Windows Version 6.0)

but prevents anyone saving changes to the file, unless he or she knows the password. Passwords entered into these boxes will again appear as a series of asterisks. An × in the Read-Only Recommended box indicates that it is advisable to read but not to amend the file. If the user wishes to write to the file, then it should be saved under a new name, so that the original version is retained.

Giving staff different privileges or security levels, which limit access to only some files or some fields within a file, is a common method of protecting data and maintaining confidentiality. The most senior staff would have:

- greater privileges

- a high security level

- access to all or most of the data

whereas more junior staff would have:

- fewer privileges

- low security

- access only to less important data.

As indicated earlier some staff can read the file, but not write to the file (i.e. make changes).

More sophisticated methods for restricting people's access to data and programs include identification numbers and encoded user cards. These procedures can apply to the system as a whole or to specific information banks or programs. Many organisations rank data files according to their degree of confidentiality.

Another method used to check security is to program the system to track exactly which user has logged on, to which files and for how long. This is known as an audit trail and its purpose is to check whether someone has accessed information to which he or she is not authorised.

Maintaining copyright

You are probably familiar with copyright warnings at the beginning of rental videos where it says something along the lines of 'All rights reserved. No part of this publication may be reproduced or transmitted, in any form or by any means, without the prior permission of the publisher.' This is the same for most computer programs, published text, pictures and graphic images.

Check for the symbol ©, followed by a date and sometimes a name, like at the beginning of this book. This indicates that a work is copyright. You must understand what copyright means and respect copyright law. Copyright protects the work of authors, artists, and composers from being reproduced by anyone without permission. The only person who can reproduce a copyright protected work is the owner. This means that you cannot make multiple copies of software without the necessary licence. Copying without a licence, whether it is program or data files, is a criminal offence. As long as you ask first and are given permission, you may be able to use other people's work. If so, it is important that you include an acknowledgement.

Although copyright becomes effective when a work is created, all publicly distributed copies must contain a copyright notice, otherwise it is lost. A copyright notice is either the word Copyright or the abbreviation Copr. or the symbol © together with the name of the owner and the year of first publication. Most software has the copyright notice under 'About' on the menu bar.

One way to protect valuable computer programs from piracy, especially during the developmental stage, is to distribute copies of the work in object code. (Object code is a machine code version of the program, which is more difficult to utilise.) The company name or names of the programmers can also be written into the code in the event that a 'software pirate' denies copying. In addition copies of the software at different stages of development can be deposited with someone independent, such as the bank manager, the date being noted. This may prove valuable later if there is a dispute concerning the author of the work, or who first wrote it.

When your college or any other organisation buys software programs it is given a licence and its 'ownership' of that copy is registered with the software company. The documents that come with the software include details of the 'Grant of Licence'. Typically (although this may vary) the licence permits the owner to:

- install the software on a single computer

- make one copy of the disks as a backup only

- load the software onto the hard disk keeping the original disks for backup only.

You are not allowed to copy the software onto a network unless you purchase a network licence, which is more expensive than a single user licence.

Following the Data Protection Act

If you are in a position of trust, you must not pass on personal information, no matter how innocently. In fact you could be prosecuted under the Data Protection Act (see below).

Think about the receptionist at a local doctor's surgery. He or she will almost certainly know some of the patients personally, and will also, inevitably, be aware of the confidential medical history of those patients. Imagine this scenario: the receptionist is aware of a bad history of heart problems in members of your close family, but you are in perfect health. He or she intends no harm, but gossips about it. Your insurance company gains illegal access to this information and refuses life insurance or increases your premiums. If you discovered what information the insurance company had obtained and how it was obtained, you could sue for compensation under the Data Protection Act.

The Data Protection Act 1984 (updated in 1998) relates specifically to personal data

held on computers. It was introduced because of concerns that more and more data is being held on computers about each of us, with the potential for misuse. For example, companies have been known to sell lists of names and addresses to other companies, with the result that large quantities of unwelcome promotional literature arrive in the post (junk mail).

? Did you know?

When you're surfing the Web, many of the sites you visit send you a cookie. A cookie is a small amount of information that is copied to your hard disk. One of its uses is to help identify you the next time you visit that site. For example, if you shop for music online, the music store website would use a cookie to store information about your favourite singers and groups, then it might later use that information to recommend particular CDs.

Personal information has always been held on paper, but now that it is stored electronically, it is so much easier for information to be passed from one computer to another, possibly with disastrous consequences. Some people are anxious that sensitive personal details are held on computer without their knowledge, and could be more easily obtained than from a manual system. Part of this anxiety stems from lack of understanding of computers – people often feel threatened by things they do not understand. Other people feel that it is all a fuss about nothing, that if you are not doing anything illegal, there is no need to worry, and in fact the more information available on computers, the easier it is to catch criminals.

In 1984 the Data Protection Act was passed to protect the rights of individuals against misuse of personal data held on computer. After several years of practical experience with the Act, it was updated in 1998 and the changes came into force in March 2000. Under the Act any organisation holding personal data in a computer system must register with the Data Protection Registrar, stating clearly what details are to be included and for what purpose.

The Council of Europe Convention on Data Protection has developed eight Data Protection Principles which are central to the purpose of the Data Protection Act. The (1998) Principles are:

1   'Personal data shall be processed fairly and lawfully and, in particular, shall not be processed unless at least one of the conditions in Schedule 2 is met, and in the case of sensitive personal data, at least one of the conditions in Schedule 3 is also met.'

    Note that Schedule 2 gives details on the conditions of processing, e.g. that the person has given permission for the data processing to go ahead. Schedule 3 gives details on what sensitive information is, e.g. the racial or ethnic origin of the person.

2   'Personal data shall be held only for one or more specified and lawful purposes and shall not be further processed in any manner incompatible with that purpose or those purposes.'

3   'Personal data shall be adequate, relevant and not excessive in relation to the purpose or purposes for which they are processed.'

4   'Personal data shall be accurate and, where necessary, kept up to date.'

5   'Personal data processed for any purpose or purposes shall not be kept for longer than is necessary for that purpose or those purposes.'

6   'Personal data shall be processed in accordance with the rights of data subjects under this Act.'

? Did you know?

While the Principles recognise your right to know what information is held on computer about you and to have any errors corrected, exemptions from the Act include: personal data kept for purposes of national security, medical and social service records, some police files and details kept on a home computer, such as an address list of your friends, or a list of their birthdays.

7   'Appropriate technical and organisational measures shall be taken against unauthorised or unlawful processing of personal data and against accidental loss or destruction of, or damage to, personal data.'

? Did you know?

One of the major concerns of parents today is that children will be exposed to pornography or be contacted by paedophiles on the Web. Programs like NetNanny provide two types of limit to the sites children can visit. The first is a filtering system that works by refusing access to any site with the key words you have entered – for example, 'pornography', 'adult', 'x-rated'. The disadvantage with filtering is that any site containing those keywords, including educational or other sites, cannot be accessed.

The second type of system is called blocking. This works by allowing you to type in the address of any site you wouldn't like a child to visit, then refusing access to it. The problem with this system is that there are so many undesirable sites, you could spend months entering all the addresses. However, some public organisations, such as libraries, provide lists of ready-entered sites to block.

Another concern is the availability of pornographic material on disks, but in reality this is simply a new version of old problems – pornography in art, literature, films, videos. It is not possible to prevent misuse of computers, any more than it is in any other area of life. It is up to each individual to take responsibility for his or her own attitude.

8 'Personal data shall not be transferred to a country or territory outside the European Economic Area, unless that country or territory ensures an adequate level of protection for the rights and freedoms of data subjects in relation to the processing of personal data.'

Full details of the Act can be found at http://www.dataprotection.gov.uk/eurotalk.htm

Inevitably there has to be trust in and reliance on the users of ICT, especially in a business environment. Most people are in fact quite honest, and have no intention of defrauding their employer or disclosing confidential information. It is, however, essential to take security issues seriously, so that you do not *unintentionally* give access to uncensored or private materials to someone else. Also, if you *accidentally* discover uncensored or private materials, you must not take advantage of the opportunity, and it may be appropriate to report that a breach of security has occurred.

Ensuring that the information you produce is accurate and readable

The most sophisticated ICT system in the world, which uses all the modern methods of data capture and is capable of applying all the processes that you will learn about in this book, is completely useless if the data entered into the system is not accurate in the first place. A common phrase used in the computer world is, 'Garbage in, Garbage out.'

In a manual system accuracy relies heavily on the operator to proofread and check visually, whereas a computerised system can build in accuracy checks to *reduce* the risk of errors. The word 'reduce' is used very deliberately, because mistakes can still be made, but the

more built-in checks available, the less chance of errors.

Validation

The word valid simply means suitable. So, if you say something is valid, you are saying it is suitable for its purpose. For example, if you mix all the right ingredients for making a cake, but try to bake it in a fridge, you will not make a cake! If you try to play CDs on a tape deck, you will not succeed in producing music! These are extreme cases, however, they demonstrate that the fridge and the tape deck are not suitable or valid for what you want to do.

The same applies to a computer system. If you try to do something that isn't valid for a particular system, then it will not work. So, you need to check what is valid for the system. There are two very important ways of doing this: type and range checks.

Type check

A data type can be a number, text, a choice, etc. If you select numbers for the design, then you cannot use another kind of data type, e.g. letters. We can use these data types in databases (see Unit 2). If a field (a blank space on the screen) has been designed for numbers, the computer will not accept letters in that field. If a field has been designed to accept a certain range of colours – red, blue, green, yellow – it will not accept any other colour in that field. Clearly, it is still possible for the data entry clerk to make errors but some errors will be immediately apparent.

Range check

If a field in a database has been designed as a number field, it is possible to include a further check as well as the type check. The field can be limited within a set *range*, by giving a minimum or maximum figure or both. Sometimes only a minimum level or only a maximum level is appropriate for the particular field, rather than both, but in every case some data entry errors will be signalled by the computer – often by a bleep and an error message on screen saying something like, 'data not within acceptable range'. See Unit 2 for more details.

Verification

The word verify means to check that information is correct. Sometimes this is carried out quite simply by the operator reading the entries and checking them again against the original document. Sometimes a second operator will read the data out loud from the original document to the first operator, who checks on screen that the entries match. This is particularly useful for numerical data, as it is notoriously easy to make keying in errors with numbers and these cannot be spotted just by proofreading, whereas spelling or grammatical errors, or words missed out or repeated, will be noticeable.

Verification can also be undertaken by one operator keying in the data once and another operator keying it again. Any differences are indicated by the computer and a check can be made against the original document to establish whether the first or second entry is the correct one. It is an excellent method of ensuring accuracy, but it is time-consuming and expensive, because the information is entered into the computer twice and two people are paid for the same work.

Spell checks

Another useful method of verification is to spell check the work. In writing, especially formal writing such as business letters, mistakes are simply unacceptable. So it is important to get into the habit of using a spell check in your work *now*. If a business letter, presentation or proposal contains

spelling or grammar mistakes, many readers will think that the author is either ignorant or just too lazy to check, and that he or she probably does not know how to do the rest of his or her job well either.

So always use spell checks to detect words spelt incorrectly and words that have been repeated (for example, 'and and'). Spell checks are not only available in word processors, they are also available in most other applications such as spreadsheets and email. They work by checking the words you have written against a list in the computer's dictionary, then any words not matching are queried and possible alternatives are suggested.

But beware! Although spell checks are one of the most popular and useful verification features, they do not understand what you are trying to say and so they can be wrong. This means that it is still important for the operator to have a reasonable level of spelling! The words 'a lot' – meaning 'many' – are frequently mistyped as 'alot'. When this happens the spell check will suggest 'allot' – which means 'to give a share'. Even though the sense is wrong this alternative is usually accepted.

Here's the spell check of the sentence:

'Alot of people go two clubs too meet there friends'.

Figure 9 A spell check

The spell checker may not always correct 'there' for 'their' or choose the correct version of 'to', 'two' or 'too'! And sometimes a spell checker will suggest that a word is incorrect when you know it is correct. This often happens with proper names, for example 'GNVQ' or 'Patel', though you may be able to add these words to a computer's dictionary to fix the problem.

In the spell check screen above, the computer picked up only the first error. Think of your spell check verification as an assistant and remember that the final decision on whether a piece of work is accurate or not, is *yours*. Try this example for yourself.

Grammar checkers

A further verification check is the grammar check feature. Grammar checkers tend to be rather less popular than spell checkers because the suggestions they make can be difficult to understand if you don't already have a good knowledge of grammar. However, when you go on to the section on grammar checkers (see p. 34) in Unit 1, you will learn how to set up your grammar checker in a way that will really help you with language style. Meanwhile, and as a starting point, the best way to use a basic grammar checker on default settings is to draw your attention to possible mistakes.

Here's what the grammar checker has to say about the sentence in Figure 10 explaining how the checker works:

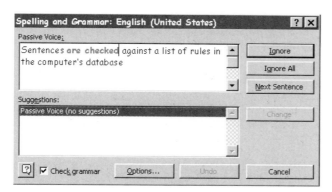

Figure 10 **A grammar check indicating passive voice**

'Sentences are checked against a list of rules in the computer's database.'

The Suggestions box tells us that the verb is in the passive voice. This is a helpful suggestion if you remember what the passive voice is. If, like many people, you don't, it can be confusing. So try to rely on your sense of what sounds right, or when possible, ask for another opinion. (In fact, modern writing mostly avoids the passive voice because it is impersonal and so doesn't communicate directly with the reader. A better sentence would be: 'The application checks words against a list of grammatical rules.')

Here is a simpler example of how a grammar checker can be really useful in helping you clearly with typical mistakes such as this sentence:

'They ate there dinner.'

This time the checker (Figure 11) shows correctly that 'there' should be changed to 'their'.

Figure 11

Correctness

Correctness means checking data to ensure that it is meaningful. It is perfectly possibly to use all the validation and verification techniques available in a modern computer, but still produce meaningless information. (Garbage out!) If an error is suggested in both spelling and grammar verification checks, it is probable, but not definite, that you have made a mistake. You need to look at the suggestions given, and try to decide what is the correct version.

You must proofread your documents for errors, first on screen and then on the printed copy. Once data has been entered into the computer, none of us is keen to have to read it all again, especially if it is a long report, but there is no other way to ensure that the data makes sense. Often our thoughts and ideas run faster than our fingers can type, so words are omitted or repeated, or the sense is muddled and can be improved with some minor changes.

With numerical data, the number entered might be in the acceptable range, but inappropriate. For example, a database of children's records in a primary school might include fields for the year group and dates of birth from which a child's age is calculated. The age field has a range check from 4 to 11. One record lists a child in the reception class, but aged 8. The reception class is for 4–5 year olds, therefore one of the entries must be wrong. Both fields contained valid data – reception is a suitable choice for the year group, and 8 is within the range for ages – however, the data is not correct. This is where the power of the computer is so useful. The data can be corrected easily and swiftly, without starting all over again.

Basic proofreading symbols

After you have proofread your document on screen, you should print out a hard copy and do your (hopefully!) final proof on paper. This is because reading on a screen and reading from a piece of paper are different – you may see errors on the paper that you didn't catch on screen. Even if you are sure there are no errors, it may be useful to have your work re-read by 'different eyes': the eyes of your

parent/guardian. When you created the document it was very much through your own eyes, so having it reread by someone else is a chance to see the impact and effectiveness of your work on them. There may be no errors as such, but perhaps someone else can show you a more effective or more interesting way to get your message across.

When you are proofreading, look for errors in these three main categories:

- 'Typos'   Misspelt words, punctuation errors, wrong numbers, repeated words or phrases.

- Layout errors   Text, numbers or graphics in the wrong place (including captions and headings), incorrect line spacing, and missing items.

- Wrong fonts   Mistakes in how you have used font styles, sizes, bold, italics, etc.

For important documents it's best to read your work several times, each time focusing on one of the areas above.

You may also find basic proofreading symbols useful, especially when you're producing documents as part of a team. Here are four of the most useful:

Instruction	Mark in the text	Mark in the margin
Leave unchanged	.... Under what you want to remain	stet
Insert the copy in the margin	⋏	New copy and the symbol ⋏
Delete	/ through characters /-------/ through item	ℛ
New paragraph	[	NP

Following safety at work procedures

Like your college, most ICT working environments are relatively safe. Even so, you should take care of your classmates, colleagues and yourself so that you avoid physical stress, eye strain or safety hazards. You should also be aware of the main laws governing safety at work.

As the use of computers has become more widespread, concerns have been voiced from time to time about the health and safety of the operators and the stress suffered by them through the course of their work. The main worries relate to physical stress caused by uncomfortable seating, unsuitable desk and VDU position, and unsuitable keyboard position. These can lead to backache, eye strain, headaches and migraine, RSI (repetitive strain injury) and radiation, especially in the case of pregnant women using VDUs. These problems can generally be avoided if sensible precautions are taken.

 ACTIVITY

Go to http://www.microsoft.com/products/ hardware/ergo/default.htm. Here you will find an interesting and useful site about the Healthy Computing Guide that includes moving images.

Backache

Backache can usually be prevented by suitable seating, good posture and taking a break from time to time. Chairs should:

- be capable of swivelling

- have a movable base – i.e. castors

- have an adjustable back rest to give support where needed.

In addition an operator should not be expected to sit working at a VDU for hours without a break, and indeed should take responsibility for changing his or her posture – perhaps taking a walk in the lunch break to exercise and relieve the muscles.

Eye strain and headaches

Problems with eye strain or headaches are likely to occur *only* if the VDU is fuzzy, flickers or is in a poorly lit position. The EU directives require that:

- the screen should not flicker, nor reflect light

- the angle, brightness and contrast of the screen must be adjustable

- desks and keyboards should have a matt finish to prevent reflection of light and to avoid glare

- lighting should ensure correct contrast between the screen and the general background

- VDU operators must have the right to a free eye test before commencing VDU work and regularly afterwards.

Repetitive strain injury

RSI is caused by making the same or awkward movements continuously. This problem may affect keyboard operators working continuously for long periods of time. The tendon sheaths in the hand, wrist or arm become inflamed, causing pain, numbness and swelling which if untreated can result in permanent disability. Ironically, it is believed that the light touch required by the modern keyboard, compared to the much heavier keys of old fashioned typewriters, may aggravate the problem.

To prevent or reduce the risk of RSI, keyboards should:

- be separate from the VDU

- be adjustable so they can lie flat or slope at an angle of approximately 10 degrees

- have concave keys that reduce the risk of the fingers slipping off them and reduce shock on the fingertips, fingers, wrist and arms.

Radiation

There are concerns about the risk of radiation from working with VDUs, and it has been suggested that pregnant women have suffered miscarriages as a result of being exposed to radiation from VDUs. Special shields can be attached to the VDU to protect users from radiation. However the evidence indicates that the risk from radiation is less than from natural sources.

Safety at work and the law

Your college and tutors care about your health and safety. In the workplace, your employer may not have the same high standards. Many young people continue to be hurt or disabled by accidents at work which are the result of irresponsible employers. No job is worth risking your health for. Hazards such as electrical faults, fire or obstruction are just as relevant when working with computers as in any other area of employment. The Health and Safety at Work Act 1974 (HASAWA) and the Control of Substances Hazardous to Health Act 1989 (COSHH) require all employers to ensure that your place of work is a safe environment.

These Acts include the provision of:

- safe entrances and exits including fire escapes

- safe equipment – electrical equipment must be checked regularly, cables should be insulated from electrical supplies and, like other equipment, should be laid out to avoid the possibility of someone tripping

- safe storage for hazardous substances and warning signs indicating their location

- a statement in writing on the organisation's health and safety policy

- training for staff – their rights, obligations, fire drills

- accident investigation procedures.

It is not just employers who have responsibilities. As an employee you will have responsibilities for yourself and your workmates.

Employees also have a duty to follow safe working practices. For example, they should:

- report/deal with (as appropriate) any hazards, such as trailing wires, obstructions – especially to fire exits

- not lift heavy equipment

- know the fire drill

- take suitable breaks

- know and use correct posture at the keyboard.

This is the end of your Preparatory Unit. As you work through the other units in this book, please ensure that you apply good practice and standard ways of working to all your GNVQ studies. Return to this unit to refresh your memory as often as you need to.

Presenting information

This unit is about recognising that different documents have different purposes, and that they use different styles to achieve those purposes. After studying this unit you should be able to:

- write original documents in styles that suit your readers

- improve the accuracy and readability of the documents you create

- improve the quality of presentation in the documents you create

- choose and apply standard document layouts.

In order to do this you need to learn about the following:

- the different styles of writing

- the different types of information you may need to communicate to your reader

- document layout and the different ways of presenting information.

In this unit you will learn how to create a variety of documents, using different styles of language, different types of information and different layouts that are appropriate to the documents' purposes. You will study a range of documents as used in organisations and compare these with the style and layout of the documents you create.

CHAPTER 1.1 STYLES OF WRITING AND PRESENTATION

In today's job market, employers look to recruit people who have good, general qualities as well as the professional skills needed for a particular job. As you advance through your career, you are likely to compete for jobs with other people who have the same or similar professional qualifications. When this happens, the employer will look carefully at a person's good, general qualities – qualities such as good IT skills (you will already have an advantage there!), being a hard worker, being a fun person to work with and having good communication skills.

Good communication skills are speaking and listening and, especially, writing skills. Good writing skills are essential because most people in the workplace are now responsible for producing their own correspondence. ICT has made it much easier and swifter for everyone to produce his or her own quality, written communications, and so this is now the preferred way of working for many organisations. This chapter will help you achieve good written communication skills.

To be able to write well depends mostly on selecting the best style for the type of document you are creating, and there is a wide range of different document types you may may be called upon to produce. Here are some examples:

- A letter replying to a job advertisement.

- A glossy advertisement for a new brand of cosmetics.

- A table of results for a sporting activity.

- An agenda for a meeting for a sports and social club.

- Minutes of a meeting for a sports and social club.

- A note to the milkman to order some milk.

- An advertisement to sell second-hand goods.

- A formal invitation to a social event.

- A letter to a newspaper.

- A form on which someone enters information (for example, a fax header page that must be completed with the sender's and receiver's details).

- A report of a local council planning meeting.

- An e-mail to a company asking for information about a product.

The starting point for creating any of these is to decide the document's purpose and who the reader(s) will be. You will then be able to decide the correct document style (letter, agenda, advert and so on) and, finally, the language style. By language style we mean *formal* (such as a letter replying to a job advertisement) or *informal* (such as a note to the milkman).

Fortunately, most computer software can help you select the correct document style. For example, you can create different styles of documents by choosing a suitable template (see below). Many computer programs also have tools to help you with the style of your language, such as AutoCorrect, spellcheckers, grammar checkers and thesauruses.

The starting point

Before beginning to create any type of document, always ask yourself these three basic questions:

1   What is the purpose of the document?

2 Who will read it?

3 What is the most suitable way to communicate the purpose to the reader?

Purpose

Each of the documents listed above has a specific purpose, and that purpose affects the writing and presentation style. The purpose of the formal letter replying to the job advertisement is to get a job (or at least an interview). The purpose of the glossy advertisement is to attract buyers' attention. The purpose of the sports results table is to make it easy for someone to read each team's scores.

So the purpose of your document is what you want it to achieve and what results you want from the person or people who read it. When creating a document you must always check the work you are producing against your purpose. Each word, sentence and paragraph should contribute towards the purpose you have in mind.

Reader(s)

The next question you need to ask yourself is who your reader(s) is(are): who is going to read your document? Your job application, for example, will be read by your prospective employer. So you need to make the right impression – you need to show you can use an appropriate document style (in this case a formal letter and CV), and that you can use the appropriate style of language (formal, to the point and clear).

Communication style

Once you know your document's purpose and you have a good idea of who is going to read it, you can choose the most suitable type of document and style of communication.

Document types

The ICT skills you gain as a result of this course should equip you to work in a wide variety of industries and organisations. Whatever type of industry you work in, you will soon come to recognise the various types of documents used in your organisation, and these types of documents will share the same features as similar documents used in other organisations. Because document types are standard and because everyone uses these, they make communication easier. The following are some of the most widely used document types:

Business cards	E-mails	Fax header pages
Memos	Agendas	Newsletters
Minutes	Itineraries	Business letters
Publicity flyers	Reports	

You will soon learn to identify all these document types by the position and layout of each document's basic features. Letters, as you will already know, have the writer's address in the top right-hand corner and the signature at the bottom left. Business cards have the staff member's name in the centre and his or her job title underneath. The layout of these basic features is the document's style.

House style

Many organisations specify a 'house style' for their documents, which you should follow closely. The idea of a house style is to produce a standard, easily recognisable 'look' for an organisation's documents. This look or image gives the customers (and staff) a sense of organisational unity and efficiency – of everyone working together to produce a high-quality product or service.

Many organisations pay a great deal of attention to, and invest a lot of money in, their house styles. If you have received different letters from the same organisation, compare the layout of the letters. You will notice that, although they may be written by different people on different equipment, they all have the addresses, dates and references in the same position and they all use the same font (the style of the lettering used in the organisation's documents). The same is true for logos (those symbols, initials, little pictures, etc., organisations use instead of their full names which we can recognise at a glance) – these are always in exactly the same place and are exactly the same colour and shape.

Marketing departments make sure the house style is followed by designing a standard letter template everyone in the organisation uses whenever he or she writes a letter. A *template* is a blueprint (or standard pattern) for the text, graphics and layout of a document. A fax template, for example, will contain the company's name, a position for the date and placeholders (boxes to fill in or blank lines to complete) to indicate where to

type the recipient's name, address, fax and phone numbers. It might also include a space to indicate how many pages long the fax is, and a box where the sender can key in or write the message.

Standard documents

You will already know the basic layout of some documents, such as the position of the addresses, date and so on in letters. The following is a detailed review of different standard document types, including examples and notes of any special considerations you should keep in mind when producing these types of documents.

E-mail

An e-mail is an informal, written electronic message and is probably the most widely used, and possibly most important, means of

Figure 1.1 The basic features of an e-mail message

communication within an organisation. E-mails are also used extensively between organisations and between individuals. E-mail format depends on the system you are using, but the most basic features of an e-mail message include the following:

- A 'To' box

- A 'Subject' box

- A textbox (see Figure 1.1).

E-mail systems offer many different options, and the ones which will be the most useful for you depends on your purpose. At work you would most likely make particular use of the following (see Figure 1.1):

- Alternatives in the address line. These alternatives include the option to send a copy of the e-mail to someone else other than the person in the To line (called CC – carbon copy – an expression from the days when carbon paper was used to make copies) and BCC (blind carbon copy – a way of sending someone else a copy without the addressees – the people named in the To line – knowing you have sent a copy of the e-mail to someone else).

- The Address button. This takes you to your professional and personal address books, which saves you having to key in someone's full address every time you send him or her a message. Another advantage of address books is that they help prevent you from making mistakes, such as a wrong spelling or putting the dot in the wrong place, which would mean your e-mail is returned, unsent, by the system's administrator.

- The Attachment button. This allows you to attach (i.e. send with your e-mail) copies of file(s) stored on your computer system – text, sound or graphics, or all three.

Business letter

A business letter is a formal, written communication from one company to another. Business letters have standard features. These include the following:

1 Company logo, address, phone and fax numbers, e-mail address, etc.

2 Reference numbers.

3 Date.

4 Name and address of the recipient (the person the letter is being sent to).

5 Greeting/salutation (Dear . . .).

6 Reference number and/or the subject of the letter.

7 Content of the letter.

8 Complimentary close (Yours . . .).

9 Signature of the person sending the letter.

10 Name and position of the person sending the letter.

11 A note of copies or enclosures (things included in the envelope with the letter).

 ACTIVITY

Study the business letter in Figure 1.2. Using the numbered list above, see if you can identify the different parts of a business letter. (It may help if you put a number next to each feature that corresponds to the numbers above.) Next, read the following notes and compare these with the business letter in Figure 1.2.

- Formal business letters are usually created in the 'fully blocked style' (see Chapter 3) – everything is aligned to the left margin.

- Fully blocked style usually adopts 'open punctuation' where there is no punctuation (commas or full stops) in the reference, date, address, after Dear X or in the closing section of the letter. Punctuation is used only in the main body of the letter.

- You will notice that blank line spaces are left at certain points in the letter – mostly just one line space although five spaces are usual between Yours sincerely/faithfully and the name (to allow room for the signature). If a letter is very short it may be spread out with more spaces – but do *not* put extra blank lines in the recipient's address.

- The name of the town/city (but not the county) should be in capitals.

- The post code should be on a new line but, if this is not possible because the letter will not quite fit on the page, allow six spaces between the name of the town/city/county and the post code.

- The opening salutation must match the complimentary close:

If you open with . . .	you must close with . . .
Dear Sir/Madam	Yours faithfully
Dear Mr/Mrs/Miss/Ms (followed by the person's name)	Yours sincerely

- Do not use first names unless you know the person well and normally use his or her first name in conversations with that person.

- In the complimentary close, use a capital 'Y' and a small 'f' or 's'.

- The first paragraph of the body of the letter should briefly introduce the letter's topic – this may be about a letter received or perhaps about a response to an advertisement for a job. Suitable opening sentences you could use often begin like this:

  – Thank you for your letter of (date) . . .

  – Further to our recent telephone conversation . . .

  – I am writing to . . .

  – With reference to your advertisement for the post of IT Co-ordinator in the 'Anytown Herald' . . .

- In the next paragraph(s) you can expand more fully on the reasons for you writing the letter.

- The final paragraph should conclude the letter. It will often say something like:

  – I look forward to hearing from you.

  – Please contact me if you require any further information.

COMPUTER CONSULTANTS LTD

108 King Street, Anytown AT2 3RJ
Tel 01329 549261
Fax 01329 319734
e-mail: compcons@server.co.uk

Our ref PG/KL/129
Your ref KW/PB

21 February 200-

Mr J Wilkins
Purchasing Manager
Datalink Ltd
19 Harwood Place
HIGHTOWN
MG2 6MT

Dear Mr Wilkins

Multi-purpose filing cabinets

Thank you for your letter of 20 February enquiring about our new range of multi-purpose filing cabinets.

I confirm these can be fitted with pull-out racks to hold computer print-outs and special sections for disk storage. Delivery is usually within ten days of receipt of order.

I have pleasure in enclosing a copy of our catalogue and price list. Should you require any further details, please do not hesitate to contact me.

Your sincerely
COMPUTER CONSULTANTS LTD
P Graham

Peter Graham
Sales Manager

Enc

Figure 1.2 The layout of a typical business letter

– Thank you for your interest in our organisation.

• If any items are enclosed with the letter, the word 'Enc' should be keyed in at the very end, allowing one clear blank line space. This is to remind both you and the recipient there should be something enclosed with the letter.

 ACTIVITY

Your tutor will give you a copy of a business letter to study. Look at this carefully and identify the standard features of a business letter and their position on the page. Next, make a note of any of the features discussed in the list above.

 ACTIVITY

Using the sample business letter you have been given as an example, prepare a business letter as follows.

You work for a local telecom company and have just received an enquiry asking for details about the mobile phones your company sells. Your letter should point out that your company has just acquired a new range of mobile phones and that you are enclosing a brochure about these.

Memo

A memo is a brief document that is used to communicate with colleagues in the same

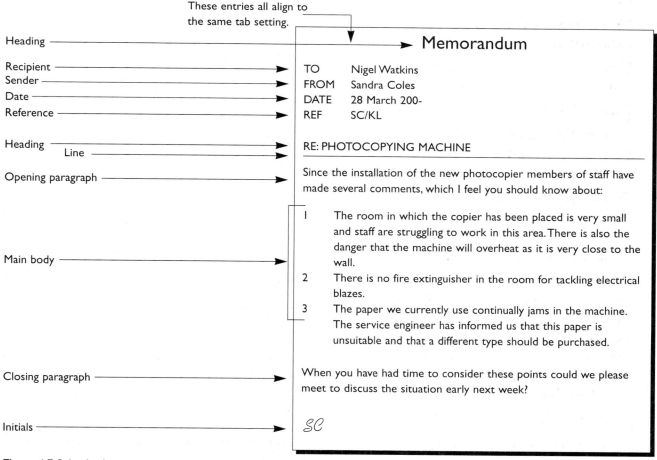

These entries all align to the same tab setting.

Heading

Recipient
Sender
Date
Reference

Heading
Line

Opening paragraph

Main body

Closing paragraph

Initials

> **Memorandum**
>
> TO   Nigel Watkins
> FROM   Sandra Coles
> DATE   28 March 200-
> REF   SC/KL
>
> RE: PHOTOCOPYING MACHINE
>
> Since the installation of the new photocopier members of staff have made several comments, which I feel you should know about:
>
> 1   The room in which the copier has been placed is very small and staff are struggling to work in this area. There is also the danger that the machine will overheat as it is very close to the wall.
> 2   There is no fire extinguisher in the room for tackling electrical blazes.
> 3   The paper we currently use continually jams in the machine. The service engineer has informed us that this paper is unsuitable and that a different type should be purchased.
>
> When you have had time to consider these points could we please meet to discuss the situation early next week?
>
> *SC*

Figure 1.3 A typical memo

25

office or organisation as yourself.

The following are the features you will find in a typical memo (see Figure 1.3):

- The heading 'Memorandum' is normally centred, although it can be blocked to the left.

- The recipient and sender's names, the date and heading all line up (are aligned at the same tab stop).

- The main body of the memo is written under a line, but it is not essential to have a line across the page – this simply makes for better presentation.

- The body of the memo is usually short and less formal than a letter.

- The sender's initials should be handwritten at the end of the memo.

Note that, unlike business letters, memos do not have a salutation or complimentary close. This may seem unfriendly but, remember, a memo is often to or from people in the same organisation who would probably know each other quite well.

ACTIVITY

Your tutor will give you a copy of a memo to study. Look at this carefully and compare it with points listed above.

ACTIVITY

Using the copy of the memo you have been given as an example, prepare a memo as follows.

The department of the company you work in has just taken delivery of a new photocopier. Write to your departmental manager, Freda Cookson, to say the new machine has been installed and that all departmental staff have been trained in the proper use of the copier.

Agenda

An agenda is a list of subjects to be discussed at a meeting. The features of a typical agenda are as follows (see Figure 1.4):

- Apologies for absence (from people who will not be able to attend the meeting).

- Minutes of last meeting (a summary of the points discussed at the last meeting).

COMPUTER CONSULTANTS LTD

A meeting of Computer Consultants Ltd will be held on Monday X August 200- in the Board Room at 3.00 pm.

AGENDA

1   Apologies for absence

2   Minutes of last meeting

3   Matters arising from minutes

4   Staff holidays

5   How often computer passwords should be changed

6   Personal use of e-mail during company time

7   Update on the company's new website

8   Any other business

9   Date and time of next meeting

FREDA COOKSON
Departmental Manager

Figure 1.4 An agenda for a meeting

- Matters arising from minutes (an opportunity to discuss those issues raised at the last meeting and to check that any action that should have been taken as a result of that discussion has been carried out).

- List of items (to be discussed at this meeting).

- AOB (any other business – a point in the meeting where people can bring up issues not listed in the agenda and have these discussed if there is the time).

- Date and time of next meeting.

 ACTIVITY

Your tutor will give you a copy of an agenda for a company meeting. Study this carefully and compare it with the features listed above.

Minutes

The minutes are the details of what was agreed at the meeting. These are listed under the same headings as the agenda. The minutes will include the following features (see Figure 1.5):

- The date of the meeting.

- A list of people who attended the meeting.

- A list of people who were absent from the meeting.

- A note about matters arising from the previous meeting.

- A summary of what was discussed (and who said what) and the points for action (including AOB).

- The date and time agreed for the next meeting.

Minutes of meeting of Computer Consultants Ltd on Monday X August 200- at 3.00 pm in the Board Room

Present: Mr Smith (chair), Ms Marley(secretary), Ms Cookson, Mr Li, Mr Crane.

1 *Apologies for absence:* Mrs Jenkins, Mr Patel.

2 *Minutes of last meeting:* Previous minutes approved.

3 *Matters arising:* None.

4 *Staff holidays:* Ms Cookson will be away XX August–X September.

5 *Changing passwords:* It was agreed that office passwords should be changed every three months because of the increase in temporary staff. Action: Mr Li to notify Technical Support by end of next week.

6 *E-mail use:* Senior management have decided that e-mail is not to be used for personal reasons during working hours, except in emergency.

7 *Website:* Mr Crane reported that Marketing expects to complete the final graphics by the end of the month, and requests a finalised fee schedule for next year. Action: Mr Smith to provide fee schedule to Marketing by the end of this week.

8 *AOB:* The question of which company is the best Internet provider was raised again. As time ran out, this item will be forwarded to the next meeting.

9 *Date and time of next meeting:* X September, 10.00 am–noon.

Figure 1.5 The minutes of a meeting

 ACTIVITY

Look carefully at Figure 1.5. Note the layout of the main features.

Did you know?

Some organisations require detailed minutes showing what was said and who said it. This makes minute-taking very difficult and time-consuming. Consequently, most organisations require just a brief summary of the discussion, together with any follow-up (action) points.

ACTIVITY

Your tutor will give you a copy of some company minutes. From these minutes, work backwards to see if you can prepare the agenda the minutes are based on.

Report

A report is a detailed description of an investigation and the results of this investigation. There are four basic sections in a report:

- Introduction – setting the scene of what has been investigated.

- Method – the way the investigation was carried out.

- Findings – perhaps arranged under relevant headings.

- Conclusions or recommendations (recommendations are the courses of action that be undertaken as a result of the report's conclusions).

For example, you might be asked to investigate and report on the most appropriate scanner for your company to purchase. You would set out information about the different types of scanner – their specifications and price – and information about your company's needs. You would then write a conclusion saying which scanner (judging from the information you have supplied) would be the best buy.

Newsletter

A newsletter is a publication that provides staff with general information about the organisation and perhaps about out-of-work activities (sports and social events, etc.).

Newsletters are not as standardised as other company documents. This is because they can make use of many different stylistic features and because they are specific to a particular organisation. You will, however, usually find these basic features in a newsletter:

- Headlines.

- Photographs.

- Articles.

- Text arranged in columns.

 ACTIVITY

Your tutor will give you a copy of a company newsletter. As you already know, there is a very wide range of newsletter styles. The style you would choose depends on the three basic questions you ask when creating any document. Before going on, make a note of what those questions are and check these with your tutor.

Next, as you look through the newsletter, see how many of the stylistic features listed above you can spot. Note any differences you can see in these. Then make a note of what you think the person(s) who created the newsletter would have answered to your three basic questions. Check these with your tutor.

Invoice

An invoice is a statement of how much money is owed for goods or services. They are sent out by companies to customers to say how much is owed for goods or services already received. When you go to the shops to buy something, you usually get a receipt. A receipt is similar to an invoice in that it shows you how much you spent on what and when you spent it. Businesses, on the other hand, will order goods or services but will pay the invoice they receive with those goods or services later, at an agreed time, usually 30 days.

Invoices usually have the following features (see Figure 1.6):

- The sender's logo, address, phone and fax numbers and e-mail address.

- The addressee's details.

- References, such as an order number.

- The date.

- Items (descriptions of goods or services).

- Amount of money owed for each item.

- Taxes (VAT, if applicable).

- Total amount owed.

ACTIVITY

Look through a computer magazine and choose anything costing less than £1,000 that you would like to buy. Using Figure 1.6 and the list of features above, try to produce the invoice you would expect to receive if you were to buy these goods.

ACTIVITY

Your tutor will give you a copy of an invoice. Study this carefully and compare it to the invoice you have prepared.

Templates

One of the most useful tools to help you produce a document is a template. Templates are standardised document types, such as letters, fax cover sheets or invoices. Most word processing programs include templates that provide you with a ready-made layout to work within. More sophisticated packages provide 'wizards' that will help you develop a template according to your own, special needs. Some offer 'style galleries' that work out an appropriate style based on the information you feed into the computer.

Templates hold a surprising amount of information. For example, an organisation's house style for a letter template might hold the following information:

- *Standard information* – such as the company's logo, address, telephone, fax and e-mail numbers.

- *Position on page* – such as the location for the recipient's name and address, for the date, for references and for salutations.

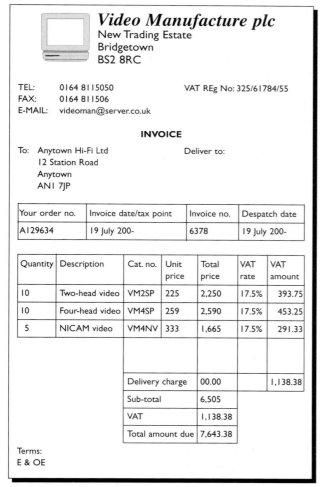

Figure 1.6 An invoice

Video Manufacture plc
New Trading Estate
Bridgetown
BS2 8RC

TEL: 0164 8115050
FAX: 0164 811506
E-MAIL: videoman@server.co.uk

VAT REg No: 325/61784/55

INVOICE

To: Anytown Hi-Fi Ltd
     12 Station Road
     Anytown
     AN1 7JP

Deliver to:

Your order no.	Invoice date/tax point	Invoice no.	Despatch date
A129634	19 July 200-	6378	19 July 200-

Quantity	Description	Cat. no.	Unit price	Total price	VAT rate	VAT amount
10	Two-head video	VM2SP	225	2,250	17.5%	393.75
10	Four-head video	VM4SP	259	2,590	17.5%	453.25
5	NICAM video	VM4NV	333	1,665	17.5%	291.33
		Delivery charge	00.00			1,138.38
		Sub-total	6,505			
		VAT	1,138.38			
		Total amount due	7,643.38			

Terms:
E & OE

- *Other detail* – such as font type and its correct size.

While most word processing applications come with basic templates, more sophisticated packages include a wide range of template types. It is unlikely you will have all the following templates available in your college, but here is an example of templates from a spreadsheet program that shows some of the types available and examples of their uses:

- Invoice (to prepare an invoice).

- Loan Manager (to work out the interest you save by paying back part of a loan).

- Purchase Order (to prepare a purchase order).

- Personal Budgeter (to itemise family income and expenses).

- Car Lease Manager (to compare car lease options).

- Expense Statement (to itemise work-related expenses).

- Business Planner (to analyse projected income, expenses and other company finances).

- Sales Quote (to prepare price estimates for goods and services).

- Timecard (to track hours studied by students or worked by employees).

Even when a program offers different styles for the same document type, many people still prefer to create their own document templates because they may want to develop and use a company house style or to personalise their documents. You will find out how to do this in Unit 3, Chapter 3.3.

Standard paragraphs

Once an organisation has set up its letter templates, it will need to create standard paragraphs for use in these letters. A college, for example, deals with thousands of applicants for its courses. Some are rejected immediately and some get through the full application and interview process finally to join a class. At each stage of the process, the college has to send out letters to the applicants: you may have seen this type of 'We regret to inform you' or 'We are pleased to inform you' letter. To save the word processing operator keying in the same information again and again, he or she simply inserts the standard paragraphs that have already been created, keying in the information for each individual applicant in the appropriate places.

Letter templates help reduce errors, but when only one or two paragraphs are different, it is easier to use what are called paragraph macros, than to prepare different templates. To do this different standard paragraphs are pre-written then assigned to buttons or keystrokes. The user chooses the appropriate paragraph and then simply inserts it into a basic letter template to produce the right letter. You will learn how to create macros in Unit 3, Chapter 3.3.

Getting started: creating your document

Sometimes you know the purpose of your document, who will read it and why, and you're familiar with a wide range of tools to help you create your document. But you just can't seem to get started. Don't worry, that is usually what happens – even to people who have many years' experience of writing. There's even an expression for it: 'writer's block.' Fortunately, there is a way around this block.

Most people find writing much more difficult than speaking, and think of writing and speaking as two different things. But they are not – in fact, they're really very similar. Both use words and sentences to express ideas. So if you have trouble getting started, try telling yourself (or an imaginary colleague or friend) just what it is that you want to say. Be careful not to get carried away and have the conversation with yourself out loud – you will get some peculiar looks!

Don't worry about your style or using the right words or anything like that – just say it in your head (or out loud if you're really sure no one else is around). Then, write down just what you said. Now you will have your first draft. With the help of the next section, you will be able to polish up what you said and wrote.

Language style

Choosing the right language to use is very important as it will ensure your document gives the reader the right message and the right impression about yourself. Language can be any of the following styles:

- Formal (e.g. for a job application letter, a letter of complaint, a company report).

- Informal (e.g. for letter to a friend, a party invitation, a note for the milkman).

- Persuasive or forceful (e.g. for an advertisement, a direction sign).

- Suited to the age of the reader (e.g. a children's book, a newspaper).

Most word processing applications have basic tools to help you with your style of language, such as spellcheckers, AutoCorrect, grammar checkers, thesauruses and readability statistics.

Formal v informal

Your basic choice of language style is between formal and informal. For example, a letter written to an employer applying for a job should be formal. The style has to help you achieve the purpose of the document, which is to persuade the reader to give your application serious consideration. It would not be an appropriate place to make a joke or to use the informal phrases we often use in conversation. A letter that starts with 'Dear Sir, I am writing to you to apply for a position with your organisation' is likely to create a very different impression from a letter that begins 'Hi, I'd really love a job with you lot!'

On the other hand, if you are inviting people to a party then 'Hi, I'd really love you to come to my party!' is more informal and friendly than 'Dear Friend, I would be most pleased if you could attend my party'. However, this more formal style might not be wrong if it creates a tone that is right for your purpose: perhaps you're getting married soon, and so a formal party invitation is the more appropriate style.

As you will gather from this, the distinction between formal and informal styles is not clear cut. It is a very gradual change from one to the other, with very formal at one end and very informal at the other. The best way to learn about style, therefore, is to make a point of always looking at the level of formality in any documents you come across. And remember, always keep your document's purpose and your reader(s) in mind, then choose what you think is the right level of formality.

The right words

Choosing the right words is probably the most important part of creating the right style of language.

When we are stuck for the right word, a thesaurus can be really useful, especially a thesaurus that is part of the word processing application we are using. A thesaurus is a list of words. The list is organised into groups of words that have the same or similar meanings (known as synonyms). For example, 'massive', 'huge', 'enormous', 'giant', 'tremendous' and 'colossal' would all be in a group of words meaning very big. If you were writing an advert, for example, 'very big' would not attract much attention, whereas the other words would be much more dramatic.

The two most frequent occasions you will want to consult a thesaurus are when you want to avoid using the same word twice in one sentence, and when you are looking for a more appropriate word that might better suit your reader(s). You might, for example, be writing a memo to your supervisor that says: 'The Internet can help our organisation research information on printers and it can also help with scanners'. Rather than use the

Figure 1.8 'Help' as a verb

word 'help' twice, highlight it, click on Tools, Language, Thesaurus, and you will see the box shown in Figure 1.7.

Because you are using 'help' as a verb, click on the first verb in the lower left panel (Meanings). Then in the right panel (Replace with Synonym). The program will suggest a list of words with similar meanings to 'help' (see Figure 1.8).

The third option ('assist') is probably the nearest, so you can click on it and then on the Replace button. Your sentence will now be better written.

The first word 'aid' and the second word 'abet' would not be good choices because they are too formal and are mostly used in legal contexts – you have probably heard the phrase 'aid and abet' used by lawyers or the police. 'Abet' is, however, a good example of how you should choose your words to suit your readers. If you were completing a legal report, perhaps describing a crime you have witnessed or you were working for a legal company, 'abet' might be a better word than help. Bear in mind that, generally speaking, the more unusual a word is, the more formal it is.

Technicalities

As an ICT specialist, you must bear in mind that a great deal of ICT language is highly specialised. Many of those 40,000 technical words referred to above are information

Figure 1.7 Looking up the word 'help'

technology words. Most people do not understand what a tape streamer is so, unless you are writing to another IT specialist, it is better simply to say a 'backup tape'.

The use of acronyms (words made from the initial letters of other words, e.g. RAM – random access memory) is even more confusing. If you need to use acronyms such as ISDN (integrated services digital network) or OCR (optical character reader), write them out in full the first time you use them. You can then use the acronym as many times as you like in the same document.

The right spelling

Good spelling is essential to good written communication. Today's software applications, with their powerful spelling checkers, means readers are less and less tolerant of mistakes. As you will already know from the Preparatory Unit, mistakes in business communications are taken as a sign of sloppiness or laziness, and no organisation wants to employ the sort of person who makes such mistakes.

Most applications that have spell checkers offer two ways to check your spelling (and grammar):

1   *As you type*: the program automatically checks the words as you type them and underlines possible spelling mistakes. If you decide it really is a mistake, you can right click your mouse to display a shortcut menu and then select the correction you want.

2   *When you have finished creating your document*: the program searches through the entire document looking for possible mistakes. Each time it finds a possible error, you can correct it or ignore it and continue with the check.

If you use technical or specialised words the spelling checker does not recognise – such as

acronyms or proper names – you can use custom dictionaries to check their spelling. You can add these technical words to a built-in custom dictionary or you can create your own dictionaries. The spell checker won't then question those words again unless you've made a mistake in spelling them. It is also possible to buy extra or supplementary dictionaries, such as dictionaries of other languages or medical and legal dictionaries.

AutoCorrect

Another feature of most word processing applications you may find useful is AutoCorrect. Autocorrect (see Figure 1.9) corrects errors as you key in – for example, if you type TWo INitial CApitals, or forget to begin a sentence or a day of the week with a capital letter. They are also very useful for correcting simple keying-in errors and will usually have a list of common mistakes and the correct spellings to replace them with – for example 'abbout' with 'about', 'adn' with

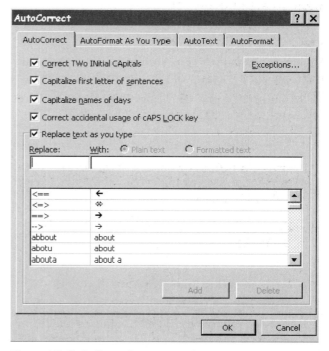

Figure 1.9 AutoCorrect

'and', 'acommodate' with 'accommodate'. You can even get them to change a ':)' into a '☺'.

Grammar checkers

As you will already know from the Preparatory Unit, most applications can assist you with grammar as well as with your spelling. It is worth your while to learn when and how to use grammar checkers because they can help you with typical difficulties encountered in the use of English, such as the following:

- Making sure your sentences have subjects and verbs that agree.

- Finding out the level of reading difficulty of your work.

- Writing most of the time in the same style.

- Detecting sentences that end with two full stops.

- Detecting missing capital letters at the beginning of sentences.

You can usually choose and set a writing style, and specify grammar and style options (see Figure 1.10).

If grammar isn't your strongest point, the best way to use grammar checkers is *selectively*. The following are some of the more popular features you should be able to make good use of:

- *Sentence length*: grammar checkers will tell you when a sentence is too long. Long sentences are usually considered bad style. This is because it might be difficult for the reader to remember the beginning of the sentence by the time he or she gets to the end!

- *Passives*: grammar checkers draw your attention to the use of passives. A passive is a way of using a verb when you don't say who performed an action. Passives are mostly used in more formal styles. For

Figure 1.10 Grammar settings

example, compare 'A goal was scored' (passive) with 'Michael Owen scored a goal' (active).

- *Subject/verb disagreements*. For example, 'she walk down the street' instead of 'she walks' – an easy enough mistake to make!

- *Commonly confused words*: grammar checkers can detect those words many people confuse. Here are three typical examples:

  – *Advice/advise*. We use 'advice' (a noun) when we mean 'suggestion' or 'guidance' – for example: 'Could you give me some advice on cellular phones?' We use 'advise' (a verb) when we mean 'to suggest' or 'to give advice to' – for example: 'Could you advise me on cellular phones?'

  – *Its/it's*. We use 'its' (a pronoun) when we are indicating possession, as in 'its processor is really fast'. We use 'it's' (a contraction) when we mean 'it is' – for example: 'It's an expensive piece of equipment.'

– Principal/principle. We use 'principle' (a noun) when we mean a rule or a standard – for example, the principles of the Data Protection Act you studied in the Preparatory Unit. We use 'principal' (an adjective or noun) when we mean 'main', 'the most important' or 'the head of a school or college'.

Customised spelling and grammar checkers

To improve the accuracy and speed of a spelling and grammar checker, you can set the spelling and grammar options to suit your needs and can make use of specialised dictionaries (see Figure 1.11).

Readability statistics

Another useful writing tool is to check how readable your text is. This check provides you with readability statistics – information about the reading level of your document (i.e. how difficult or easy your document will be to understand by your intended reader). Two of the most common ways of assessing readability are the Flesch Reading Ease score and the Flesch–Kincaid Grade Level score. These scores are based on the average number of syllables per word and the number of words per sentence. The bigger the words and the longer the sentences, the more difficult the text is to read.

The Flesch Reading Ease score

This score rates text on a 100-point scale. The higher the score, the easier it is to understand the document. For most standard documents, you should aim for a score of approximately 60–70.

The Flesch-Kincaid Grade Level score

This score rates text on a US grade-school level. If you want to use and understand this score, add 5 years to the US grade and that will tell you roughly how old the students are. For example, in the eighth grade, students are around 13 years old.

A Flesch-Kincaid Grade Level score of 8.0 means that a 13–14-year-old (an eighth grader) could understand the document. For most standard documents, you should aim for a score of approximately 7.0–8.0.

Figure 1.11 Setting the spelling and grammar options

Figure 1.12 Readability statistics

Figure 1.12 shows my computer's assessment of this part of this chapter.

Text is probably the most important type of information you will need to use in your work. So keep in mind:

- your purpose

- your reader(s)

- your style of communication.

In the next chapter we look at other ways of presenting information that will be of great help in getting your message across successfully.

CHAPTER 1.2 TYPES OF INFORMATION

After words or text, the main types of information you will be dealing with are numbers and graphics. Most information – in electronic or paper form – integrates text, numbers and graphics to make documents easier to understand.

Making a document easier to understand depends in part on how these types of information are organised and presented, and on what form they take. It is sometimes much easier, for example, to explain something by drawing a diagram than by trying to find the right words to describe it. Numbers are often easier to read and interpret when they are expressed in charts, graphs or tables. This is why nearly every page you look up on a web site, in a magazine or in this book contains different types and forms of information, combined to make the pages easier to read and understand.

Using different forms of information helps you to get your readers' attention, keep your reader interested and to make your point more easily or clearly. Because different forms of information are so widely used in documents, it is important to select those that are best suited to the purpose, the reader(s) and which clearly illustrate the points being made.

This chapter will familiarise you with the different forms numerical and graphical information may take. It also describes how you can organise and present different types of information in the most effective ways to get your message across.

Tables and charts

Numerical information is rarely presented in its 'raw' form, that is, as lists of numbers. Where there are a lot of figures, when comparisons need to be made or when people need an overview understanding of information, it is better to use charts. For example, Figure 1.13 is a list of computer system sales over the past 12 months and Figure 1.14 is a chart giving the same information.

It is easier to see the picture the chart represents than to try to form a picture in your mind from the list of numbers. It is also easier to interpret what the numbers are saying: you

Computer Sales

Month	Sales
Jan	23
Feb	25
Mar	23
Apr	17
May	15
Jun	13
Jul	13
Aug	12
Sep	26
Oct	33
Nov	30
Dec	34

Figure 1.13 Computer sales: 'raw' figures

Figure 1.14 Computer sales: column chart

can see that fewer computers are sold in the summer months than in the winter. Why do you think this is so? Perhaps the cold winter weather keeps people indoors but, in the summer, people prefer to spend their money on holidays. Why do you think most computers are sold in October, November, December and then sales drop again in January?

> ## ? Did you know?
>
> Although specialised charting software is available, most people use the charting function in spreadsheet programs to create their charts. In Unit 2 you will study spreadsheets in detail.

Tables and charts are interesting ways to present your information. Once you are comfortable creating them, you should use them whenever they are appropriate to make your information easier to understand.

Tables

Tables are rows and columns of data that allow readers to see and compare information quickly and easily. For example, when data are arranged chronologically (in date order) – such as the number of people using the Internet over a five-year period – tables show trends (patterns of increasing or decreasing activity). The data for the activity under the heading 'Line graphs' on page 39/40 are arranged chronologically (by year). Similarly, the data for computer sales in the table in Figure 1.13 are in chronological order (by month).

At the top of each column is a heading which describes the contents of that column. The title of a table is placed above the table or is the first row of the table.

Most word processing programs allow you to draw or insert tables easily. You can choose the number of columns and rows, borders and shading and other details, or you can use AutoFormat (see Figure 1.15).

Use tables when you want to set out details that fall under the same categories. Refer back to the example of a report in Chapter 1.1 which recommended which scanner your company should buy. The considerations were specifications and price. This is good data for a table because the specifications for each scanner fall under the same categories (e.g. their speed, size, weight, etc.) but are different for each scanner (e.g. A is this fast, B is that fast). The same is true of price: they all have a price but this is different for each scanner.

When you create a table, be sure to show only the data you need for your purpose. Monster tables with 20 columns and 30 rows are unreadable! Give the table a title. It is also a good idea to explain what the data mean in the text just before you insert the table. This makes it much easier for the reader to understand the table than if you say nothing at all and leave him or her to figure it out for him or herself.

Charts

The main types of chart are:

- line graphs
- column graphs
- bar charts
- pie charts
- flow charts
- pictograms.

The following is a description of each type of chart, an example of their use and the main reasons for using them.

Line graphs

A line graph is a diagram showing the relationship between two varying quantities (or variables). Each variable is measured along one of a pair of axes which are at right angles to each other. The axes are referred to as the y and x axis. It's easy to remember which is

Click on the up and down arrows until you find the style of table you want. Click on this style

A preview of your chosen style appears in this box

If you put a tick in any of these checkboxes, AutoFormat will apply these styles to the parts of the table ticked in the **Apply special formats to** section of the dialogue box

Figure 1.15 AutoFormat

which because the tail of the y goes in an up/down direction. It is also important to label what the x and y axes represent. For example, Figure 1.16 is a graph that shows the rates of use of photocopies in different departments (marketing and production) over a six-week period. The y axis variable is the number of copies made and the x axis the number of weeks. By plotting (marking) the graph with the number of copies each department has made each week, you can join these points up by drawing lines across the graph that help the reader see at a glance the trend or pattern in photocopier use. Notice the legend at the right side of the graph: this tells the reader which line represents which department.

Use line graphs when you want to:

• illustrate trends or patterns

• make a straightforward comparison between different things on the same graph.

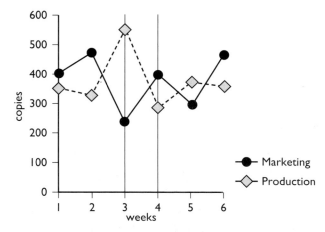

Figure 1.16 Photocopy use by two departments, marketing and production

ACTIVITY

The following data come from a survey into people who are connected to the Internet. The numbers are in millions, and 1996–1999 are estimates. Present this information as a line graph.

1990	7
1991	8
1992	10
1993	12
1994	15
1995	19
1996	28
1997	37
1998	52
1999	74

Column and bar charts

Column charts use vertical columns and bar charts horizontol bars to show specific figures at a particular time or to illustrate comparisons among items. The chart at the beginning of this chapter (Figure 1.14), showing computer sales by month, is a typical column chart. It compares sales during the different months.

Like line graphs, column and bar charts use axes. In the example in Figure 1.17, the y axis represent the % of processor sales, and the x axis represents the type of processor. Column charts (and line graphs and pie charts – see below) often use colour, shading or line style (solid or dashed), which you will need to explain in the legend. The example in Figure 1.17 uses shading and has a legend that explains the shadings represent different brands.

Use bar or column charts (as you would graphs) when you need to present an overview

of information rather than the exact detail. In our example, you do not see the exact percentages as you would in a table, but you do see the overall picture in a more interesting and dramatic form than in a simple table.

ACTIVITY

The following data come from a survey into the number of people planning to take courses in different software programs in the next 12 months. Present it as a column chart, using the computer sales chart as your model.

Word	77
PowerPoint	23
WordPerfect	60
Visual C++	11
PageMaker	53
CorelDraw	44

Pie charts

A pie chart is a circle divided into sections that represent different quantities. It shows the proportional size of the different items that make up the whole (the slices of the pie). It always shows only one type of information. As pie charts are drawn as circles with each wedge showing a proportion of the whole, the figures they present can be expressed as percentages.

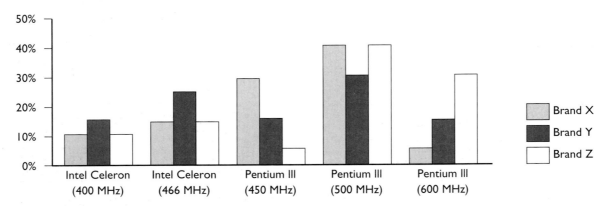

Figure 1.17 Processor sales by type for three different brands in the year 2000

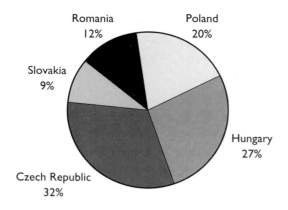

Figure 1.18 Pie chart showing the use of mobile phones in some eastern European countries

Flow of documents between customer and supplier

Figure 1.19 A flow chart illustrating the different stages in ordering goods

The example in Figure 1.18 shows the distribution of mobile telephones in some eastern European countries. The data series (the information displayed) is mobile phones. Each wedge represents the usage in a different country, and is also expressed as a percentage of the total use in those countries.

Use pie charts when you want to show the relationship of one part to the whole, or when you want to emphasise a particular section of your data.

Flow charts

A flow chart is a diagram that shows the movement of things or people through the different stages or processes of a series of events. Anything that occurs in a sequence can be described in a flow chart. For example, when one company (the customer) orders goods from another company (the supplier), a purchase order is sent to the supplier's sales department. The sales department enters the order into the computer system, which informs the accounts department, so that an invoice (a bill) can be issued, and the warehouse so the staff know they have to pack the goods for delivery, including the delivery note. The goods are sent to the customer, where the delivery note is checked to make sure everything ordered has been

received. The purchaser's accounts department is informed so that the bill can be paid when the invoice is received. It's quite hard to follow this in words, but the diagram in Figure 1.19 illustrates this much more clearly as a flow chart.

Use flow charts as alternatives to numbered lists or as alternatives to text that would otherwise repeat such words as 'then', 'after that', 'next', etc. Also, use flow charts as a particularly useful way to illustrate a sequence that has different alternatives. Explaining how to 'cut and paste' is a simple example (see Figure 1.20).

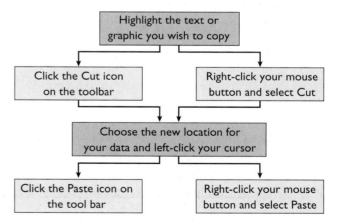

Figure 1.20 A flow chart showing alternative ways of doing the same thing

Pictograms

Information can also be displayed in a picture diagram (called a pictogram or a pictograph). Each picture represents an item. For example, in Figure 1.21, software is represented by a picture of a floppy disk. A pictogram may show increasing numbers by the enlargement of each illustration or by increasing the number of illustrations. It may also need a key to show what information each picture represents.

Pictograms are often used where readers have difficulty in dealing with numbers or where detailed statistics are not necessary. They are also used to show general information in a visually striking way – for example, in a sales presentation.

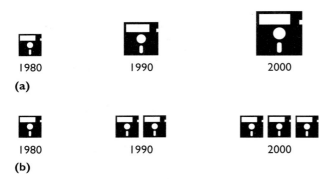

1980   1990   2000

(a)

1980   1990   2000

(b)

Figure 1.21 Two ways of showing increasing sales of software by pictogram: (a) by increasing the size of each illustration; (b) by increasing the number of illustrations

After you have selected the most appropriate chart, you must be careful to transfer your data to the chart accurately and correctly.

Computer graphics

Producing graphics (i.e. the drawings or artwork we often see inserted into documents) is not as difficult as you might first think. And it's fun – you don't need to be a professional graphics artist or technical draftsperson to produce and use them in your documents.

ACTIVITY

The Preparatory Unit explained the importance of keeping your own customised reference log. In this chapter you are going to practise using a reference log. Open a new file in a graphics program and save this as your Graphics Reference log. In the activities that follow, save only the results of the particular activity you have just finished – do *not* print out at this stage. Also, don't forget to make full use of the Help functions in your application to guide you through the activities, if necessary.

There are two basic ways to create graphic images on a computer – bit map and vector. A bit map graphic is a pattern made up of dots. A vector graphic is made up of unconnected elements, such as lines, curves, circles and squares. Graphical user interfaces (GUIs) and paint programs are examples of bit map applications. Technical drawing software, computer aided design (CAD) and illustration packages are examples of vector applications. Charts and slide show presentations, on the other hand, use both methods.

Bit map graphics

Bit map graphics treat images as collections of dots (or *pixels*) rather than as solid shapes. Each bit in a bit image corresponds to one pixel (short for picture element) on the screen. Because computer screens have high resolutions, it is difficult to see the way an image is constructed from pixels. However, if you can zoom in to view a bit map image to an increased size of at least 200%, you should just be able to make out the bits.

You can see the individual pixels in a bit map image more easily on a (non-high definition) television screen, particularly in information service graphics such as TeleText and Ceefax. When you begin to work with them, you will find clearly constructed pixel images in Paint programs – they usually include a facility that allows you to change a paint pattern or a small section of a drawing, pixel by pixel.

Did you know?

On the black and white screens of older computers, the bit values in a bit image were either 0 to display white, or 1 to display black. The pattern of the 0s and 1s that made up the bit image, specified the pattern of black and white dots that made up the screen graphic. To display shades of grey or colour images, two or more bits are required. For example, two bits for 4 colours, four bits for 16 colours, and sixteen bits for 256 colour displays.

Vector graphics

In vector graphics (often called object-orientated graphics), objects are treated as collections of lines rather than as patterns of individual dots. Hence you can treat one individual part of an image as a complete unit – for example, you can change the length of a line or enlarge a circle as an independent element of the complete image.

Vector images are described mathematically as sets of instructions to create the objects in the image. For example, the position, length, and direction in which lines are to be drawn. This make it much easier to magnify, rotate and layer object-orientated graphics than bit map graphics.

Graphics software

When you open a graphics design program, it usually displays an area on the screen for you to create your design in and several sets of tools at the top, bottom or side of the screen (see Figure 1.22). These tools will help you to produce your desired graphical design. The basic tools are line, shape, text, brush and a colour palette. Other tools allow you to specify the appearance (attributes) of each component of the graphic and of the entire image itself. Attributes include fill (colouring or shading an entire component or image), style (for example, bold, italics, underline), line thicknesses, colours and shades, height and width.

You also have access to manipulation tools, such as for sizing and moving objects, and to standard editing tools, such as for copying,

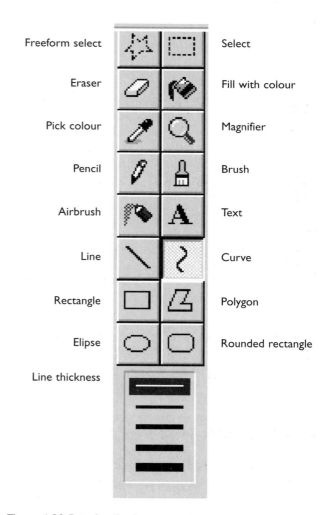

Figure 1.22 Drawing tools

cutting and pasting. Before you examine and experiment with different graphic components, you need to acquire a clearer understanding of the basic image attributes you will be using.

Image attributes

Most programs allow you to choose the attributes you wish to give to images or components before, during or after you have created the different components or image. The main attributes you will be working with are colours and sizes.

Colours

Colours (and shades) are available in the colour palette, which is usually a separate toolbox. Colours can be used for text, single lines, outline shapes and for filling backgrounds and shapes.

Did you know?

Most programs include a custom colours option which allows you to create a colour of your own choosing that is not already available on the colour palette. To use it, select the colour you want to customise then choose Edit Colours. You will see a chart where you can define the colour you want by moving the cross-hair shape around. There are two stages in customising a colour: RGB (red, green, blue) and HLS (hue, luminescence and saturation). When you have achieved the colour you want, save it to the custom palette.

You can colour shapes and backgrounds with solid or shaded colours, patterns and even textures. To fill an area or object with

Did you know?

Design specifications for manufacturing state tolerances. Tolerances refer to the maximum errors in size that a manufactured article may have, or the size of the graphic image that is required.

colour, select the fill icon, choose a colour then click in the area or object you want to fill.

ACTIVITY

Open your Graphics Reference log, key in the word 'Colours', draw a few shapes in different colours and fill two of them. Next, choose a colour and experiment with customising it. Save your customised colour to the custom palette and then save your document.

Sizing

You can usually move and reshape an image or any of its components by dragging its resize handles (see Figure 1.23). Resize handles appear around an image in a framework when you select an image by clicking on it. To resize the height, drag the handles at the top or bottom of the frame. To resize the width, drag the handles at the sides

Figure 1.23 Using a sizing frame

of the frame. Resizing in this way will alter the proportions of your image. To resize an image while maintaining its correct proportions (its *aspect ratio*), drag from a corner of the frame.

To move an entire image, do not use the handles but click anywhere in the border. Then drag the image to the position you want.

ACTIVITY

Open your log and type a new heading – 'Sizing' – under your colour experiments. Open a ClipArt file, choose a picture and insert two copies of it side by side. Click on the object to activate the sizing handles then experiment with different sizes. Save your file. Do not print at this stage.

Graphics tools

The main tools you will be working with to construct graphic components are the text, line, shape and brush tools.

The text tool

The text tool is used to key in and arrange text. The standard way to use this is to select the icon and create a text frame by dragging the mouse pointer diagonally. Next, choose the font, size and style you want. Then, click inside the text frame and key in the text.

Once you have entered your text you may want to move or enlarge the text frame or change the colour of the text. To write text on a coloured background, select the foreground icon from the colour palette, then choose your colour. By selecting the background icon and then a colour, you can change the background colour.

ACTIVITY

Open your Graphics Reference log. Use the text tool to write the main heading 'Graphics Reference' at the beginning of the document. Choose an appropriate font, style and size for this heading. Move or enlarge the heading text as necessary. Next, go to the end of the document (under your sizing experiments) and key in the heading 'Text Tool'. Put it into a different font, style and size from the main heading, and then into your custom colour. Save your work at regular intervals in the correct directory, using a suitable filename, and make a backup copy. Do not print at this stage.

The line tool

The line tool draws straight lines from the point where you click to start, to wherever you drag the mouse and click again to finish. The standard way to use the line tool is to select the icon, choose how wide and what colour your line will be, then draw it. In many graphics programs you can add arrow heads and make a line dotted, dashed or a lighter shade.

ACTIVITY

Try it yourself. Open your Graphics Reference log, enter the heading 'Lines' and draw three lines. One should be on its own but the other two should be joined at right-angles. All three should be different colours. Do not print at this stage.

The shape tools

Basic shapes are constructed using the rectangle, circle and polygon tools. These shapes are created in the same way: select the shape tool icon from the toolbox, choose the thickness of the outline, its style and a colour. Then, to draw the shape, drag the mouse pointer diagonally in the direction you want.

? Did you know?

You can use the shift key to straighten up a wobbly line. Select the line then use the Ctrl key plus the cursor arrows. This will allow you to move the line up, down, etc., in small movements.

Rectangle tools usually offer a choice of a square-cornered or a round-cornered shape. To draw a perfect square, in most programs you press and hold down the Shift key while dragging the mouse pointer. An ellipse is an elongated circle, like a rugby ball. To draw an ellipse, select the ellipse tool then follow the standard shape procedure as described above. For a perfect circle, follow the square procedure.

In most graphics programs you can draw a polygon with either the polygon tool or with a Freeform – a freehand drawing tool. Poly, incidentally, means many, so a polygon is a shape with many sides. If you use Freeform you can add text then group them so that they move, rotate, flip and resize together. Either way, start by following the same procedure as for the other shapes.

If you want to fill any of these shapes with colour, choose the colour, select fill, then click inside the shape.

 ACTIVITY

Experiment with drawing shapes. Open your Graphics Reference log and key in the new heading 'Shapes'. Then:

- produce at least one rectangle, square, circle, ellipse and polygon
- use different outline colours, thicknesses and styles
- use different fills and two (labelled) custom colours.

Next, copy, paste and resize two of your shapes underneath their originals.

When you have a drawing that illustrates each shape and attribute clearly, make a backup copy but do not print at this stage.

The brush tool

You can use the brush tool to create a range of different-sized and shaped brush strokes. To paint with a brush, select the brush tool, then choose the size and shape you want and the colour. To paint, just drag the mouse pointer.

Most graphics programs include an airbrush effect with adjustable spray areas. The effect is very similar to using a spray can from different ranges, and it is particularly useful for creating graffiti-like effects. The procedure for spraying is the same as for brush strokes.

 ACTIVITY

Open your Graphics Reference log. The new heading is 'Brushes'. Produce a drawing that clearly illustrates the different styles of brush strokes you can use and the effects you can achieve with the airbrush. Save your work but do not print at this stage.

ACTIVITY

Finally, look back at all the work you have done for this chapter. How well do you think you have achieved what the activities asked you to do? Where could you make improvements? Once you are satisfied with your work on screen, print out a hard copy. Keep your Graphics Reference log in your working file for future reference.

Combining information types

When you insert a graphic object, such as a piece of ClipArt into a document, it is normally out of proportion with the rest of the document. Sizing the object will bring it into proportion. Click and drag the sizing handles to bring the object to the correct shape and size. Sizing is also important in tables, as we will see in the next chapter.

To resize a column (or row) in a table, you drag the cell border in the direction you require.

? Did you know?

To place a graphic exactly where you want it on the page, it is easier in most programs to put it into a frame and then move the frame. This is because a frame moves text out of its way to one or more sides, whereas a graphic just lays on top of text. (Your computer system might require you to use a text box rather than a frame.)

When you have drawn a graphic object or imported (inserted) one into a document, you may need to rotate it (turn it round). Graphics packages usually include rotation and flip features. You highlight the object and select the degree of rotation you require. Rotating 180° is the same as turning the object upside down, which you can usually do with the Flip command.

CHAPTER 1.3 DOCUMENT LAYOUT AND PRESENTATION

To produce good basic documents as well as those with more interesting or unusual features, you need a working knowledge of page layout. Page layout means the structure or the basic appearance of each page of a document. All documents require that each of its pages has a structure. The simplest and most common document structure is a rectangle containing all the text. The position and size of the rectangle are determined by the top, bottom and side page margins, as shown in Figure 1.24.

More complicated page structures might divide the text into columns or sections, like a newspaper. Charts, graphics and photographs are then placed into the sections and sized to fit exactly. The correct sizing helps to create a sense of order and makes the page easier for the eye to read or scan through.

Pages on websites and in magazines and similar documents often position graphics so that they run over the margins into other pages. The basic page structure is still there but, by placing some elements outside the basic order, you can catch and hold your reader's attention – the unusual effect makes the page more vibrant to look at (see Figure 1.25).

As you already know from Chapter 1.1, many organisations have a house style – rules that state the size and position on the page of headings, graphics and other features. House styles also include rules about the layout of documents.

 ACTIVITY

In this chapter you will learn about and practise the conventions involved in standard document layouts. As part of that practice you will produce a Layout Reference log, similar to the one you produced in Chapter 1.2. Save your work as you go along but print it only when the log is complete.

Note: To find out about the activities in this chapter use the Help function on your word processing program.

Common standard layout features

Your choice of layout features always depends on – you've guessed it – your document's purpose and its readers. Sometimes using fewer features will allow you to convey your message in a more direct, simpler style (and this will save you time). On other occasions (such as a web pages or newsletters), using a wide range of features helps you to keep your reader's attention and interest for longer. Word processing applications, including those you might use for the Internet, have many different layout features. This chapter covers the following:

Figure 1.24 Basic page layout

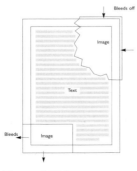

Figure 1.25 A more dramatic page layout

Page attributes · Indents
White space · Line spacing
Tabulation · Bullets and numbering
Page breaks · Font styles and sizes
Special symbols · Justification
Page numbering · Contents and indexes
Headers and footers · Column layouts
Borders and shading · Margins

Page attributes

Page attributes are a page's orientation (which way up it is) and the *size* of paper the page (i.e. text) will fit on to. Orientation can be either portrait or landscape (see Figure 1.26). To remember which is which, just think of the way up a portrait, such as a passport photo, usually is. Although portrait is used for most documents, landscape can be very useful for graphics and for spreadsheets. In most word processing applications, you will find the commands for selecting both page orientation and page attributes under Page Setup in the File menu.

The paper size you print to depends on the capabilities of your printer or online photocopier. The following are the standard paper sizes:

- A4 210×297 mm (by far the most widely used)
- B4 257×364 mm
- Letter $8.5 \times 11''$
- Legal $8.5 \times 14''$

Line spacing

Line spacing is the amount of space left between each line of text. The standard line spacing options are single, one and a half and double (see Figure 1.27). Most word processing applications are set by default to single line spacing as this is by far the most commonly used line spacing. One and a half and double line spacing are used to draw the reader's attention to a portion of text or when you need to leave plenty of space in a document so that its author can make amendments to it by hand.

ACTIVITY

Open a new file in a word processing application and key in the main heading 'Layout Reference'. Save it as Layout Reference in an appropriate folder. Key in the heading 'Line Spacing' and then the following text:

```
Line spacing is the amount of
space left between each line of
text. The standard line spacing
options are single, one and a half
and double. This is an example of
single line spacing.
```

Using a cut and paste method, copy the text twice more.

Find out how to adjust line spacing in the application you are using. Then adjust the spacing of the second copy of the text you have keyed in to one and a half line spacing. Adjust the last sentence of the text to say this is now in one and

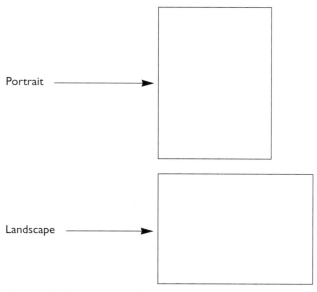

Portrait

Landscape

Figure 1.26 Page orientation

a half line spacing. Do the same for double line spacing. Check your work and save.

Page breaks

When you are keying in text and you get to the bottom of the page, your word processing application will automatically start a new page for you – a page break. However, there will be occasions when you want to start a new page before you reach the end of the page. For example, it is not good page layout to have a heading at the bottom of a page but no text after it – a heading should always be followed by a few lines of text. To overcome this problem, you could insert a page break before the heading so that the heading moves over to start a new page and, therefore, is followed immediately by its text.

Page breaks the application inserts automatically for you are called *soft* page breaks. Page breaks you insert yourself are called *hard* page breaks.

 ACTIVITY

Find out how to insert hard page breaks in the application you are using. Open your Layout Reference log and position the cursor on a new line at the end of the last piece of text you keyed in. (This should be after the paragraph that ends with the words 'This is an example of double line spacing'.) Key in the next heading 'Page Breaks' and the following text:

```
This is an example of a hard page
break.
```

Leave one blank line and then insert a hard page break. Your cursor will then jump to the start of a new blank page, leaving your new heading and text on the previous page. Key in the next heading 'Justification and Alignment' ready to start the next activity.

Justification

Fully justifying text means making both the left and right margins even. If you put a ruler down the sides of text that is fully justified, you will find that both the left and right sides of the text are absolutely straight. The 'blocked' appearance fully justified text gives makes a document look very formal. Today, most business documents are produced using a justified left margin but an unjustified right margin. This means the left margin is straight but the right margin is 'ragged' – the lines do not all end at the same place as with a justified right margin.

Figure 1.27 shows a dialogue box where you can set the justification of your text. Before you can apply justification to text, however (or apply any of the options shown in the dialogue box in Figure 1.27), you must first choose which text you want to apply this to by selecting (highlighting) it. You will see a preview of the style you have chosen in the box at the bottom of the dialogue box.

Left align means that your text lines up to the left of your document, right align means that it lines up on the right and centring, not surprisingly, means that it is centred on the page. (For information on indentation, see below.)

 ACTIVITY

Open your Layout Reference log and start a new line after the heading 'Justification and Alignment' you keyed in in the last activity. Find out how to justify, left align, right align and centre text in your application. Key in the following text:

```
Fully justifying text means making
both the left and right margins
even. If you put a ruler down the
```

Select the style of indentation by choosing from the options in this box

Set the justification you want by clicking on the arrow and choosing from the list displayed in this box

Increase or decrease the indentation by clicking on the arrows in these boxes

Set the line spacing by clicking on the arrow in this box and choosing from the options displayed

Figure 1.27 Paragraph dialogue box

sides of text that is fully justified, you will find that both the left and right sides of the text are absolutely straight.

Using a copy and paste technique, copy this text three times and apply a different alignment to each. Save your work

Headers and footers

Headers (see Figure 1.28) are at the top of a page, before the first line of text. They are used to repeat information on each page, such as a document or chapter title, or to repeat graphics (such as a company logo). A document footer (see Figure 1.28) is at the bottom of each page after the last line. It is usually used to show such information as page numbers and perhaps the name of the document's author and the date the document was created.

Headers and footers can be printed on the first page, all pages, or every even or odd page. You can adjust the style of headers and footers in the same way as you would any other text, and centre or align them with the left or right margin. You can adjust the space

Header

Document Layout and Presentation

Footer

Layout Reference Log
My Name
September 200-

Figure 1.28 Header and footer

ACTIVITY

Open your Layout Reference log and enter the next heading 'Headers and Footers.' Find out how to insert headers and footers in the application you are using. Insert the header **Layout Reference** and put it into a different font (type style) from your main text. In the footer, insert the month and year and *Your own name* **Publications**. Use the same font as in your header. Then save the file.

Margins

Margins (see Figure 1.24) are the distance between the text and the edges of the page. In most word processing programs you adjust the margin by dragging the margin boundaries on the ruler, using the mouse. Alternatively, you can go to Page Setup (see Figure 1.29), adjust the measurements by

from the edge of the page of a header or footer by choosing Margins in the Page Setup dialogue box (see Figure 1.29).

Use this box to adjust the space above or below the headers and footers

Click on these arrows as appropriate

Use this box to set gutter margins

Put a tick in this checkbox if you wish to set mirror margins

View the effects of your changes here

Use this box to choose which part of your text to apply the changes to – the whole document or a highlighted section only

Figure 1.29 Page Setup dialogue box

clicking on the up and down arrows as appropriate and you can view the effects of your changes in the Preview box.

When you are binding several pages together, for example in a report, brochure or booklet, use gutter and mirror margins (see Figure 1.29). Gutter margins run down the centre of an open booklet. They add extra space to the centre or inside margin so that it is still easy to read the end of the lines in the middle of the finished booklet. When you print documents on both sides of the paper, mirror margins ensure the margins mirror each other: they have the same width.

ACTIVITY

In your Layout Reference log, enter the new heading – 'Margins'. Find out how to adjust the left and right margins in the application you are using. Key in the following text:

```
Margins are the distance between
the text and the edges of the
page. In most word processing
programs you adjust the margin by
dragging the margin boundaries on
the ruler using the mouse.
```

Select the text you have just keyed in by highlighting it (otherwise you will change your entire document). Adjust the margins at both the left and right sides of the new text. Check your work and save.

Indents

There are three types of paragraph indent, all of which can be increased or decreased in width. (You can do this using the Indentation boxes in the Paragraph dialogue box shown in Figure 1.27). Figure 1.30 is an illustration of each type of indentation.

Figure 1.30 Indents

Did you know?

Many people confuse indents with margins. They are not the same. Left and right margin settings specify the distance between the text and the edges of the page. An indent is the distance between the text and the margins. (You should be able to tell the difference between indents and margins by studying Figure 1.30 carefully.)

ACTIVITY

Open your Layout Reference log and enter the next heading 'Indents'. Look up how to indent paragraphs in the application you are using. Key in the following text:

```
Margin settings specify the
distance between the text and the
edges of the page. An indent is
the distance between the text and
the margins.
```

Using a copy and paste technique, copy the text once more. Put a first line indent into the first copy of the text and a hanging indent into the second. Check the indents have come out as you specified and save your work.

Tabulations

Tabulations (better known as tab stops or just tabs) are standardised distances across the page, usually set by default at every ½ inch, where you can line up columns of text or numbers, etc. By using tabs you will ensure that text or numbers inserted at different points across the page will all line up correctly. In most word processing programs you can change the tabs on the horizontal ruler, and you can specify whether you want them left, centre or right aligned or decimal (see Figure 1.31).

A special type of tab (useful for directing the reader's eye across the page in a contents list, for example), is a leader character. This is a solid, dotted or dashed line that fills in the space usually left blank when you press the tab key – for example:

'Unit 1 ---------------- Presenting Information.'

You will practise using this later in this chapter.

? Did you know?

Less experienced ICT users often position text by pressing the space bar. Then, when they want to make changes, it takes a long time to delete all those spaces. Make sure you use tabs and indent settings correctly so that you can easily make changes as and when necessary.

123	123	123.99	123
12345	12345	12345.99	12345
1.99	1.99	1.99	1.99

Left-aligned tab   Right-aligned tab   Decimal tab   Centred tab

Figure 1.31 Tabulations

ACTIVITY

In your log enter the new heading 'Tabulations'. Find out how to set tabs as left, centre or right aligned in the application you are using. Key in the following text:

```
Tabulations (better known as tab
stops or just tabs) are
standardised distances across the
page. By using tabs you will ensure
that text or numbers inserted at
different points across the page
will all line up correctly.
```

Copy the example in Figure 1.31 using the tabs shown. Check your work and save.

Font styles and sizes

You can change the font (the style of the lettering) and the font size of any amount of selected text, and even of single characters. In business documents, however, your choice of font and font size should be guided by clarity. When the font is easy to read, the message gets across. No matter how interesting or attractive you think a particular font is, always ask yourself if it is easy to read. The same applies to using a range of fonts – limit yourself to as few as possible. Look at this example:

How ᵉᵃˢʸ do you find **it** to <u>read</u> **this sentence**?

Does it look professional and attractive, or does it look clumsy and amateurish?

As well as font types and sizes, most word processing programs offer a choice of font styles and effects. The most common styles are *italic*, **bold**, ***bold italic*** and <u>underline</u>. The most common effects are as follows:

- ~~Strikethrough~~
- SMALL CAPS

- Superscript

- Subscript

- ALL CAPS

Figure 1.32 shows a dialogue box where you can choose font styles and sizes as well as apply some of these effects.

ACTIVITY

Open your Layout Reference log and enter the next heading 'Fonts'. Find out how to change font type, size, style and effects in the application you are using. Key in what you have learnt using different fonts, sizes, styles, etc. For example:

To change font type   Select . . .

To change **font size**   Select . . .

To change *font style*   Select . . .

To change font effects   Select . . .

When you finish, save the file.

Page numbering

You would think that page numbering was a simple matter of inserting a number instruction in the footer, then right aligning it. In fact, there are many options: you can place numbers in the header or footer, left, centre or right align them, and can change their fonts (see Figures 1.33 and 1.34).

You can also include text with page numbers, for example 'Page 3'.

If you click the Format button, another dialogue box appears (see Figure 1.34). You can choose to start numbering on a page other than the first page of your document – that is, you can specify which page to start

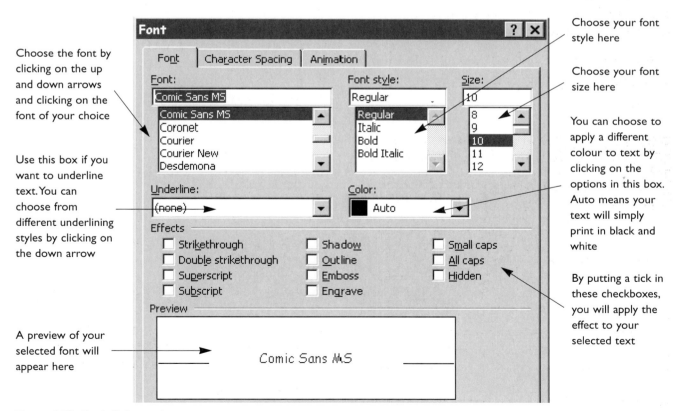

Choose the font by clicking on the up and down arrows and clicking on the font of your choice

Use this box if you want to underline text. You can choose from different underlining styles by clicking on the down arrow

A preview of your selected font will appear here

Choose your font style here

Choose your font size here

You can choose to apply a different colour to text by clicking on the options in this box. Auto means your text will simply print in black and white

By putting a tick in these checkboxes, you will apply the effect to your selected text

Figure 1.32 Font dialogue box

Click on the down arrow to choose the position on the page for your page numbers

Choose how you want to align your page numbers here

If you put a tick in this checkbox the first page of your document will have a page number (usually 1). You might decide not to number the first page – for example, the first page of a two-page letter

You will see a preview of your chosen style in this box

This allows you to select a style as shown below.

Figure 1.33 Page numbers dialogue box

If you tick this checkbox (to include the chapter number with the page number), you can choose from the heading styles listed on the right. A separator is the character that will separate your chapter number from the page number

Click on this arrow to display the different number formats and choose from the options displayed

If you put a dot in the first bullet your page numbering will continue from where you left off numbering your document. If you put a dot in the second bullet, you can specify at which number you want the page numbering here to start from

Figure 1.34 Page Number Format dialogue box

numbering at. This is particularly useful if several people are working on a long document. You might also want to change the page number format so that different sections of a document, such as the introduction, main content and appendices, are numbered differently.

Check the introduction for this book – are the page numbers in a different style?

ACTIVITY

Open your Layout Reference log and type the new heading 'Page Numbering'. Look through the options available on the program you are using for formatting numbers and make a note of them in your log. Then choose a format and place your numbers in the right-hand corner of your footer. Save your work.

Earlier in this chapter you learnt about leader characters. You are now going to create a Contents list for your log using leader characters. First, find out how to insert leader characters in the application you are using then go back to the very first page of your log and, after the main heading 'Layout Reference', insert a new subheading 'Contents'. Next, leave a few blank lines after this heading and then insert a hard page break so the subheading 'Line Spacing' moves to a new page. (Your page numbering should automatically adjust itself to take account of the new page you have created.) Now position your cursor on the second blank line after the heading 'Contents' and create a right tab near the right margin.

Copy in all the subheadings you have included in your log so far leaving a clear line between each entry, and use leader characters after each heading so that you can insert the relevant page number at the end of each entry. (You will learn more about contents and indexes later in this chapter.)

Column layout

There are three basic types of column layout; newspaper columns, positioned columns and columns in tables (see Figure 1.35).

Most word processing programs enable you to arrange all or part of your document in newspaper columns. The text flows from the bottom of one column to the top of the next. You can also place lines between the columns. When you use columns, make sure you highlight the section of text you want in columns before executing the command. Otherwise you may put your entire document into columns.

When you need to adjust the amount of space between your columns, or the width of a selected column, drag the column marker (the line separating the columns) to its new position.

(a)

(b)

(c)

Figure 1.35 Basic column types: (a) newspaper columns; (b) positioned column; (c) table columns

A positioned column (see Figure 1.35) is when a graphic or a heading text takes up the first, narrower column and the main text takes up the other, wider column. Positioned columns are useful for inserting company logos and side headings, and for making circulars, etc., more interesting through the use of photographs and graphics.

 ACTIVITY

Open your Layout Reference log. Go to the Help menu to find out how to make newspaper columns. Key in the heading 'Columns', and then key in the entire paragraph above that begins 'Most

word processing programs enable you to arrange all or part of your document . . .' Convert your paragraph to three newspaper columns. Save the file.

Now add the new heading and its page number to your contents list.

White space

Areas of your document where there is no text or graphics are called white space. White space in a document is not necessarily a bad thing: a common mistake in document layout is to include too much information so that the page looks cluttered and too busy. This makes the page more difficult to read.

As telecommunications make more and more information available – faxes, e-mails, the Internet – it is increasingly important to design your pages in a way that allows readers to access the information they want quickly. People have neither the time nor the

patience to work through irrelevancies, and will likely pass over crowded documents to find another source of information.

Bullets and numbering

If you want to include a list in your document, you could either number each item in the list or give each item a bullet (see Figure 1.36). To do this, select Bullets and

Click the appropriate tab to select your choice of list

Click on one of the basic styles offered

Click here to customise your list once you have chosen a basic style from the alternatives offered

Figure 1.36 Bullets and Numbering dialogue box

Numbering from the Format menu. You can add bullets or numbers to individual sentences or a complete list (after you have selected these by highlighting them) either by clicking the bullet or number options in the dialogue box or by right-clicking your mouse and choosing from the options displayed in the menu. As you can see from Figure 1.36, choosing Bullets and Numbering from the menu bar allows you to select a style from the ones offered or you can customise the list to your own requirements.

Did you know?

In Word, if you begin a paragraph with a hyphen, the program automatically converts the paragraph to a bulleted item when you press enter to end the paragraph.

 ACTIVITY

Open your Layout Reference log and add the heading 'Bullets and Numbering'. Key in a short list of your favourite sports, film or pop stars and select the list by highlighting it. Click on the Format button and then on Bullets and Numbering. Choose a basic list style. Then click on the Customise button and experiment with the options shown (you will see the effects of your experiments in the Preview box). When you are satisfied with your customised list, click OK to apply it to the list of names you have keyed in. Save the file. Remember to add this new section to your Contents list.

Special symbols

You will sometimes need to insert a symbol or special character into a document that you cannot insert from those characters available on your keyboard – for example, © (the copyright symbol), é, Å, etc. To do this, position your cursor in the document where you wish to insert the symbol and, from the Insert menu, choose Symbol. The Symbol dialogue box will appear (see Figure 1.37). Choose your special symbol by clicking on it, click on Insert, then click on Close. The symbol will now be inserted into your document.

 ACTIVITY

Key in the heading 'Symbols' into your Layout Reference log. Find out how to open the Symbol dialogue box in the application you are using. Open this and then select Windings by clicking on the arrow in the Font box (see Figure 1.37). Select a few of your favourite symbols and insert these into your document. Copy the Windings symbol dialogue box into your document. Save your file. Don't forget the Contents!

Contents and indexes

Textbooks such as this one have a contents list at the beginning. Websites usually have contents buttons on their first pages. Many sites are also designed so that the contents list is on the screen somewhere at all times, no matter what page you go to.

Content lists show you the organisation of a document and help readers find their way around. They also serve as a sort of summary, showing you the main topics of the document. Whenever you prepare a document of several pages or more, such as a report or newsletter, you should add a contents list. If your document is very long, you may find it easier to use a 'create a table of contents list' wizard, if your word processing application offers you this facility.

Click on this tab to display a list of commonly used symbols and for a list of keyboard shortcuts you can use to insert these symbols

If the symbol you require is not in the options shown, click on this down arrow to display even more symbols!

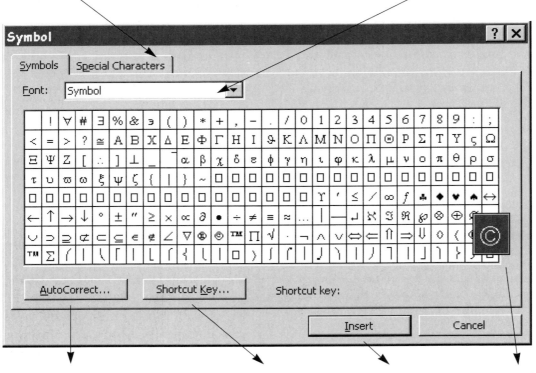

You can use this button to add your symbol to your AutoCorrect list. For example, when you key in a capital C, you can specify in Autocorrect to replace this with ©

You can use this button to create keyboard shortcuts to insert the symbol you have chosen

Click on Insert to insert your symbol, then on Close

When you have selected your symbol by clicking on it, it will appear larger like this

Figure 1.37 Symbol dialogue box

Much the same is true of indexes. Indexes are alphabetical lists of names, subjects, etc., with page numbers, and are usually positioned at the end of a book. Preparing an index manually is a long and difficult task. Most Help functions allow you to find what you need through the contents or the index. Use the Contents when you have only a general idea of what you're looking for. Use the Index when you know exactly what it is you're after.

Some word processing programs help you to prepare an index electronically. To do this you have first to mark the index entries in the document – the words or phrases you want to include in your index. Once you've marked all the index entries, you can choose an index design and finish the index from there. The program will collect all the index entries together, sort them into alphabetical order and give them the relevant page numbers.

Borders and shading

Borders are the edges or lines around a table, a paragraph or a selected piece of text in a document. You can add a border to any or all sides of an object or to any or all sides of each page in a document. As you can see from Figure 1.38, you can choose different border settings and you can also choose your border's line style, width and colour.

You can use shading to fill in the background of a table, a paragraph or of selected text (click on the Shading tab shown in the dialogue box in Figure 1.38 to open the shading options). The choices for shading usually include colours and how light or dark you would like the shading to be (expressed as a percentage, where jet black is 100% and

Click on the up and down arrows to view border styles, then click on the style of your choice

A preview of your border appears here. You can remove or add sides either by clicking on the preview of your chosen style or by clicking on the four little buttons round the preview

Click here on the border setting you wish to use

Click on this button to view the colours you can apply to your border. 'Auto' means the border will be applied in simple black and white

Choose the width of your border here

Use this box to choose where to apply your border

If you click on this button a dialogue box is displayed where you can alter the position of the text in your selected border

Figure 1.38 Borders and Shading dialogue box

light grey is 5%). Be careful not to use too dark a background because it can make the object or text difficult to read. You can also choose to shade with lines (e.g. diagonal, horizontal, grid and so on).

ACTIVITY

In your Layout Reference log, add the heading 'Borders and Shading'. Find out how to add a border in the application you are using. Key in the following text:

Borders are the edges or lines around a table, paragraph or a selected piece of text in a document.

Put this text into one narrow column. Now add a border of your choice to the text.

Find out how to add shading in the application you are using and then key in the following text:

You can use shading to fill in the background of a table, a paragraph or of selected text.

Again, arrange this text as a narrow column and apply a shading of your choice. Check your work and save. Have you remembered to alter the Contents?

ACTIVITY

Look through your Layout Reference log carefully and make any improvements you think necessary.

- Have you included everything on the contents list?

- Are the headers and footers positioned well on the page?

- Are all the page breaks in the correct places?

- Is the page numbering correct?

Don't forget to use all the tools available to help you improve your log – spell check, grammar check, Print Preview, etc. When you have made all your improvements to your log and you are happy with it, print it out and resave it. Keep your Layout Reference log in your working file for future reference.

After studying this unit you will be able to:

- understand what information handling means and how it is used

- create a database to store and process records

- create a spreadsheet to store and process numerical information

- search, sort, explore and predict information

- discover trends and patterns from numerical information

- understand and develop good practice and standard ways of working with ICT.

You will need to learn about:

- information handling

- handling techniques

- designing information handling systems

- database methods

- spreadsheet methods.

To do this effectively you will need to use standard ways of working, which has already been covered in the Preparatory Unit. Keep referring back to this unit to make sure you are using correct procedures.

Unit 2 will be assessed through your portfolio work. You will need to produce a relational database and a spreadsheet to meet the needs of a given business situation. You will be expected to:

- identify the requirements of the user

- set up a system to meet those requirements

- enter appropriate data into the system

- check for accuracy

- search the system to find specified information

- print out the results of the search.

You will need to make notes which:

- explain the purpose of the system – i.e. the user requirements

- show the planning stage *before* you actually set up the system
- describe the system you create – this might include screen dumps as well as annotated printouts
- demonstrate the operation of the system – printouts of information requested.

You must also produce an evaluation of your work, e.g.:

- How successful are your database and spreadsheet?
- Which aspects would you retain?
- What improvements or changes would you make?
- How effectively do they meet the user's needs?

You are expected to use a wide variety of information sources to obtain data, but you can undertake this as a team and pool your resources. However, the design and implementation of the system must be the *individual* work of each student.

CHAPTER 2.1 INFORMATION HANDLING

During the course of your studies, in your future employment and, indeed, in life in general, you will need to find all kinds of information. One of the benefits of computers is that they can give you access to vast amounts of data (from which it is possible to discover all kinds of information) *very quickly*. But what do we mean by the words **data** and **information**?

Data and information

Data are small, individual details such as a second name, a first name or a date of birth. *Information* is what can be discovered from the data. For example, if the coach of a karate club wanted to start a junior league for players under the age of 16, this information could be found out by checking the dates of birth of the members in the database – the data (Figure 2.1).

Data		Information
Names	Dates of birth	Names of members eligible to join the junior league
Smith, John	31/01/37	No
Patel, Nisha	23/10/88	Yes

Figure 2.1 Data and information

It would be perfectly possible to find this same information from a manual system (from record cards, for example) but if there were two thousand members in this club it would be very time-consuming to search through the cards manually, whereas a computer system could find the information very quickly.

Sources of information

The sources of information are very varied – people, written publications of all kinds, television and radio, computers. The method of obtaining information will, of course, vary depending on what you need to know. Table 2.1 looks at some examples related to the specific sources mentioned in the standards concerning your programme of study.

Did you know?

For the first time, in March 1999, '11 musicians in five countries united on the Internet to record a single in a record time of one hour, as a Megalab charity fund-raising stunt'. (*The Daily Telegraph,* 18 March 1999).

More than 70,000 Web sites are added to the World Wide Web every hour. Internet traffic is doubling every month, and it is estimated that revenue from electronic transactions could reach £2,000 billion by 2003 (from *The Daily Telegraph,* 25 January 2000).

ACTIVITY

1   Design a simple questionnaire to find out what types of information sources people use and which ones they prefer to use. Your first question might be 'What different kinds of sources can you think of which provide you with information?' You might then compile a list of possible sources and ask 'Which of the following sources of information do you use: regularly, occasionally or never?' Then conduct a survey amongst approximately six people you know, choosing people in different age groups. Compare the results with the rest of your class. Did you find that most people in a

Source	Information available
People	This may not seem an obvious source of information, but when you enrolled for this course you had to give details about yourself, such as your name, address, date of birth and so on.
	Have you ever been stopped in the street to answer questions for a market research survey? The answers given are analysed to provide information on all sorts of topics, e.g.:
	• which football team you support
	• who your favourite pop star is
	• where you usually buy your groceries
	• for whom you will vote in the next election.
	Have you ever asked people for information, e.g.:
	• A tutor when you applied for this course?
	• A friend or member of your family about what it is like to work for a particular company, if you were thinking of applying for a job with that company?
Books	Encyclopaedias, reference books or textbooks provide information on virtually anything you could wish to know about. You are already using this textbook as the source of information for the GNVQ in ICT.
	Contents pages or the indexes in books can be very useful to help you find the information you want.
Directories	Probably one of the most frequently used directories is the telephone directory. You might wish to look up a personal telephone number (which would be listed alphabetically) or you might want to find the names of local driving schools, in which case the classified sections in the *Yellow Pages* are invaluable.
Computer databases	Virtually all businesses, schools and colleges have computerised databases which contain details about customers, students, staff, orders received, products available, goods sold, etc.
Television, radio and newspapers	All three give us the news, weather reports, sports results but, whereas a newspaper is up to date only at the time of going to press, television and radio can supply the latest details.
	If you wanted to check football or tennis results, you might look at Ceefax or Teletext (which are examples of *public databases*) or you might prefer to look in a newspaper because it will give a more detailed report about the match.
Timetables	You may have a printed timetable for your local train station. This is a very convenient way of checking what time the next train leaves. However, if you want to travel from London to Chester, you aren't likely to have this timetable available. You could look it up on the Internet – www.railtrack.co.uk – or you might go to the station to book your ticket. The ticket officer used to look in an enormous book giving all UK train times. Nowadays he or she is more likely to check via the computerised database.
	Travel Agents will look up flight details on a computerised timetable and, if you decide to book, the reservation can be made immediately.
CD-ROMs	A wide variety of CD-ROMs are now produced for use with computers, e.g. software such as Microsoft Office, computer games, encyclopedias, some newspapers (regularly updated) and study aid CD-ROMs on all kinds of topics. Most libraries will have copies of these CD-ROMs.
	Imagine you are writing an essay on Shakespeare's *Hamlet* and want to check the rest of the famous quotation 'To be or not to be'. If you ever had to find information like this at school, you will know how time-consuming it is to search through a play or book to find an exact reference. How much easier and quicker it is to use a CD-ROM to search for that phrase.

▶

Source	Information available
	If you were researching a famous person, how much quicker it would be to use *The Times Newspaper* CD-ROM rather than looking through back copies of newspapers in libraries to find relevant articles.
	A CD-ROM called *UK – INFO DISK* holds addresses and telephone numbers for the UK. This can be a very useful tool for companies searching for potential customers but, on a more simple level, it can be used to find post-codes or telephone numbers (unless the number is ex-directory).
	Suppliers sometimes provide customers with a CD-ROM (giving details of products and prices) to help with ordering. TESCO Direct provides a CD-ROM which enables you to download from the Internet the goods available and their prices. You can then make your selection off-line (so you are not paying for Internet time whilst you make your selection) and, when you are ready, you upload your order which will be delivered at a time of your choice the following day.
Instruction manuals	Products such as irons, kettles, washing machines, etc., usually come with an instruction manual. Software for programs such as Word also come with instruction manuals, but more and more these days the hard copy manual is very slim or even non-existent. Nowadays, the program documentation is more likely to be included in the CD-ROM, together with the help files, or further assistance can often be found on the Web. Sometimes the help files are not very user-friendly but this situation is improving.
Magazines	There are magazines for every conceivable interest a person might have. Articles are written on every subject from makeup to home improvements, pop stars' weddings to the funerals of the famous. Most magazines also include relevant advertisements. For example, the wide variety of magazines that are available on computers include advertisements for all kinds of hardware and software, but you would not expect to see advertisements about jewellery or clothes.
Class notes	Your teacher/lecturer will undoubtedly expand on the information given in this textbook from his or her own knowledge and experience. He or she will brief you on assignments, often giving additional pointers on the tasks. You are unlikely to remember these tips unless you make notes at the time.
The Internet	This source has deliberately been left to last in the list as, arguably, it can provide information that is available from all the other sources except your own class notes.
	The Internet expands daily and more and more businesses have established their own Web sites. It can be used to find information, to book hotels or holidays and, as already mentioned, to order goods that are delivered to your door.
	You can find out about everything, from the First World War to volcanoes, from the results of NASA's latest space exploration to the most up-to-date medical research.
	The Internet is a bonus to those who are housebound, enabling them to keep in touch with the outside world.

Table 2.1 Sources of information

particular age group prefer the same type of information source?

2   Look in a newspaper for the football results – or for the results of any sport of your choice – and compare the information you find against that which is available on Teletext or Ceefax.

3   Find out which CD-ROMs are available in your school or college library. Make a list of the ones that may be useful to you in your GNVQ studies. Select one and print out a topic of your choice.

4   Choose a famous person who interests you and search *The Times Newspaper* CD-ROM to find articles on that person. Print at least three of these.

5   Search the Internet for the following Web sites:

- www.vauxhall.co.uk – select a car and print out the relevant information.

- www.railtrack.co.uk – select a major town in another part of the country as your destination and find out which trains you could catch from your local station to arrive at your chosen destination on a weekday by 5.00 pm.

6 Using the Internet, find out about the Jorvik Centre in York.

Design of an information handling system

The efficiency of a computer system depends on the way the data has been organised or structured. When a computer-based system is either being designed or modified, it is very tempting to start designing the system or to make changes to the system without giving some thought to what you want the system to do or achieve. This approach is rarely successful and, the more complex the system, the more important it is to *think* and *plan* **before** launching into the design. This planning and thinking stage is known as systems analysis. Systems analysis involves the following stages:

1 *Initial study:*

  - What is the purpose of the system – what data do we need to enter into the system?

  - What are the needs of the users – what information do they need to obtain from the system?

  - What processing is required – what kind of searching, sorting or calculating will be needed?

2 *A feasibility study* It may be very expensive to introduce or update a computer system and, therefore, it is important to compare costs and benefits – including the cost of hardware, software and training.

3 *Systems investigation and analysis* The detailed stage where the system is *designed* to achieve the objectives already set out in the initial study.

4 *Implementation* Only at this stage is the actual ICT system set up. This stage also includes testing the system to check it does what it was intended to do.

5 *Maintenance* It is important to maintain the system in order to:

  - resolve problems which occur, despite earlier testing

  - address changing needs

  - take advantage of improvements in hardware and software as and when these become available.

Once the ICT system has been established it will be necessary to undertake the following:

1 Identify and collect the required data – this may be existing data taken from a manual system already in use or new data (e.g. the name and address of a new customer).

2 Enter the data into the system, proofread the data to check for accuracy and edit the data as necessary.

3 Process the information required from the data.

Handling techniques

In the next three chapters, we are going to look at three different computerised methods of handling data which you must be able to *use*:

- record-structured databases

- spreadsheet (number-structured) databases

- hypertext databases.

In order to fulfil the requirements for Unit 2, you are also expected to *design*:

- record-structured databases

- spreadsheet (number-structured) databases.

However, before you can design an effective system, you need to learn more about databases and spreadsheets.

CHAPTER 2.2 DATABASE METHODS

What do we mean by a record-structured database (usually referred to simply as a database)? A database is any organised collection of data or information. It might not be very well organised, but your personal address or telephone book is a database. Card index systems or filing cabinets are also databases. The more phone numbers or other information you add to your database, the more space you need and the harder it is to find the precise piece of information you want. Imagine the amount of information kept by government agencies such as MI5, the CIA or Interpol. Even small businesses will need to store and access databases of information. For example, a local newspaper will have a database on subscribers, advertisers, writers and so on. A computer-based system can store vast amounts of data in its memory, organised for easy access by authorised users.

In today's world, data about us will be held in numerous databases, often without us even realising it. Have you ever done any of the following:

- Subscribed to a magazine?
- Opened a bank or building society account?
- Applied for a driving licence?
- Paid for goods or services with a debit or credit card?
- Applied to a college?
- Joined a club or society?

If you have done any of the items in this list then details about you will be stored in a database file.

In simple terms a database is a store of *related* data. In an address book you will have the same types of data for each person, such as:

- last name
- first name
- address
- telephone number
- and, possibly, date of birth.

These days we tend to think of databases as existing only in computers, but databases have always existed. It used to be commonplace in offices to use card index boxes (Figure 2.2). Each card would be written out with the same kind of details, just like in an address book, and most often filed in alphabetical order. This too is a database.

Figure 2.2 A paper-based card index system

ACTIVITY

Think about an employment agency. What details do you think the agency might need to obtain from someone who wishes to register with them?

The following index card has been started for you, but what other details would be useful?

Last name:	First Name:
Street:	
Town:	

So what has changed? If you can simply flick through a set of cards in a small box sitting conveniently on your desk, why bother with a computerised database? Table 2.2. lists some of the advantages of computerised databases and some of the disadvantages of paper-based card index systems.

Let's look at a computerised database in more detail.

Database structure

A database consists of a *file* which contains many *records*.

Records

Each record includes the *fields* into which will be entered the appropriate *data*. Each record contains the same fields but, sometimes, a field is left blank in a particular record (e.g. if someone does not have a telephone, then the field for telephone number will be left blank).

A database file is in effect a collection of records (see Figure 2.3).

Cover the diagram in Figure 2.3. See if you can label the record in Figure 2.4.

Tables

A database record can be designed in the style that bests suits you – just as forms for different purposes are designed and laid out differently. When you look at a record on screen, you see just one record at a time (known as Form View) – just like looking at one card from a card index box. However, there may be times when you need to do more than simply view one record at a time. You might, for example, want to see a list of the records arranged under the different field names, or a list of certain selected fields only. In a computerised database it is possible to have such a list by using Table View. In this

Computerised databases – advantages	Card index systems – disadvantages
A vast amount of data can be stored on one disk	You would need many, many boxes to store the same quantity of data
Records are entered once but can be *searched* in all kinds of ways (e.g. alphabetically, numerically, selectively, by date, etc.)	If the index cards are stored alphabetically but you would also like them in, say, order of age, *a second set of cards* would need to be written and stored in date order
Searching is fast – even in a huge database	Searching can be very slow
Data can be lost but could be retrieved if backups are kept	Cards are easily lost, filed in the wrong place or mislaid
Can perform calculations (e.g. you could ask the database to calculate the VAT on a price and give the cost price, VAT and total price. If the rate of VAT changes, it is quick and easy to update this)	The calculations would have to be written out manually. It is difficult and slow to update records

Table 2.2 The advantages of computerised databases and the disadvantages of paper-based card index systems

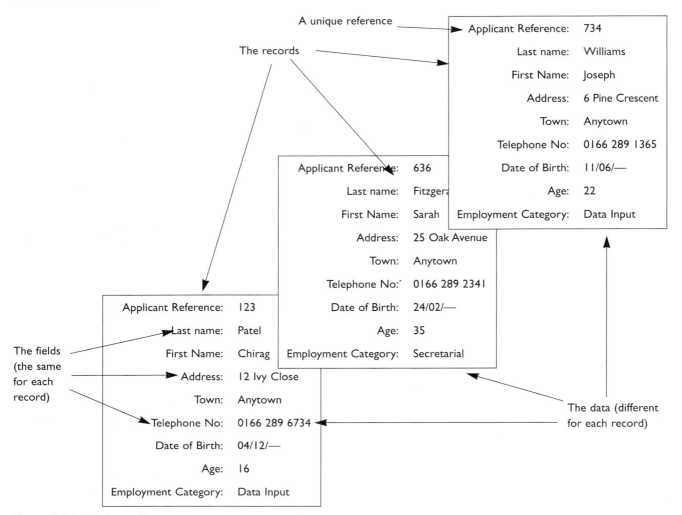

Figure 2.3 A database file

Note: See if you can label Figure 2.4.

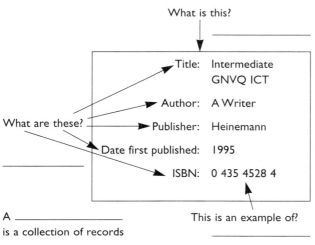

Figure 2.4 A diagram to complete

format each *row* is equivalent to one *record*, and each *column* is the equivalent of one *field*. You can choose whether to display all the fields in the row or just those required on this particular occasion (e.g. you might just want names and telephone numbers). In Table View, the three records shown in Figure 2.3 would appear like Figure 2.5.

This is much more convenient than looking at each individual record, especially if there is a large number of records relevant to a particular search. In practice, of course, an employment agency would probably have

The column headings are the field names

Applicant Reference	Last name	First Name	Address	Town	Telephone No	Date of Birth	Age	Employment Category
123	Patel	Chirag	12 Ivy Close	Anytown	0166 289 6734	04/12/–	16	Data Input
636	Fitzgerald	Sarah	25 Oak Avenue	Anytown	0166 650 2341	24/02/–	35	Secretarial
734	Williams	Joseph	6 Pine Crescent	Anytown	0166 289 1365	11/06/–	22	Data Input

} rows

Figure 2.5 Database records shown in Table View

hundreds of applicants listed in its database rather than just three as shown here.

Let's imagine that a new job as a data input clerk becomes available for a school leaver. It would be possible to *ask* the database for a list showing just the names and telephone numbers of relevant applicants who were aged between 15 and 20 years. This is known as a *query*. The resulting search might look like Figure 2.6.

Last name	First Name	Telephone No	Age	Employment Category
Patel	Chirag	0166 289 6734	16	Data Input

Figure 2.6 The results of a query

ACTIVITY

In a sophisticated database, the age field would *not* be entered as a number but would be calculated from the member's date of birth and today's date, which would be permanently stored in the computer. Why would this be a better way of recording the members' ages, rather than simply keying in their age?

Figure 2.7 shows the differences between Form View and Table View when looking through a database file.

Table View

One table
↓
Many rows
↓
Specific fields
↓
Data

Applicant Reference	Surname	First Name	Address	Town	Telephone No	Date of Birth	Age	Employment Category
123	Patel	Chirag	12 Ivy Close	Anytown	0166 289 6734	04/12/–	16	Data Input
636	Fitzgerald	Sarah	25 Oak Avenue	Anytown	0166 650 2341	24/02/–	35	Secretarial
734	Williams	Joseph	6 Pine Crescent	Anytown	0166 289 1365	11/06/–	22	Data Input

Figure 2.7 Form View and Table View

Database design

Students on an ICT course understandably like to get their fingers on the keyboard/mouse. They don't really want to *write* anything! However, as we have already seen, when planning a computerised database it is very important *to think carefully* about the design *before* you start creating the fields. For example, it would be perfectly possible to create every field as text because text allows you to enter *both* letters and numbers into a field. However, if you did use all text fields you would not be able to make calculations (such as finding out the VAT on the price of an item). You would similarly not be able to use dates of birth to search for people in a particular age range. You would not be able to search easily for a particular category, such as 'data input' shown in Figure 2.6. To be able to do these tasks, the field for the price of the item would have to be *numerical*, the field for dates of birth would have to be a *date* field and it will be much easier to find a category if they were specified in a *choice* field. Let's look at this in more detail.

Setting up a computerised database

Once you are clear about the purpose of your database, you have to decide on the following:

1 *The fields you need* In other words, the *names* of the fields (e.g. last name, date of birth, etc.). The name of the field indicates which data should be entered into it.

2 *The data type for each field* You could just use text for everything in your database because text will accept both letters and numbers. However, as we have just seen, your database would be much less effective when it comes to searching and it would not be possible to do calculations.

3 *The length of the fields* In other words, how many characters are you going to

allow in a particular field? With fields such as names and addresses, obviously you need to allow enough space to enter a long name or long street reference (although it is possible to increase the length of the field later, if necessary). On the other hand, you would not design a field with decimal places for the price of a house – house prices are not quoted as £56,789.58p, but a price field for items in a stationer's shop would be quite different, and so decimal places would be appropriate. Hence you might fix the length of the field for a house price at seven digits, which would allow a price up to £9,999,999. For stationer's items, you would probably fix the length at three spaces to the left and two to the right of the decimal point, which would allow prices up to £999.99.

It is good practice to have just enough space for the data you wish to enter but not to allow more space than necessary, as extra, unused space can waste the memory capacity of the computer.

Field data types

Table 2.3 lists some typical fields that are useful in a database (please note, however, that you may not find all these data types in the database program you are using).

ACTIVITY

Look back at the index card given in the activity earlier in this chapter. Include the extra fields you have identified and decide what type of field they should be and their length. Plan this out on *paper* – a form to assist you is available in the tutor's resource file. Your database will, undoubtedly, be much more effective and less likely to require changes if you do take this planning stage seriously. You will then be ready to create the database file.

Type of field	Purpose	Advantages/possible uses
Text/character (Sometimes called alphanumeric)	Any data (letters, numbers or symbols on the keyboard) can be entered into a text field	• Names/addresses • Where you might need to include extra detail/description
Numerical *Integer*	Whole numbers (the number of digits can be restricted to a specified length, e.g. 3. This will limit space to a maximum of three digits, e.g. 156)	• Restricts data entry to whole numbers • Cannot enter more than the specified number of digits • Reduces the risk of errors • Can be listed in numerical order • Can ask for a list of items above/ below or equal to a specific number
Decimal	Numbers with decimal places (you can usually decide on how many digits to the right and how many to the left of the decimal point, e.g. 15.67)	• Suitable for money where prices include pence (£15.67) • Measurements (4.25 km)
Currency	Can be set as an integer or with decimal places	Would show only the currency specified (e.g. £5.67, $287, € 18)
Counter or Autonumber	A numeric value. As each new record is entered the counter automatically selects the next number in the sequence	• Suitable for a member ID, student ID or account no., etc. • The operator does not have to enter the number and, if a number has already been used, the computer will not allow you to use it again • Ensures that each member's ID, account no., etc., remains unique
Formula	The database can use a formula to make calculations for you	Given the cost price the database can calculate automatically, e.g.: • VAT • total price
Range check	A lower and/or upper limit	If items are priced in a range of £20–£50: • lower limit can be set at £20 • upper limit set at £50 • entries outside that range will not be allowed • reduces the risk of errors
Date	A typical date format will be prepared, e.g. --/--/--	• Restricts data entry to 1–31 for the day and 1–12 for the month • Reduces the risk of errors • Can be used to calculate a person's age, which will be automatically updated once his or her birthday has been passed Can search for: • birthdays in a given month • those older or younger than a given age • birthdays between particular dates

▶

75

Type of field	Purpose	Advantages/possible uses
Time	A typical time format will be prepared, e.g. --/--/--	• Can be used where employees are paid by the hour • Hours worked can be calculated from the times the workers clocked on and off • Wages can be calculated on the basis of the length of time worked

Choice
  Yes/no
 	
  Male/female
  True/false
 	
  Colours
      Red
      Blue
      Green
      Yellow
	Data entry is limited to yes or no – no other entry is allowed
	
	Data entry is limited to the predetermined selection
		• Speeds up data entry
		• Can search for all the 'yes' or all the 'no' entries
		
		• Can search for specific entries, such as 'male', 'true' or 'green'

Table 2.3 Fields used in databases

Relationships

Just as a book is divided into chapters, when a database is designed it is usual and indeed good practice to divide it into two or more sections known as *tables*. These tables are *related* or connected to each other, and this saves having several separate files or one huge file. A database for a manufacturer would have many related tables but let's consider just two related tables, one for 'Customer' and one for 'Order'.

The 'Customer' table would include the following fields:

• Account No (a unique reference number)

• Name

• Address

• Town

• Post Code

• Telephone No

• Contact Person

The 'Order' table would include these fields:

• Order No (each order would have a unique reference)

• Account No (a unique reference number)

• Date of order

• Catalogue Reference (each item in a catalogue has its unique reference)

• Description

• Price

• Quantity

In order to be able to connect the tables it is essential that one unique field is repeated in each of the linked tables. Look again at the examples opposite and you will see that the fields for Account No link the tables (this field, and *only* this field, occurs in *both* tables). Figure 2.8 also illustrates the way these two tables are linked.

When tables are linked in this way, it is possible to search each table separately or to

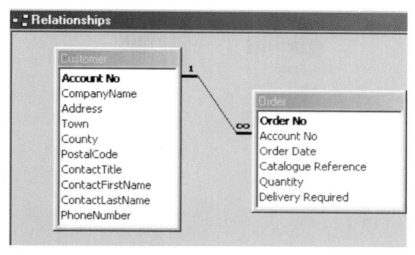

Figure 2.8 The relationship between two tables in a manufacturer's database

select fields from both tables. From the *data* in these databases it would be possible to find out *information*, such as:

1   the contact person for a given customer

2   the name of the customer who placed a particular order

3   the items ordered by a particular customer over a period of, say, 6 months

4   the items included in a particular order.

(*Note*: For purposes of understanding database relationships this explanation has been limited to two tables but, if you study databases at a more advanced level, you will learn about the more complex relationships that would exist in, for example, a manufacturer's stock file.)

Did you know?

The sophisticated facilities of modern databases assist the police in fighting crime. Whereas at one time only the basic details of a criminal would be entered into the records system, nowadays it is possible to link records concerning crime, custody details and other intelligence details. The system also has the ability to record a criminal's photo, so the arresting officer can easily check someone's identity and hence tell whether he or she is a known criminal. Details on known criminals can be immediately e-mailed to other police officers who may have a special interest in that person (taken from *IT Training*, 14 July 1999).

Key fields – primary and foreign

We have already seen that each record in a database usually has one unique field which identifies that record as different from every other record in the file or, in table format, that identifies each row from every other row. This field is known as the *primary key*. No doubt when you enrolled at school or college you were given a student ID number, which is different from every other student ID number. It is essential that the primary key is unique, otherwise the computer will not be able to identify the exact record required. Records are automatically sorted in order of the primary key.

When this unique field is used in another table it is known as a *foreign key*. Look again at the example of the manufacturer's database to identify the primary and foreign keys (see Figure 2.9).

Table	Primary key	Foreign key
Customer	Account No	
Order	Order No	Account No Catalogue Reference

Figure 2.9 Primary and foreign keys

ACTIVITY

1   Refer back to Figure 2.5. Decide which other tables might be included in the employment agency's database.

2   Identify the fields required in these tables and then decide:

- the field data type and length
- the field length
- the primary key for each table
- the key field that would link the tables together
- the foreign keys in the tables, if any.

Entering data and editing the database

Once you have created the fields and built the relationships, you are now ready to enter the data. Just as with a word processor, editing a database is usually much easier than editing a manual system. From time to time you may need to:

- add new fields or change existing ones
- amend (change or alter) a record – e.g. if an address changes
- append (add) a new record – e.g. a new customer

- delete (remove) a record – e.g. a product is discontinued.

If you need to amend or delete a record, it is very easy to find the correct one in a computerised system – you simply enter suitable data (e.g. an account number) into the correct field and *ask* the computer to search the database. It will very quickly locate the record required.

When you add a new record to the database, it will automatically be filed in the correct order of the primary key. Any fields that have been indexed (see 'Selection of index key' below) will also be updated automatically.

Searching the database

Searching the database to find specific information is known as submitting a query. The query defines the parameters (i.e. what you need to know). The result of your query may be presented on screen or printed on paper. Figure 2.6 is an example of a database query. To obtain this information from a manual system where the applicants' cards were filed alphabetically, it would have been necessary to:

- look at each individual card
- check whether the category of job on each card was 'Data Input'
- remove the cards or write down the names and telephone numbers
- refile the cards (with every danger that cards will be lost or filed in the wrong place).

Imagine how long this would take if the employment agency had 500 applicants on its books! A computerised database will use the same criteria but will find the information very quickly. Remember, though, that if you design the database using only text fields,

Applicant Reference	Last name	First Name	Address	Town	Telephone No	Date of Birth	Age	Employment Category
636	Fitzgerald	Sarah	25 Oak Avenue	Anytown	0166 650 2341	24/02/–	35	Secretarial
123	Patel	Chirag	12 Ivy Close	Anytown	0166 289 6734	04/12/–	16	Data Input
734	Williams	Joseph	6 Pine Crescent	Anytown	0166 289 1365	11/06/–	22	Data Input

Figure 2.10 Database sorted in alphabetical order of last name

Applicant Reference	Last name	First Name	Address	Town	Telephone No	Date of Birth	Age	Employment Category
636	Fitzgerald	Sarah	25 Oak Avenue	Anytown	0166 650 2341	24/02/–	35	Secretarial
734	Williams	Joseph	6 Pine Crescent	Anytown	0166 289 1365	11/06/–	22	Data Input
123	Patel	Chirag	12 Ivy Close	Anytown	0166 289 6734	04/12/–	16	Data Input

Figure 2.11 Database sorted in descending order of age

searching for information will be very limited. When a query is made, fields such as date, number or choice will give you the opportunity to search for information as shown in Table 2.3. Let's now look in more detail at the different ways we can search the database.

Sort by selected key field

This simply means presenting a query in a particular order – e.g. alphabetical, numerical or in order of date. The order can be *ascending* (lowest to highest), i.e. A–Z or 1–100, or *descending* (highest to lowest), i.e. Z-A or 100-1. The query illustrated in Figure 2.5 might have been requested *in alphabetical order of surname* (the selected key field), in which case the report would have looked like Figure 2.10.

Alternatively, the query might have been requested *in descending order of age* (the selected key field), in which case the report would have looked like Figure 2.11.

Sometimes sorting has to be undertaken on two fields. For example, in a telephone directory, the *primary field* would be the last name but, as you know, many people have the same last name. In order to print the directory in alphabetical order, first names or initials are used as the *secondary field*. When the database is sorted into alphabetical order, the primary field of last name will be considered first, so that Brown comes before Evans, comes before Smith, etc. Then the first names or initials will be taken into account. In this way Smith, Alan, will be listed before Smith, Andrew (see Figure 2.12).

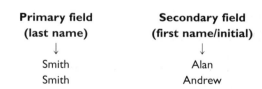

Figure 2.12 Sorting on two fields

ACTIVITY

Look at the index at the back of this book. Can you find any examples where the list has been sorted using two fields?

Relational operators

If you search a database using relational operators, you will be looking for a number greater than, less than or equal to:

<	less than
>	greater than
=	equal to
< >	not equal to
< =	less than or equal to
> =	greater than or equal to

(If, like me, you confuse the signs for *greater than* and *less than*, try to remember that **less than** < points to the **left**.)

The example in Figure 2.6 used relational operators, because the criteria for selection was applicants aged *greater than 14 and less than 20*. Using these criteria only applicants aged 15, 16, 17, 18 or 19 qualify.

Using the relational operators listed above limits the selection to the particular relational operator chosen.

Logical operators

When you search a database using logical operators, the criteria for selection is *and*, *or* or *not*. The computer checks to see whether it is *true* or *false* that any of the applicants, for example, match the criteria. If a *true* match is found, then the records will be displayed. Again the search shown in Figure 2.6 required applicants of a specific age *and* those who were suitable for a Data Input post. By including *and*, *or* or *not* in the search criteria, the selection is limited by the particular logical operator used.

Selection of index key

When you read a novel you generally start at the first page and carry on until the end (unless you like to cheat!) but, as you well know, a textbook is different and the reader often wants to look something up without reading all the previous pages. At the back of this book you will find an alphabetical list of the topics covered in the book and the page number where that topic can be found – the index. Without an index it would be very difficult to find a particular topic. Basically, the index makes it much quicker to *search* the book for the information required.

An index in a database is much the same. A field in a database can be indexed by categories. For example, 'category of job' would be a suitable field to index. Although indexing can speed up searching the database, it is not wise to index too many fields as each index will automatically be updated when records are added to or removed from the database, which might slow down the process. Choose fields to index that are likely to be used frequently in searches.

 ACTIVITY

Once again look back at the employment agency database. Which of the fields would be suitable to index?

Complex searches

A complex search is one where two or more criteria have been used for the search, as in Figure 2.6. The three criteria used in this search were applicants:

1 for Data Input jobs

2 aged >14

3 but < 20.

CHAPTER 2.3 SPREADSHEET METHODS

What do we mean by a number-structured database (usually referred to simply as a spreadsheet)? The main purpose of a spreadsheet is to store numerical data, and to make calculations using these data. Just as in a database, any other combination of numbers and non-numeric characters is treated as text. For example, '45 High Street' – the house number as part of an address – is considered to be text. The spreadsheet screen is divided into rows and columns, creating cells that look very much like the Table View in a record-structured database. Each row and column in a spreadsheet is unique so each cell can be identified rather like a map reference. The data is entered into the cell – the data might be a row or column heading, text, a date or a number.

Spreadsheet programs make financial tasks (such as calculating how much money you have) much easier. You might use a spreadsheet to work out how much spending money you'll have for your holiday: you can enter all the income you expect between now and July and also make deductions for your spending before July. You can then 'play around' to see what happens if you halve the money you plan to spend on clothes, or do two hours overtime on five Saturdays, or work on bank holidays. You wouldn't have to do all the sums again because the spreadsheet would recalculate for you. A business might use a spreadsheet to calculate the difference between how much money it receives from sales and how much it spends. The difference is the profit.

Sophisticated programs can link one worksheet or one file to another so that when you change the numbers on one sheet, the numbers in linked worksheets or files are updated automatically. For example, you might have one sheet showing the money you have saved and spent this month. When you get to next month you might want to carry the total over to a new sheet for the new month. You can use the program to link the two worksheets automatically. This means that, if you change a number in one month, the next month will also change.

Let's look at the structure of spreadsheets in more detail.

Cell format

This textbook could have been printed using a very small font without the use of **bold** or *italics* to emphasise headings and subheadings. The content would be the same, but it would be so much more difficult to read. An interesting, professional presentation is far more appealing to the reader. This is arguably even more important in a spreadsheet, because the majority of the data in it will be numerical. It becomes much easier to read the spreadsheet if attention is giving to formatting the cells in an appropriate manner. Just as in word processing software, you can enhance the text in a spreadsheet by:

- bold

- italics

- underline

- varying the font size for main or subheadings

- using different font styles.

(See Figure 2.14 version 2.)

In addition, you can improve the appearance of the spreadsheet by:

- centring a heading both horizontally across cells, or vertically within cells

- centring headings across columns

- adjusting the cell width or row height

- wrapping text within a cell to avoid having an extremely wide column, or using a vertical heading (see Figure 2.13)

- placing borders around or using colour for significant cells – e.g. ones with totals

- using shading or colour for the background of significant cells.

(Look again at Figure 2.14 version 2.)

When designing your spreadsheet you should also pay attention to the following:

- How many decimal places do you need, if any?

- Do you wish to show the currency symbol?

- If yes, is it too cluttered to show the £ sign everywhere, or might it be better to use it just for the totals?

- Showing negative numbers in red – which can be set automatically.

(Figure 2.15 illustrates some of the above points.)

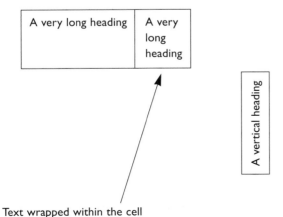

A vertical heading

Text wrapped within the cell

Figure 2.13 Wrapping text

Imagine you are starting up your own business making sandwiches to sell in local offices. You decide on a selection of sandwiches, and you wish to keep track of how many of each type you sell and how much revenue you earn from them. Figure 2.14 could be the start of simple business accounts using a spreadsheet program. You will notice that Figure 2.14 (Version 1) shows the spreadsheet with no attempt to improve its presentation, whereas Version 2 is a modified form of the same spreadsheet illustrating many of the points mentioned above.

Figure 2.15 shows the same spreadsheet with the totals and averages calculated through formulae entered as follows:

- cells F3 to F9 add up the number of sandwiches sold for the three months

- cells G3 to G9 multiply the price per sandwich by the total sold

- cell G10 adds up the total sales

- cell G11 calculates the average weekly sales.

ACTIVITY

1 Create a spreadsheet like the example in Figure 2.14. Don't forget to:

- format the cells with shading and borders as shown

- centre the main heading 'Select Sandwiches – Quarterly Sales' across columns A to G

- create formulae as indicated – check your results against the ones shown in Figure 2.15.

2 Save the file as **sandwich**.

Version 1 (notice that many of the column headings are too long to fit in the cells)

Version 2

Figure 2.14 Two versions of the same spreadsheet. Notice the difference between the two versions. In Version 1 there has been no attempt to improve the presentation by formatting the text, or by using borders or shading, compared to Version 2, where the formatting facilities that have been used enhance the appearance

Column headings formatted vertically and angled

Formulae here

Figure 2.15 The same spreadsheet when formulae have been entered

Technical terms

Formula

A formula is a sequence of values (numbers), cell references (e.g. D4) or operators (e.g. addition or multiplication) that produces a new value from existing values. The important point to remember is that, in Excel, *a formula always starts with an equals sign (=)*. This tells the spreadsheet that a calculation needs to be performed – not a number entered. A formula is used to make calculations – adding (+), subtracting (-), multiplying (*), dividing (/), finding the average or a percentage. The spreadsheet can do everything you can using a calculator – *but so much more.*

Formulae enable you to make a wide range of automatic calculations that take place instantaneously. You could key in a very simple formula, such as:

Formula	Result
=5*55	275

but, more typically, cell references are used in formulae. For example, in Figure 2.15:

The formula in cell F3 is   =SUM(C3:E3)
The formula in cell G3 is   F3*B3

Although formulae range from the easy to the very complicated, the basic formula types are used over and over again. It is worth getting to know some of these (see Figure 2.16). As long as you write the formula correctly, the results are never wrong. However, you need first to decide what you need to do *manually* and then find the most suitable formula.

The big advantage with formulae is that the spreadsheet will automatically recalculate if any changes are made in the data. For example, if the price of the chicken tikka sandwiches increases to £2.00, the value of the total sales will immediately increase. When you enter a formula into the spreadsheet the result is shown in the cell, but the actual formula used shows in the status line (see Figure 2.17).

Arithmetic operators

Formulae use what are called arithmetic operators and comparison operators (you will find out more about comparison operators

later on). This sounds complicated but it's quite straightforward. Arithmetic operators perform basic mathematical operations, such as addition, subtraction, division and so on. Look at Figure 2.16 where the following formulae have been used:

to	add	Cell D8	=D6+D7
	subtract	Cell D10	=D8–D9
	divide	Cell D11	=D10/12
	multiply	Cell D4	=B4*C4
	percentage	Cell D7	=D6*17.5%
		Cell D9	=D8*5%
	sum (total)	Cell D6	=sum(D3:D5)

Data View

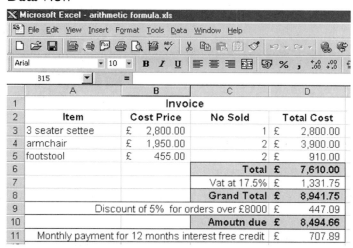

Formula View (to show the formulae in Excel, from the Tools menu, select: Options and click on the Formula box)

Figure 2.16. The basic arithmetic formulae that are most commonly used

ACTIVITY

1 Create a spreadsheet like the example in Figure 2.16 so that you can practise using the various formulae. This time the invoice should be for:

- 2 two-seater settees – £2,500 each
- 3 lampshades – £350 each
- 1 armchair
- 2 footstools.

Make sure you format the cells by using bold, shading and borders to improve the presentation.

2 Open the spreadsheet you saved as **sandwich**:

- Insert a new column for April sales.
- Enter the following data and notice that the totals and average will automatically recalculate:

	April
Egg Mayonnaise	334
Corned Beef & Salad	218
Ham & Tomato	256
Cheese & Pickle	160
Chicken Salad	345
Bacon Lettuce & Tomato	245
Chicken Tikka	321

Add a formula to calculate the monthly totals

3 What would be the benefit of keeping accurate sales of each type of sandwich, especially when setting up a new business?

4 What further improvements or additional information could be included in this spreadsheet to make it more useful?

Status line

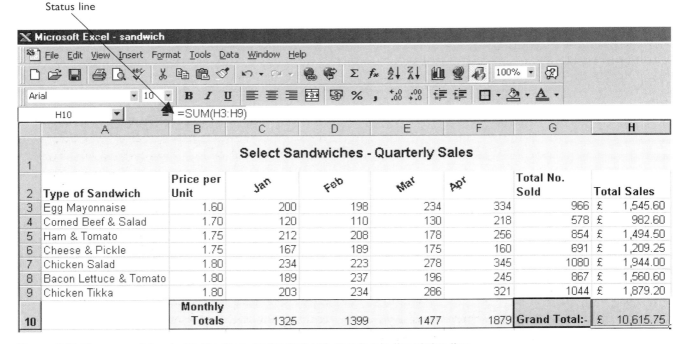

Figure 2.17 The spreadsheet with the formula for Cell H10 showing in the status line

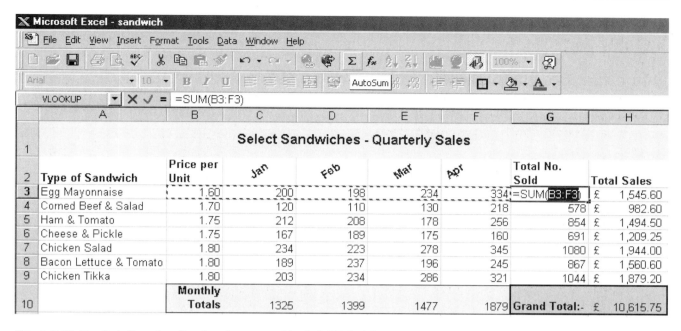

Figure 2.18 The AutoSum function has been used in Cell G3, but it has selected the range B3:F3, which includes the price of the sandwiches. In fact, only the range C3:F3 is necessary to obtain the total number sold. To correct the error you can enter C3:F3 yourself or scroll across cells C3 to F3

Function

Spreadsheet functions are simply formulae prewritten into the software, which you can use either on their own or as part of a more complex formula. The two you are going to use now are **SUM** and **Average**.

SUM

If you are using Microsoft Excel at your school or college, you will find the AutoSum icon Σ on the tool bar. If you wish to find the total of a column or row of figures, you select the cell at the bottom of the column or to the right of the row, simply click on the icon and the formula will be written for you. Did you use AutoSum to find out how many sandwiches are sold in each month or did you key in the formula each time? Do be careful when using AutoSum. It is important to check that Excel has selected the range of cells you require (see the example in Figure 2.18).

Average

When you calculate the average, you are not trying to establish the correct number but what is typical of a group or situation. You do this by adding up all the relevant totals, and dividing by the number of totals. For example, if you wanted to find the average age of the students in your group, you would add up all their ages and divide by the number of people in the group. Or if you wanted to check how much you spend on entertainment each week, you add up the total spent each week and divide by the number of weeks.

Figure 2.19 Finding the average: goals scored and sales to date

Figure 2.20 The formula view for finding the average

Figure 2.19 illustrates the point. You will notice that the record sales were never actually £4,423.43 but this was the average or typical sales, and clearly it is not possible to score nine-tenths of a goal, but on average My Town United scored nearly two goals each week.

Figure 2.20 illustrates the formula for calculating the average rather than the *result* of the formula shown in Figure 2.19. If you were working out yourself the average goals scored by My Town United, you would need to add up the total of goals scored (13), check how many games have been played (7), and then divide the total by the number of games played to obtain the result (1.9). The advantage of using the average function available in the spreadsheet is that these various stages are all worked out automatically for you.

Relative cell reference

One of the advantages of using a spreadsheet is the spreadsheet's facility to copy formulae across columns or down rows. It is very convenient to copy the formula rather than having to keep entering it again and again. For example, if you needed to have totals down several rows or across several columns, you can simply enter the formula into the first cell and then copy the formula across to the last column or down to the last row. The spreadsheet will automatically change the formula to give the correct cell reference.

Figure 2.21 shows Select Sandwiches' spreadsheet in Formula View. Notice the formulae in columns F and G. After entering the formula =F3*B3 in cell G3, it can be copied down the column, but the spreadsheet automatically changes the cell reference to

The total number sold for all types of sandwiches have now been included in Row 10. Notice how the formula references change as they are copied down Columns G and H and across Row 10

	A	B	C	D	E	F	G	H
1			Select Sandwiches - Quarterly Sales					
2	Type of Sandwich	Price per Unit	Jan	Feb	Mar	Apr	Total No. Sold	Total Sales
3	Egg Mayonnaise	1.60	200	198	234	334	=SUM(C3:F3)	=G3*B3
4	Corned Beef & Salad	1.70	120	110	130	218	=SUM(C4:F4)	=G4*B4
5	Ham & Tomato	1.75	212	208	178	256	=SUM(C5:F5)	=G5*B5
6	Cheese & Pickle	1.75	167	189	175	160	=SUM(C6:F6)	=G6*B6
7	Chicken Salad	1.80	234	223	278	345	=SUM(C7:F7)	=G7*B7
8	Bacon Lettuce & Tomato	1.80	189	237	196	245	=SUM(C8:F8)	=G8*B8
9	Chicken Tikka	1.80	203	234	286	321	=SUM(C9:f9)	=G9*B9
10		Monthly Totals	=SUM(C3:C9)	=SUM(D3:D9)	=SUM(E3:E9)	=SUM(F3:F9)	Grand Total:-	=SUM(H3:H9)

Figure 2.21 The spreadsheet in Formula view

=F4*B4, =F5*B5 and so on. A similar change occurs when formulae are copied across columns. The formula to calculate the total number of sandwiches sold in January was entered in cell C10, i.e. =sum(C3:C9). As the formula was copied across the columns, the cell reference automatically changed to =sum(D3:D9) and to =sum(E3:E9). The spreadsheet assumes that, as the formulae are copied from cell to cell, the formulae should be *relative* to, not the same as, the previous cell.

Absolute cell reference

Sometimes you may want to refer to a particular cell address many times. Therefore,

when you copy the formula, the cell address needs to remain the same – the technical term for which is *absolute*. For example, you might have one cell containing the rate for VAT (the government's value added tax on items we buy). When we purchase goods we are not interested in how much of that money has to be given to the government but, clearly, it is essential for the shopkeeper to know this.

Figure 2.22 illustrates this point. The rate for VAT is 17.5% and is entered into cell B3, and the amount of VAT to be paid is calculated in column C. You will notice that the formulae show $ signs before the B and

The formula reference for cell B3 does not change as it is copied down the rows because the $ sign (B3) indicates that this reference should remain fixed or *absolute*

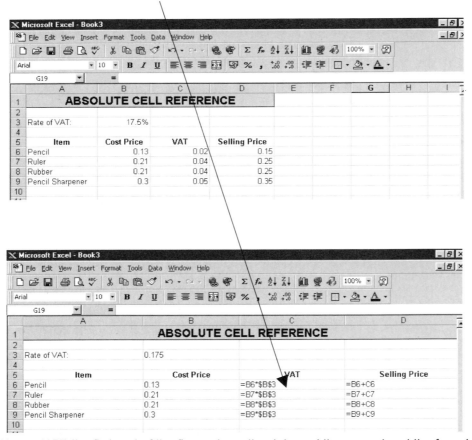

Figure 2.22 Working out VAT: the first part of the figure shows the data and the second part the formulae

the 3 in the cell reference. These signs are used in Excel to indicate that, when copying the formula, this cell reference must not be changed. Although in the small example shown it would be very quick to key in the formula on each new line, in a commercial spreadsheet you might be copying the formula down hundreds of rows. The other benefit is that, if the government changes the rate of VAT, it is a simple matter to enter the new rate in cell B3 – all cells depending on that formula will, automatically change.

ACTIVITY

Copy the spreadsheet shown in Figure 2.22 but experiment with the formulae:

1 At first, enter the formula in cell C6 as B6*B3. Copy the formula down the four rows. You will notice there are errors in the results.

2 Go back to cell C6 and change the formula to B6*B3. (Note: In Excel, a quick way to add the $ signs is to place the cursor in front of the cell reference on the status bar, in this case B3, and to press the function key F4.) Copy the formula down the four rows. This time you should find the results match those in Figure 2.22.

3 Imagine that the rate of VAT has been changed to 22%. Change the rate in cell C6 to 22%. You should find that the columns for VAT and Selling Price will automatically recalculate.

Comparison operators

Comparison operators, as the name suggests, compare two values to determine whether something is true or false. Comparison operators in a spreadsheet are just the same as those we have already looked at in the previous chapter on databases, but in a spreadsheet these are typically used with the If function (see below):

>	greater than
<	less than
=	equal to
>=	greater than or equal to
<=	less than or equal to
<>	not equal to

If . . . then . . . else

We often make statements like 'If it's fine, *then* we'll have a barbecue'. The implication is that if it's not fine we will do something *else*. Effectively, we are making a condition and, depending on that condition, a certain action will follow. Notice that the words '*If it's not fine, we won't have a barbecue*' were not actually said, but the listener would realise the implication. To understand this more clearly, look at Figure 2.23.

The condition	True or false	Action
It is fine	True	We'll have a barbecue
It is fine	False – i.e. it is not fine	We won't have a barbecue

Figure 2.23 If . . . then . . . else

Spreadsheets do exactly the same thing: you can ask the spreadsheet to provide answers depending on a certain condition. If that condition is *true*, the spreadsheet performs a particular action; if the condition is *false* the spreadsheet performs a different action. For example, a manufacturer offers a discount of 2% to customers who order more than £20,000 of goods (i.e. *if* sales are greater than £20,000, *then* pay a discount of 2%, *else* pay nothing.) (See Figure 2.24.)

Data View

Formula View

Figure 2.24 Customers who earn a discount

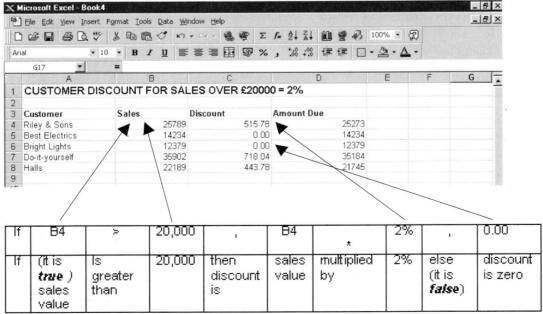

If	B4	>	20,000	,	B4	*	2%	,	0.00
If	(it is **true**) sales value	Is greater than	20,000	then discount is	sales value	multiplied by	2%	else (it is **false**)	discount is zero

Figure 2.25 The spreadsheet formula

You will notice that in the Discount column in Figure 2.24, those customers whose sales are greater than £20,000 have received a discount, but those whose sales are less than £20,000 have not. You can see from Formula View that the formula in Cell C4 is =IF(B4>20000,B4*2%,"0.00"), which was then copied down the column (using the relative cell reference). The formula is explained in Figure 2.25.

In other words, *if* it is *true* that the value in Cell B4 is more than 20,000, *then* multiply the value in Cell B4 by 2% to calculate the discount payable. *If* it is *false*, i.e. less than 20,000 (*else* or otherwise), enter 0.00 in the cells. In Column D the discount is deducted from the sales to give the amount due.

It is also possible to use the If function to display text rather than to make a calculation, as shown in Figure 2.26 .

You will notice that the two examples show different statements in cell A10. The formula in Cell A10 is:

=IF(E20<100,"YOU NEED TO DRAW MONEY FROM THE BANK", "Enough Money in the Account"

The formula is saying that *if* the balance at the end of the week is less than £100, *then* the statement **YOU NEED TO DRAW MONEY FROM THE BANK** will appear on the screen, but the implication is that if the balance is more than £100 (*else* or otherwise), the statement **Enough Money in the Account** will appear.

ACTIVITY

I   Create a spreadsheet like the one shown in Figure 2.24 using the following formula in cell C4:

=IF(B4>20000,B4*2%,"0.00")

Make sure you copy the formula *exactly*, including commas, inverted commas and brackets as shown.

The formula in D4 should be =B4-C4.

Copy the formulae down the rows and compare your results with Figure 2.24.

Example 1

	A	B	C	D
1	PETTY CASH - DAILY EXPENDITURE			
2	DATE	RECEIPTS	EXPENDITURE	BALANCE
3	06/03/2000	150.00		150.00
4	07/03/2000		45.00	105.00
5	08/03/2000		25.78	79.22
6	09/03/2000		14.89	64.33
7	10/03/2000		34.21	30.12
8	Balance at the end of the week:-			30.12
9				
10	YOU NEED TO DRAW MONEY FROM THE BANK			

Example 2

	A	B	C	D
1	PETTY CASH - DAILY EXPENDITURE			
2	DATE	RECEIPTS	EXPENDITURE	BALANCE
3	13/03/00	150.00		150.00
4	14/03/00		5.00	145.00
5	15/03/00		16.23	128.77
6	16/03/00		4.05	124.72
7	17/03/00		12.00	112.72
8	Balance at the end of the week:-			112.72
9				
10	Enough Money in the Account			

Figure 2.26 The If function displaying text

2 Change the sales data in Column B as shown in Figure 2.25 and notice the discount and amount due changing automatically.

3 See what happens if the discount is applied to sales greater than £15,000. Change the formula and then change the amount in Cell C4 to 15000.

4 Create a spreadsheet as shown in Figure 2.26, Example 1, using the following formula in cell A10:

=IF(E20<100,"YOU NEED TO DRAW MONEY FROM THE BANK","Enough Money in the Account")

Again copy the formula *exactly*.

5 Alter the expenditure as shown in Example 2 and notice that the statement in cell A10 will automatically change.

6 You decide you only need to keep £30 in petty cash. Change the formula accordingly.

Testing the spreadsheet

Do not assume that the result of a formula is correct without checking it. For example, it may be that you made a simple keying-in error in a formula and pressed the + key when you meant to press * to multiply. You will get a result in the cell, but it will be inaccurate. Look back at Figure 2.21 (page 89) where you will see that the formula in cell G3 is =F3*B3. If F3+B3 had been entered, Figure 2.27 would have been the result.

Data to enter		Expected result	Actual result	Formula correct?
Cell B3	*Cell F3			
1.60	632	1011.20	1011.20	Yes ✓
1.60	632	1011.20	633.60	No ✗

Figure 2.27 Testing the spreadsheet

It is important that you always test your spreadsheet to check it is working as you intended. You might try checking the results of formulae on a calculator. If they do not match, you can then check to find out where the problem lies.

Graphs and charts

When reading a textbook such as this, you will almost certainly find pictures, illustrations and diagrams to help clarify the information given in the text. Graphs or charts can be very helpful tools to illustrate numerical information, and spreadsheet programs provide easy-to-use facilities to create the graphs/charts. However, it is important to check that the type of graph/chart chosen is appropriate for the data and that it is clearly labelled. The 'reader' must be able to understand the graph/chart easily and must find it beneficial to have the information presented in this way. Otherwise, it is a waste of time producing the graph.

Probably the most frequently used examples of graphs and charts are:

- column charts

- bar charts

- pie charts

- line graphs.

A well presented graph or chart might include:

- a main title

- axis titles

- axis scale labels

- data or series labels

- a legend, where appropriate.

Let's experiment with creating graphs using the very small sample of data from Select

Sandwiches shown in Figure 2.15 (page 84). The aim is to compare sales of the different varieties of sandwiches. Cells A1 to G9 were highlighted to use as the basis for the chart, column style was selected, a legend was included and main and axes titles added. Figure 2.28 shows the finished chart.

Unfortunately, the chart is not very helpful, the problem being that too many cells were selected from the spreadsheet. Before selecting the cells from which to create a chart, it is essential to decide what information you are trying to present. Given the aim of the chart

discussed above, it would have been more appropriate to select cells A2:A9 and G2:G9 (see Figure 2.29 for the result).

You will notice this time there is no legend. Since there is only one set of data for each sandwich type, there is no need for a legend to explain the different patterns in the columns. Neither is there a title for the value y axis, since the value of the axis is already clearly shown as £. Data labels are included at the top of the columns, but do you feel these are helpful, or do they clutter the graph too much? This is a matter of personal

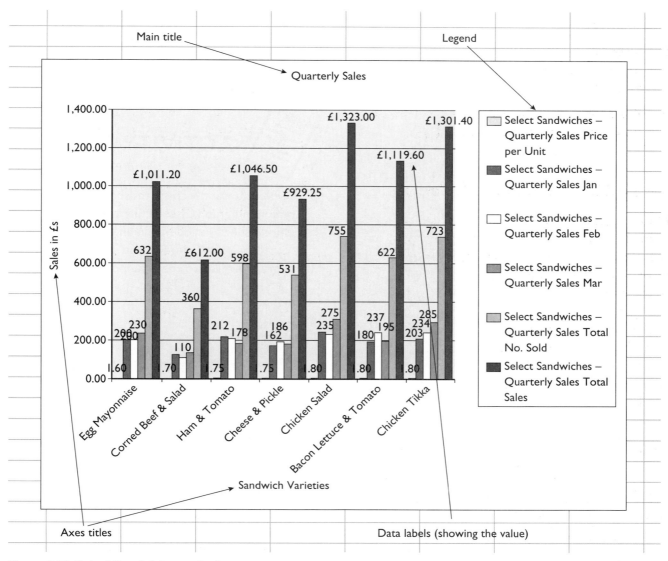

Figure 2.28 Select Sandwiches – chart

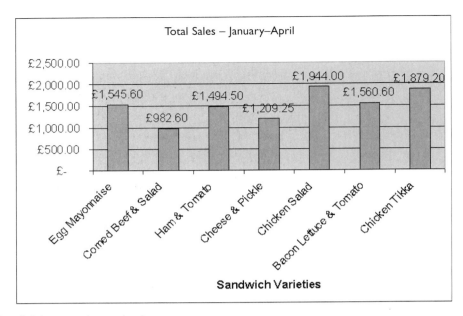

Figure 2.29 Select Sandwiches – column chart

preference, but it is important to consider these points when presenting charts or graphs.

Using the same selection of cells, Figure 2.30 shows a pie chart with percentages rather than values. Figure 2.31 shows the same information as a line graph. Which of these options do you prefer? Which represents the information most clearly?

ACTIVITY

1   Open the sandwich spreadsheet and create a column graph by selecting the whole spreadsheet. Include main and axes titles, data labels and a legend. You should produce a graph similar to the one in Figure 2.28.

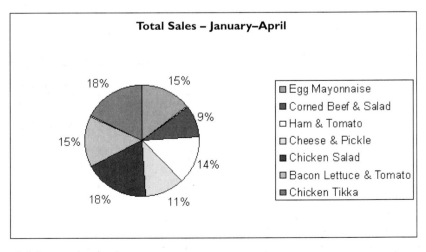

Figure 2.30 Select Sandwiches – pie chart

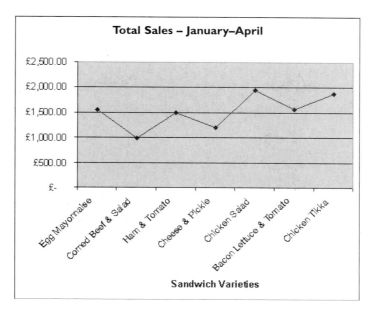

Figure 2.31 Select Sandwiches – line graph

2   Make sure you have included the data for April sales and create a second graph. If you are using Excel, highlight the cells A2:A9, press the Control key, then move the cursor and highlight cells H2:H9. (Pressing the Control key before moving the cursor to the next block you wish to highlight allows you to select non-adjacent cells.)

3   Experiment with creating different chart styles to compare the sales for the four months.

4   Create further graphs showing:

  •   the total number of sandwiches sold

  •   a comparison of the total number sold and the total value of the sales.

'What if' queries

One of the benefits of a spreadsheet is the ability to calculate easily and quickly the impact of *possible* changes. For example, there is a rumour that the government is going to increase the rate of VAT to 23%! This would have an enormous impact on businesses. A company might wish to identify how much will be involved if the rumour proves to be true. By changing the rate of VAT in the spreadsheet, the additional cost is immediately apparent.

Look at Figure 2.32 and compare it with Figure 2.22 (page 90). You will notice that the data has altered but the formulae stay the same. Try it out for yourself.

	A	B	C	D	E
1	ABSOLUTE CELL REFERENCE				
2					
3	Rate of VAT	23.00%			
4					
5	Item	Cost Price	VAT	Selling Price	
6	Pencil	0.13	0.03	0.16	
7	Ruler	0.21	0.05	0.26	
8	Rubber	0.21	0.05	0.26	
9	Pencil Sharpener	0.30	0.07	0.37	
10					

Figure 2.32 'What if' query

If you earn £12,000 a year and your boss gives you a 5% increase, you don't need a spreadsheet program to work out what the rise is worth and your new salary. You could easily use a calculator or even work it out with pen and paper! However, pay rises are often negotiated – you ask for 9%, your boss offers 3% and you meet somewhere in the middle. Here, 'what if' queries can help. Simply by changing a single variable (the %), 'what if' calculations can show you the value of the different percentages and the new totals at a glance.

Calculating the effects of different percentage increases is just one use for 'What if' queries. 'What if' is a powerful financial tool that is used in almost all organisations. The nature of each 'What if' query depends on the nature of the processing activity being resolved. In manufacturing, for example, it might be used to assess the effect on production costs if the price of raw materials changes. In tourism, it could establish the break-even point for the number of seats on an aircraft that need to be sold at a given price to recover costs. The break-even point means simply the point at which the income earned covers the costs incurred. As you can appreciate, it is crucial for a business to know whether it will make a profit or a loss. Therefore, break-even points are one of the most frequently asked 'What if' queries.

We have seen how Select Sandwiches have started to keep records in the computer on the number of sandwiches sold and the income generated, but wouldn't it be much more effective if details on costs were also included? If data on cost of ingredients, travel expenses and wages were added, it would be possible to establish the break-even point.

ACTIVITY

Include a new worksheet in your **sandwich** spreadsheet to calculate the *cost per sandwich* for the corned beef and salad (lettuce and cucumber), and the ham and tomato sandwiches, using the following data:

Item	Cost	Quantity per sandwich
Sliced loaf – 30 slices excluding crusts	50p	2
Corned beef – ten slices per tin	£1.25	4
Salad Tomato – approx. 24 slices	60p	4
Lettuce – approx. 15 portions	45p	1
Cucumber – approx. 30 slices	70p	6
Ham – ten slices per packet	£1.80	1
Low-fat spread – assumed cost per sandwich	1p	1

Is Select Sandwiches charging enough per sandwich, even before other expenses are included?

CHAPTER 2.4 HYPERTEXT DATABASES

What is meant by the term *hypertext*? Have you ever used an encyclopaedia for research? If you have, you will almost certainly discover that an encyclopaedia is not just one book, but consists of 10 or 20 volumes. Quite often, one of those volumes is an index that gives a brief description of the topic and tells you where to find more information. You then select the next volume, read a bit but find that almost certainly some further interesting detail is in yet another volume of the encyclopaedia. Wouldn't it be great if you could just point to the topic in the index making the book you need, as if by magic, pop out of the shelf and open itself at the right page? When you had finished reading that section, you could point to the next topic, and again the right volume would pop out of the shelf and open itself for you. In effect this is the service hypertext provides.

Hypertext databases are pages of information with highlighted items creating links to other pages, which provide further detail on the subject. Help files, CD-ROM encyclopaedias and the World Wide Web all use hypertext, but any type of document can incorporate hypertext. The link can be either a text-based hyperlink (usually indicated by means of a different colour) or a hyperlinked image. Think of the *hyperlink* as an invitation to visit another place. As you move the mouse pointer towards the *hyperlink*, the arrow changes to a hand and, if you click the hand on the highlighted item, the next page of information will open for you. The new page may be part of the same document, another file at the same site or it may link to any other site on the Internet. The hyperlink is the underlying code of hypertext, which contains the directory details, file details or World Wide Web address of the information, which can be accessed by clicking on the hypertext. If you click on the Back button, you return to the previous page. The concept is very simple and immensely powerful. To access the Internet you need a browser (a program that allows you to read the hypertext). Examples of browsers include Explorer or Netscape Navigator.

 ## ACTIVITY

1 Figure 2.33 is part of the help files in Microsoft Word. If you have access to Word, try it out for yourself. From the Help Menu, choose Contents and Index, select the Index tab and type in the box 'hyperlinks, automatic formatting of'.

You will notice that if you click on the word *hyperlink*, which is shown in green, you will be given a definition of the term hyperlink, as shown in Figure 2.34.

2 You may find the free On-Line Dictionary of Computing helpful in your studies. Try accessing it via the Internet at: http://foldoc.doc.ic.ac.uk If you cannot find the Web page, try searching for 'Free On-line Dictionary of Computing'.

Experiment with the hyperlinks to access different pages in the dictionary.

3 Other useful Web sites are:

- www.FixWindows.com
- www.Nowonder.com

HyperText Markup Language (HTML) is the code for writing Web pages. Originally, Web page developers had to write the HTML code themselves, but now you can buy software that allows you to design your page 'visually' and then save the file in HTML format, ready to upload to your web site. The different types of

Use automatic formatting to turn file names into hyperlinks

By using the automatic formatting features in Word, you can create a hyperlink just by typing the address of the file you want to jump to. Network paths and Internet addresses can automatically become hyperlink display text — "hot spots" — that the reader clicks to jump to the hyperlink destination.

For instance, if you are creating a Word publication that will include several Internet e-mail addresses, Word can automatically format the addresses as hyperlinks as you type. Then, when the reader of your publication clicks one of the hyperlinks, an e-mail message with the correct address already in the **To:** line is created, provided the reader has an e-mail program installed.

1   On the **Tools** menu, click **AutoCorrect**, and then click the **AutoFormat As You Type** tab.

    Show me

2   Under **Replace as you type,** select the **Internet and network paths with hyperlinks** check box.

    When you type the address of a file located on a network or on the Internet, Word changes the address to a hyperlink. The address of the file becomes the display text the reader clicks.

Note   If you want to create hyperlinks from addresses in existing documents — such as a document that's attached to an e-mail message you received — use the **AutoFormat** command on the **Format** menu. Click the **Options** button, and be sure that the **Internet and network paths with hyperlinks** check box is selected under **Replace.**

Figure 2.33 The Help file from Microsoft Word

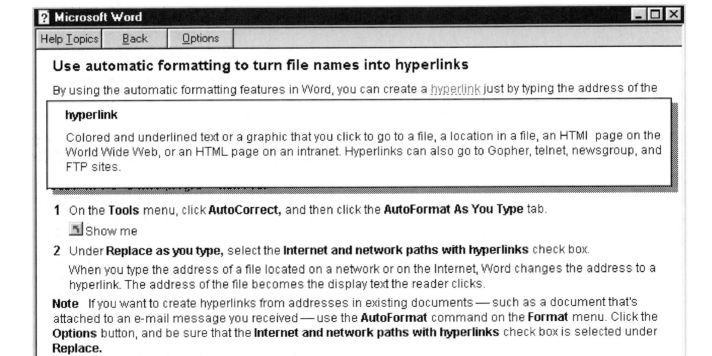

Figure 2.34 The subsequent page of the Help file from Microsoft Word, showing the definition of hyperlink

information that can be transmitted digitally have increased rapidly to include not just text and numeric data, but graphics, still pictures, sound, video and animation and, over the years, the HTML has expanded to include links to these other media. In fact the World Wide Web has become so vast that it has been necessary to provide 'search engines' to make it easier to find what you want. Search engines are indexes which work by keywords and context, and no doubt you are familiar with examples such as Yahoo or Lycos.

The Internet uses a URL (universal resource locator) or Web address to locate the Web site you wish to visit. You are probably very familiar with Internet addresses, such as http://www.bbc.co.uk http://www.qca.org.uk or http://www.heinemann.co.uk, but do you know what the different components actually mean?

http	Hypertext transmission (transfer) protocol is the Web's own method for accessing and transferring documents between different sites. It is a set of rules (the protocol) used by network servers to transmit and receive files on the World Wide Web. When you type http at the start of a Web site address, you are telling your computer to use this protocol.
://	This simply separates the transmission protocol from the rest of the address.
www	The World Wide Web is a part of the Internet whose pages are linked.
bbc qca heinemann	These are examples of the names of the Web servers that store the pages you want to look at. In this case bbc refers to British Broadcasting

Corporation, and is the name of the domain given to the BBC site. This name has been registered with the Internet Society. The other examples are:

qca (Qualifications and Curriculum Authority), the organisation which monitors educational programmes, such as GNVQs, GCSEs and A-levels and

heinemann – the publisher of this textbook.

.co .com	Indicate a company
.org	Generally refers to a charity or non-profit-making organisation
.ac	Indicates a university, college or academic body
.gov	Indicates a government department
.uk	Indicates United Kingdom
.ca	Indicates Canada
.au	Indicates Australia

This is a brief introduction to hypertext databases but you will be learning more about them in Unit 3.

? Did you know?

Various academic, research and government computer centres have been gathering information for 20 or more years and storing it on their local networks. The Internet is the means by which these various different local networks are linked together, or *interconnected*, to form an international network that has come to be known as the World Wide Web. The World Wide Web is a user-friendly way of navigating data stored on computers connected to the Internet. Because the Internet originated in the USA, American Web site addresses do not include the country reference, whereas other countries are identified.

After studying this unit you should be able to:

- understand ICT specifications for hardware and software

- select an ICT system and configure it to meet the needs of users

- write a program to improve efficient use of applications software (macros)

- write a program to display hypertext information (HTML)

- understand and develop good practice in your use of ICT.

In order to do this you will learn about the following:

- input devices

- processing units

- storage devices

- output devices

- operating systems software

- applications software

- programming languages, including HTML

- setting up and configuring a computer system.

You will be able to put into practice what you have learnt about standard ways of working and the knowledge you have gained from Presenting and Handling Information in Units 1 and 2 will also help you.

Unit 3 will be assessed through your portfolio work and you will specify suitable hardware and software to meet a user's needs, set up an ICT system and configure the software to help that user make the most effective use of the system. In addition you will have the opportunity to write some short computer programs to create macros and your own web pages.

CHAPTER 3.1 HARDWARE

If you walk round any computer superstore it can be bewildering if you don't understand the 'jargon'. How would you decide what to buy?

You would need to know about the parts you can see and touch (referred to as the hardware) and the parts you can't touch (the software).

We talk about our computers in the same way as we talk about music centres. A friend might tell you he or she has an Intel Pentium III 600 MHz processor with a 15.3 GB hard drive, 128 MB SDRAM and DVD-ROM. Change the subject, and your friend might say he or she has just bought a new mini hi-fi with double auto-reverse Dolby B NR, 2 × 90 watts RMS, 2-band AM/FM digital tuner with presets and an H+ amplifier with super woofer system.

This is the jargon. In fact jargon is simply the words that describe the components. Once you know what the different components are, what they look like and what they do, you can easily understand and use the jargon too.

The computer you are using is made up of different components that together form an ICT system. Such a system is generally referred to as a PC (personal computer). At home you will probably have a standalone system and at school or college you may be using a network.

You can't tell much about a computer just by looking at it. To appreciate the differences you need to examine its physical components and appreciate their features. These components can very simply be divided into:

- input devices that get data into the computer

- the main processor unit that manipulates the data

- the storage devices that save the data

- the output devices that display the data in soft or hard copy

- the cables and connectors that join it all together.

Let us consider each of these in turn.

Input devices

Input devices enable you to enter data, commands and programs into the computer's central processing unit (CPU) – its brain. The input devices you are most likely to come into contact with are:

- keyboard
- mouse
- rollerball
- scanner
- digital camera
- microphone
- joystick.

Keyboard

The keyboard is the most commonly used input device and is used to key in data or to enter commands to the computer. Almost all keyboards follow the standard IBM layout and design (Figure 3.1). Touching or pressing a key sends an electronic signal to the computer which interprets it as a character or function.

The keyboard is divided into four main areas:

- function keys across the top
- letter keys in the main section
- a numeric keypad on the right
- cursor movement and editing keys between the main section and the numeric keypad.

A computer keyboard is basically the same as an ordinary typewriter keyboard but it has extra keys for specialised functions. The standard layout of most typewriters and keyboards is called the QWERTY layout. The name comes from the first six keys on the top row of the alphabetic characters. Have a look next time you use a keyboard. The original design was based on mechanical considerations to slow the typist down, rather than on efficiency: the letters you would use most often were put as far apart as possible so that the old typewriter hammers (that swung up and hit the print ribbon) did not stick together.

Another keyboard has been developed – the Dvorak keyboard – which is much easier to use. Imagine a typist using a QWERTY keyboard continuously for 8 hours – his or her fingers would travel an estimated 16 miles. If that same typist was using the Dvorak keyboard his or her fingers would only travel about one mile! However, since everyone is used to the QWERTY keyboard its use is widespread and so to change it would be extremely difficult.

Figure 3.1 Keyboard

Figure 3.2 Ergonomic keyboard

Touch-sensitive keyboard

This type of keyboard is used in special situations where, for example, dirt or liquid could damage a conventional keyboard. It consists of a plastic surface where the keys are replaced by designated areas that are programmed to input commands into the computer. Overlays are put on the keyboard with symbols indicating the areas, and the commands are activated by pressure.

One particular type of touch-sensitive keyboard is known as a *concept keyboard*, and this is often used by young or disabled people (see Figure 3.3).

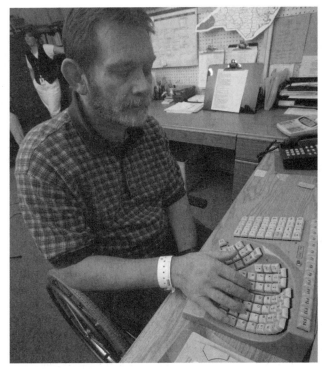

Figure 3.3 A concept keyboard

Mouse

A mouse (a computer mouse – see Figure 3.4) is a pointing device that enables you to control the movement and position of the on-screen cursor by moving the mouse around on a surface such as a desk. To select items (such as words or icons) you position the mouse pointer and press one of the mouse buttons. This produces a 'mouse click'. You might have heard the expressions 'double click', 'click and drag' and 'drag and drop'. These refer to actions you perform with the mouse. Although you can still use the keyboard for most commands, a mouse makes things much easier. You need to treat the mouse firmly to achieve the best control – remember – it can't bite you.

The standard mouse comprises casing, buttons and base. The casing is designed to be held by the fingers and thumb of one hand, with the bottom of your palm resting

Figure 3.4 A computer mouse

on a mat or other surface. The top has one, two or three buttons, each clicked for different functions. The bottom is flat and has a 'multidirectional detection device', usually a rubber ball (see Figure 3.4).

As technology has advanced, the mouse has evolved from its original design and now comes in different styles to suit different requirements. Some are ergonomically designed to fit the hand, some are programmable and most now have a wheel button on top to make scrolling and zooming easier.

The rubber ball needs to be cleaned frequently because dust and dirt can cause the mouse to stick or hang. To overcome this problem, a mouse has been developed where the rubber ball has been replaced with an optical sensor that detects motion on the desktop (see Figure 3.5). A tiny digital

Figure 3.5 Mouse with optical sensor

camera takes up to 1,500 pictures per second of the surface beneath the mouse and these pictures are translated into the movement of the cursor on the screen. You no longer need a mouse mat because the sensor works on most non-reflective surfaces – even your lap – and, as there are no moving parts, the mouse moves smoothly.

The cordless mouse (see Figure 3.6) relies on digital radio technology to send signals to a digital receiver. Radio waves enable communication with the CPU from a distance range of up to 2 metres regardless of any obstacles which might be in the way.

Figure 3.6 Cordless mouse

Rollerball

A rollerball (or trackerball) (see Figure 3.7) is like an upside-down mouse that allows the user to point to select items on screen. The user rotates the rollerball with his or her fingers instead of pushing a mouse around a desktop. It requires very little space to operate and is commonly built into laptop computers in place of the conventional mouse.

Figure 3.7 Rollerball

Scanner

Scanners read words, symbols or other graphics from a printed page and 'translate' the pattern of light and dark (or colour) into a digital signal the computer can store and manipulate.

The most popular type of scanner is a flatbed scanner (Figure 3.8) which works in a similar way to a photocopier. You put the document face down on a flat bed of glass and close the lid. The sensor moves across (scans) underneath the glass, reading the information – very much like the operation of a photocopier.

Figure 3.8 Flatbed scanner

Handheld scanners (Figure 3.9) are still in use but, as flatbed scanners are now relatively inexpensive, their use is diminishing. They are usually only a few centimetres wide, which

Figure 3.9 Handheld scanner

limits the amount of information you can scan to small areas. You use a handheld scanner simply by rolling it across the document to be scanned. The images produced are not of the same high quality as flatbed scanners.

Sheet-feed scanners (Figure 3.10) are useful in businesses where a variety of documents (from reports to receipts to business cards) needs to be scanned. They will scan black and white documents about five times faster than flatbed scanners, are quieter to run and can cope with a stack of papers, not just one at a time like the flatbed scanner.

Figure 3.10 Sheet-feed scanner

Digital camera

A digital camera looks similar to a traditional camera but, instead of recording an image on film, light intensities are converted into digital form that can be stored on a disk as a data file, similar to a Word or Excel file. In fact, you can see the photograph in the camera immediately you have taken it and, if you don't like it, you can delete it and take another picture. No processing is needed to see the image, which can be transferred directly to a computer screen where you can manipulate and edit it. When printed on special photographic quality paper, the image looks no different from a traditionally processed photograph.

Digital video cameras work in a similar way and, with DVD technology (see page 113), are likely to provide a much cheaper way of making feature films in the future.

Microphone

Microphones are sensors that detect sound, and the microphones used with computers are basically the same as any other type of microphone. At present, they are mostly used with voice recognition modules that take spoken words and translate them into digital signals for the computer. This makes it possible to operate a computer without using your hands.

Joystick

You will be familiar with a joystick if you play computer games. The handle in the centre of the joystick moves an object on screen (such as a car, plane or person) and translates the physical motion of your hand and fingers into motion on a computer screen. Buttons on the top or sides of the joystick let you perform selected tasks, such as firing. They are not used in word processing, spreadsheet or database applications but are used in some CAD (computer aided design) software.

Main processing unit

The main processing unit is housed in a case and may come in the form of a tower, a mini-tower or a desktop (see Figure 3.11). No matter how it looks, the main processing unit will comprise the following essential components:

- central processing unit (CPU)
- memory
- motherboard
- ports
- disk drives
- CD-ROM drive.

Figure 3.11 Main processing units

It may also have some additional components:

- modem
- network card.

Central processing unit (CPU)

The central processing unit (CPU) – or microprocessor – is the computer's brain. It is the component that interprets and carries out the commands you give the computer through the input devices. It fetches, decodes and executes instructions, and transfers data to and from other components.

A microprocessor is a chip of silicon composed of tiny electrical switches. These chips are usually around 0.5 cm (0.2 in) long and 0.05 cm (0.02 in) thick. The speed at which the processor carries out its operations is measured in millions of cycles or pulses per second – megahertz (MHz). The higher the number of MHz the faster the computer can process data. At the time of writing, Intel's 'Pentium III 1000 MHz' chip is the most advanced, although you would expect 600 MHz to cope with most of your everyday processing requirements. (In 1995 you might have considered a speed of 90 MHz to be adequate!) Although Intel's Pentium is probably the most well-known chip, the Intel Celeron and AMD (manufactured by Advanced Micro Devices, Inc.) are alternative cheaper microprocessors that are now being installed in new PCs.

Did you know?

Computer theft is one of the fastest growing crimes. Silicon chips are so valuable they are targeted by computer thieves who no longer bother to take the whole computer – they just take the lid off the main box, unplug the chip, put it in their pocket and walk out.

Memory

Memory is the name given to the chips inside the processing unit where data and instructions are stored for fast access. Memory is used to store the programs you use and is the working area that processes the current data (e.g. the letter you are word processing). It comprises *ROM* (read-only memory) and *RAM* (random access memory).

ROM (read-only memory) is a permanent memory that is available whether the computer is switched on or off. The start-up procedure (or boot program) – when you switch your computer on – is stored in ROM. It is installed when the computer is manufactured and can be read from, but not over-written (i.e. changed).

RAM (random access memory) is the computer's temporary working memory

where programs and data are stored when the computer is running. Windows 98 requires at least 64 MB of RAM to run efficiently and more powerful machines will have 128 MB. Some may be upgraded to 256 MB or more. Documents created in your software are stored in RAM while the computer processes instructions, but must be saved permanently on a hard or floppy disk or they will be lost when the computer is switched off. For this reason RAM is known as volatile memory. To enable the computer to run the advanced applications you are familiar with, the amount of RAM that is needed has increased from approximately 16 MB in 1995 to the 64 MB or more found in current systems. SDRAM (synchronised dynamic RAM) permits an extremely fast transfer of data between the microprocessor and the memory.

The size of data (or storage) capacity of a computer is measured in *bytes*. One byte contains 8 *bits*. Bits stands for **bi**nary dig**its** and is the smallest unit of data that can be stored. A byte is approximately equal to one single keyboard character (letter, number or special character).

We normally refer to the storage capacity of a computer in terms of kilobytes (kB), megabytes (MB) and gigabytes (GB) (see Table 3.1).

Unit	Definition
bit	Smallest unit of data with a value of 1 or 0
byte	Equal to 8 bits – approximately equivalent to one character. The letters a, b and c are represented in binary code by 0110 0001, 0110 0010 and 0110 0011
kilobyte (kB)	Equal to 1,024 bytes or 2^{10}
megabyte (MB)	Equal to 1,048,576 bytes or 2^{20} (equivalent to approximately 500 double spaced pages of text)
gigabyte (GB)	Equal to 1,073,741,824 bytes or 2^{30} (equivalent to approximately half-million double spaced pages of text)
terabyte (TB)	Equal to ~1,099,000,000,000 bytes or 2^{40}

Table 3.1 Units of measurement used for a computer's memory

Motherboard

The motherboard is the main printed circuit board of the computer, which usually forms the 'floor' of the system. All the other electrical components are plugged into the motherboard (e.g. CPU and memory). These components are linked by 'buses' which are etched into the motherboard and carry signals from one component to another.

Ports

Ports are the 'sockets' at the back of the main processor casing, which are used to attach the peripheral devices (printer, monitor, keyboard, mouse, etc.). Cables from each peripheral plug into the ports allowing data to be sent and received from the microprocessor. There are *serial* and *parallel* ports. A serial port transmits data one bit at a time. These are known as COM1, COM2 and are referred to as male connectors because they have pins. A parallel port transmits data in bytes and is therefore much faster. Parallel ports are called LPT1, LPT2 and are designated female connectors because they have receptacles for the pins.

Modem

If you want your computer to provide access to the Internet or e-mail, you will need a modem. Modems come built in to most new computers but some older computers have a separate external modem which plugs into the PC.

A modem, or **mod**ulator/**dem**odulator to give it its full title, allows two computers to communicate using the telephone system. The public telephone system was originally designed to carry sounds or analogue signals but, with the help of a modem, data or digital transmissions can also be made. (In this context the word *data* is used for anything created on your PC, from word processing, to spreadsheet, to graphics.)

The digital or on/off signals transmitted by your computer are translated by the modem into continuous signals, which can be sent down the telephone line. Another receiving modem converts the telephone signal back into digital form, which can be understood by the receiving computer. The modem translates analogue (continuous) to digital (on/off signals). If you find this difficult to understand, think of a light switch. A conventional switch is either off or on, just like the bits in computer transmission, which are either 0s or 1s. However, if you use a dimmer switch the light level can be gradually increased or decreased in a continuous movement – analogue (see Figure 3.12).

Network card

If you are at school or college your computer is probably connected to a network. Networks allow the sharing of resources and data by users and, to access the network, each PC must be fitted with a network card. This

? Did you know?

We talk about local area networks (LAN) and wide area networks (WAN). As its name suggests, a LAN system is located in a small area – usually within one building – whereas a WAN connects users over a much larger geographical area – even between continents.

Figure 3.12   A modem

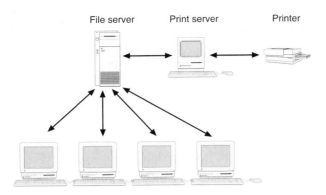

Figure 3.13 Flow of information in a local area network

is similar to a printed circuit board, which slots into the CPU, and which contains all the necessary electronics and connections to allow the PC to link into the network.

A local area network (LAN) includes a *file server*, which is a central computer that runs the network's operating system and which contains the files and programs the network users share. (See Figure 3.13.)

Storage devices

We have already looked at RAM and ROM and seen that they don't provide the means to store either the applications (e.g. word processing, spreadsheet, etc.) or the data you have input and spent time working on. Disk drives provide the means to do this.

A disk drive is a storage device that transfers data to and from a magnetic or optical disk. Your PC will probably have one hard drive (typically referred to as Drive C), one floppy drive (referred to as Drive A) and a CD-ROM drive (referred to as Drive D).

The hard drive

The hard drive is the storage area (rather like a filing cabinet) where all the applications software you use and documents you create are kept. It is the main memory of the computer. Hard drives are measured in

gigabytes (GB). The most expensive computers will have the largest hard drive – over 30 GB – but at present a capacity of 10 GB will be sufficient for most everyday processing. This is an enormous increase from 1995, when you would have expected a hard drive to be about 800 MB.

The hard drive houses the *hard disks* (see Figure 3.14), which are flat, round, rigid

Figure 3.14 Hard disk

Did you know?

The amount of work you do on your computer at home can easily be backed up on a floppy disk for safety. However, most organisations need to back up large volumes of data, and floppy disks or hard disks would not be large enough for this. Mainframe computers therefore use *tape backup* to store copies of the computer's hard disk files that can be retrieved if necessary (e.g. hard drive failure). The backup procedure is often scheduled at night when the computer is not in use.

Access to data on tape is through 'serial access', which is the reason why tape is not used for storing data that is constantly needed. Compare a cassette music tape with a music CD. If you want to find a particular piece of music on cassette you have to run through the tape until you find the right track. This is like tape backup. With a CD-ROM you can go directly to the track you want to listen to – this is like a hard drive, which has direct access.

platters that provide faster access to data than floppy disks and that are capable of storing much more data. Because they are rigid, they can be stacked so that one hard disk drive can access more than one platter (hard disk). Most hard disks have from two to eight platters.

Hard disks come in sealed units that protect them from contaminants (such as dust) that might interfere with the close head-to-disk tolerances. The read/write heads you can see in Figure 3.14 ride over the surface of the disk on an air cushion, 10 to 25 millionths of an inch deep.

The floppy drive

The floppy drive is a removable storage area which enables you to save files on to a *floppy disk* so that you can take data files between home and school or college and make backup copies of your data files as a security measure (Figure 3.15).

Floppy disks are round, flat and made of a substance called mylar. They have a magnetic surface which allows the recording of data and are covered in a protective plastic shell. The disk turns in the drive, allowing the read/write head to access the disk. Most PCs take a 3.5 inch floppy disk, which can store up to 1.44 kB of data. This is approximately

Did you know?

A zip drive is similar to a floppy drive but zip drives can store 100 MB of data, 70 times more than a floppy.

equivalent to 300 A4 pages of straightforward text. Obviously, graphic images and complex formatting will reduce the number of pages. The old 5.25 inch disk that was used with early home computers is now virtually obsolete.

Floppy disks need to be formatted before data can be written to the disk. Formatting establishes tracks and sectors into which data files are stored. Each floppy disk can be write-protected to ensure data are not accidentally erased from the disk. Care should also be taken when handling disks to protect the data. For example, the surface should not be touched, they should be kept away from extreme temperatures, not stored near magnetic fields (e.g. telephones, televisions) and kept away from dust and moisture.

The CD-ROM drive

The CD-ROM drive (compact disk read-only memory) uses the same technology as CD music disks and CD players. A laser beam reads the data from an optical disk rather than a magnetic disk. A typical CD holds

Did you know?

The new DVD-ROM (digital versatile disc, or digital video disc read-only memory) is the same diameter as a CD but holds nearly 10 times the data. A DVD can hold between 4.7 GB and 15.9 GB data and, while it requires its own drive, the DVD drive can run existing CDs. They have provided the means for digital-quality films or other home entertainments you can watch on your PC!

Figure 3.15 3.5 inch floppy disk

around 650 MB of data, which is equivalent to about 450 1.4 MB floppy disks.

The entire contents of a text-based encyclopaedia take up only 25% of one standard-sized CD-ROM. This has allowed publishers to fill up the other 75% with video sequences, animations, photographs, sound and interactive programs. The result is interactive multimedia encyclopaedias.

The CD drive has a read-only memory which means you cannot alter or store data. However, CD writers are now available that enable data to be written to CD. These enable you to make copies of music on CD and are increasingly being used for backing up hard drives.

Output devices

An output device lets you see (or hear) the results of the computer's operations – its data manipulations or calculations. For example, when you enter text through a keyboard or select a function through an icon or pull-down menu, you see the results of your actions on the computer screen.

The most common output devices are video display units (VDUs), printers and speakers.

VDU

A VDU is a computer video display and its housing. Together they are usually referred to as a monitor. VDUs display images (characters or graphics) generated by the computer's video adapter. The image on the screen is referred to as 'soft copy' – you will lose it when the computer is turned off.

Monitors come in different sizes – 15, 17, 19 and 21 inches. The size is determined by the distance between diagonal corners. Like television sets, most VDUs use a cathode ray tube (CRT) which accounts for their size.

However, the new flat screen monitors with TFT LCD (thin film transistor liquid crystal display) flat-panel displays take up less than half the space of a traditional monitor but at the moment are very expensive (see Figure 3.16).

The sharpness or clarity of the image on a VDU is determined by its resolution. Resolution is measured in pixels (short for picture elements). If you look at your computer monitor closely, you will see that the image is made up of tiny dots. Each dot is called a pixel. The more pixels per square centimetre of screen the better the resolution.

Most computers come with super video graphics adaptor monitors (SVGA) with resolutions measured in pixels across and down the screen. Resolutions vary between

Figure 3.16 VDUs

1,024 × 768 pixels, 1,280 × 1,024 and 1,600 × 1,200. The higher the number of pixels the clearer and crisper is the display.

The image on screen is referred to as a frame. A steady image needs to be constantly regenerated or updated and this is known as the *refresh rate*. An SVGA monitor is *non-interlaced* because it is refreshed or regenerated from top to bottom in one stage, frame by frame. This technique allows the easy display of changing images. Most SVGA monitors tend to have refresh rates of 70, 75 or 85 MHz – the higher the frequency, the less likelihood of flickering images. A slow refresh rate of 60 times per second (60 MHz) or less can cause headaches.

Television screens are formed of 625 separate lines rather than pixels. They have a lower refresh rate of 30 full frames or 60 half frames per second because the picture is updated in two stages. Each new frame is transmitted as two interlaced fields – first the odd-numbered lines and then the even-numbered lines. This is known as an *interlaced* monitor. Early computer displays were interlaced.

Older types of monitor are monochrome display adaptor (MDA), colour/graphics adaptor (CGA) and enhanced graphics adaptor (EGA).

Printers

If you need a permanent (or hard) copy of the information on screen you will need a printer. Today, most PCs use laser or ink-jet printers (see Figure 3.17). The quality (or resolution) of the image is measured in dots per inch (or dpi). The more dots per inch the more detailed the output. The speed of the printer is rated by pages per minute (ppm) or by characters per second (cps) – the higher the value, the faster the speed (and, of course, the greater the cost). Files containing graphics are more complex and might slow the printer down.

Figure 3.17 Printers

Laser printers are based on the technology used by photocopiers – lasers produce an image on an electrically charged drum, dry ink or toner sticks to the electrical charge and this is fixed by heat. They have a high resolution of over 1,200 dpi, can reproduce complex graphics, are almost silent and operate at a reasonably high speed of between 8 and 17 or more ppm – depending on their cost.

Ink-jet printers use liquid ink to spray characters on to a page and they provide a similar high resolution of up to 1,200 dpi and are very quiet to operate. It can be difficult to distinguish between a printout from a good-quality ink-jet and a standard laser printer. However, they operate at much slower speeds of between 6 and 10 ppm for black and white copies, but half the speed if printing colour.

Laser and ink-jet printers are known as non-impact printers because no part of the printer touches the page to form the image. An example of an impact printer, on the other hand, is the dot-matrix printer, which produces characters made up of dots using a 9, 18 or 24 pin print head. However, impact printers are noisy.

The pins hit the paper through a ribbon, making patterns of dots in the shape of letters and numbers. They can do this in different fonts and type sizes. The print quality mostly depends on the number of dots in the matrix. This could be low enough to show individual dots or high enough to look almost like fully formed characters.

Dot-matrix printers are often used to print multiple copy, preprinted forms. For instance, if you take your car to be serviced or repaired, the garage will print your invoice when you collect it. They will often have preprinted continuous NCR (no carbon required) stationery and your personal details will be printed in the appropriate places. You will be given a copy and the garage will keep a copy (see Figure 3.18). Receipts for credit card purchases are sometimes printed on NCR paper using a dot-matrix printer. You sign and then you and the shopkeeper each have a copy.

Figure 3.18 A dot matrix preprinted form

Speakers

Most computers are fitted with a small internal speaker that will beep to draw your attention if, for example, the wrong keys are pressed. On multimedia PCs additional speakers are attached to the computer to provide better quality sound. The amplifier driving external speakers is built on to the sound card or into one of the speakers themselves.

Did you know?

Some of the first PC printers were daisy-wheel. They received this name because of the shape of their print head. Their quality of print was about the same as a typewriter's but they were slow, noisy and could only deal with text rather than text and graphics.

Did you know?

Blind and partially sighted people in Preston, Lancashire, have their own cyber centre that has been established to open up the Internet to them. The computers are controlled by voice, and special software strips out unnecessary graphics and animations from web pages, leaving just text which the computer reads out loud.

Cables and connectors

The different components of a computer system are connected by cables. When a system is set up (or moved from one place to another) it is important to check that the input and output devices are connected to the main processing unit correctly or the computer won't work!

If you look at the on-screen display when your computer boots up, you will see messages that indicate the main processing unit is trying to locate/communicate with the keyboard and mouse. These may be 'keyboard detected' or 'mouse initialised'. You may also hear sounds from the printer as communication between the processor and printer is checked.

It is relatively straightforward to set the system up as hardware connections on desktop and tower cases (and on portables) are all standard. Newer computers even have easily recognisable symbols for some connections on the back of the case. For example, a mouse symbol shows you where to plug in the mouse.

We have already learnt about the cordless mouse. With the advent of digital radio technology, cables might soon be a thing of the past because, in addition to the cordless mouse, a cordless keyboard and speakers are also available.

? Did you know?

When you are looking at connectors, check their gender. Most are classified as male or female. A male connector has one or more exposed pins whereas a female connector has one or more receptacles, designed to accept the pins on the male connector.

CHAPTER 3.2 SOFTWARE

Software programs are sets of instructions that make hardware work. A computer can't do anything on its own. Instructions are input by the user, through perhaps the keyboard or mouse, and the software reacts to these instructions. This is why you shouldn't blame the computer if things go wrong. It is only doing what you (the user) have told it to do!

Whereas you can see and touch computer hardware (VDU, keyboard, mouse, etc.), you can't see or touch computer software. Some software comes ready installed on your computer (ROM) and others come on disks or CD-ROMS (operating systems and applications software, for example) that you or your computer supplier must load on to the hard drive before you can use the computer.

The different types of software include:

- the ROM (read-only memory)
- operating systems
- applications software
- programming languages.

The ROM BIOS chip

The read-only memory chip is on the motherboard and contains the instructions that enable the computer to start up or boot. These instructions are permanently stored in the computer's memory. When the computer is first turned on or restarted, it reads the start-up instructions in the ROM BIOS chip. BIOS stands for 'basic input output system' and is a set of instructions that tells the computer how to handle the flow of data between the computer and its input and output peripherals, such as the keyboard and printer.

> **? Did you know?**
>
> When we switch the computer on we have to wait for it to 'boot up' before we can use it. 'Boot' comes from the old saying, 'pull yourself up by your bootstraps'.

Operating systems

Operating systems (OS) are the software programs that control the use of hardware resources. For example, they control:

- central processing unit (CPU) time
- the allocation and use of memory
- the allocation and use of disk space
- the operation of peripheral devices, such as printers.

This makes operating systems the foundation that applications software, such as word processing and spreadsheet programs, are built on. The most common operating systems are MS-DOS, the Macintosh system (OS/2) and systems that use windowing environments, such as Windows '98.

MS-DOS was developed by Microsoft and introduced as a standard operating system in all IBM compatible computers from the early 1980s and, for many years, was the most popular system in use. MS-DOS stands for **M**icro**s**oft **D**isk **O**perating **S**ystem. It controls many internal computer functions, such as how to process data, how to manage files and how to interpret commands. It is a 'command-led' system which means that you operate it by keying in command codes. For example, keying in 'dir' at the c:\> (or command) prompt and pressing Enter will display the contents of the C Drive. The command **copy c:\letter.doc a:** would be required to copy a file called 'letter' from the hard drive to a floppy disk.

DOS was difficult to work with because commands had to be entered in an exact way and there were a lot of different codes for the ordinary everyday user to remember. You might have used a computer that required you to enter c:\>win to access Windows. If so, you were giving a command in MS-DOS to load the windows environment.

Windows was first introduced in 1985 and is now the most popular PC operating system. The name comes from the computer term 'windowing environment', which is an operating system that can divide the screen into independent areas called windows. Each window has its own frame that can usually be resized and moved around on the screen. Individual windows can contain different documents or messages, or even their own menus or other controls (see Figure 3.19).

The advantage of Windows is the graphical user interface (GUI – pronounced 'gooey'), which is a user-friendly method of showing information on screen graphically. It lets you start programs, choose commands and other options by using the mouse to click icons (symbols) and lists of menu items. You no longer need to remember complicated commands. For example, to copy a file from

Figure 3.19 The advantage of a windows environment. If you are working on more than one document you would normally have one open on screen and would switch to the other using the Window menu. Here you can see two different documents are on screen at the same time and you can work in either half of the screen

the hard drive to a floppy disk you can use Explore and drag and drop the file from one folder to another.

Applications software

Applications are sometimes referred to as packages. They are programs designed to help people perform certain types of work by manipulating text, numbers and graphics, or all three together. All the popular software applications are now written to work in the Windows environment, which is why they look very similar on screen. This makes it much easier to use the different applications.

The various types of applications software include:

- word processing
- spreadsheet
- database
- desktop publishing
- graphics
- personal organisers
- e-mail
- utilities, such as virus checkers
- programming languages.

Word processing

Word processing enables you to manipulate text-based documents – for example, you can enter text, edit and format it, change the presentation, etc. You have probably already looked in detail at many of the features available in word processing in Unit 1. The simplest features make typing and basic editing tasks, such as deleting and inserting, easier. The more complex check your grammar, find synonyms, allow you to drop text, graphics or calculations created with another program into your text, display documents in multiple on-screen windows and record macros that simplify difficult or repetitive operations (for more on macros, see page 125).

You will use word processing software to present most of your written assessments and, again in Unit 1, you have looked at the different ways of presenting information to suit the occasion.

Spreadsheets

Spreadsheets are used to process numbers in a similar way to the word processor processing text. You have seen in Unit 2 how spreadsheets can be used to enter text, numbers and formulae into cells and how those cells can be formatted to display their contents as whole numbers or currency, etc. Spreadsheets are a useful tool in producing charts and graphs which help display trends and which make comparisons clear, and are particularly helpful for financial forecasting. Charts and graphs produced in a spreadsheet can be copied and pasted into word processed reports.

Databases

A database contains data but produces information from this data as a result of the processes carried out within it. For example, the database in the public library contains the names and addresses of members, the names of authors and the titles of books. It can manipulate this data to produce information to show which library member might have a particular book on loan or how many times that book has been borrowed. You have seen in Unit 2 how a database is structured and have learnt about queries and reports. A database containing names and addresses could be used as the data source for a mail-merge letter.

Desktop publishing

Purpose-written desktop publishing (DTP) software is more sophisticated than word processing software. For example, the text for inclusion in a newsletter would be created in a word processing application, spellchecked, edited and saved. It would then be imported into the DTP program together with any graphics (that would have been created in a graphics program). The DTP software has the capability of implementing the layout you have designed.

Newspapers and magazines are produced using DTP software. To achieve the best results from a DTP application you would, ideally, use a high-resolution monitor and have access to a high-resolution, colour laser printer.

As you have seen in Unit 1, your word processing software has many of the features of DTP programs. For instance, you can combine text, graphics and page layout features to create newsletters and brochures. You can add lines and borders, change the font size and style, position and resize graphics.

Graphics

As soon as we see any of the images in Figure 3.20 we recognise them instantly. Graphics are therefore a very powerful tool to help get a message across.

Graphics are computer-generated images, such as pictures or illustrations. The range of graphics software is extensive and you have probably come across images stored in word processing software (e.g. ClipArt) and images created on the computer using lines and shapes (e.g. circles, rectangles or squares). You may also have used presentation software or scanned images in your documents.

In Unit 1 you looked at the attributes of graphics software and know that images can

Figure 3.20 A range of signs

be manipulated or enhanced. The photographic models you see on the front cover of a magazine are not always as perfect as they appear – imperfections can be removed!

Computer-aided design programs help architects and designers produce technical drawings, and other industries also use graphic applications to assist them in the design and production of their work – fashion designers and publishing companies, for instance.

Graphics files can use a lot of memory and you therefore need a computer with a powerful CPU, a large hard drive and ROM, together with a high-resolution monitor and colour printer.

Graphical CD-ROMS are widely available today, offering selections of ClipArt, garden and home design activities or designs for greetings cards, etc.

Personal organisers

We have learnt how the use of networks can enable computers to share resources and communicate directly with each other –

Figure 3.21 An electronic diary

Did you know?

An intranet is a network of computers (often in a company) that uses Internet technology (such as e-mail and browser software) but that is not part of the Internet. Employees can use the intranet to find out about the company – for example, training available, social activities or job opportunities.

either through cabling in a local area network or via a modem and the telephone system over a wide area network. As a result of this, facilities such as the *scheduler* or *electronic diary* are now useful tools in large organisations. They can be set up to offer prompts automatically to remind you of important dates or events and can provide an easy reminder of your most used telephone numbers. They enable anyone with access to the diary via the computer system to see when colleagues might be available for meetings, and can save countless telephone

calls when trying to arrange a meeting. Once a convenient date and time have been found, the meeting details can be entered in all the diaries (see Figure 3.21).

E-mail

The use of e-mail is an increasingly popular method of communication which enables people all over the world to communicate from one computer to another by using the Internet and public and private networks. E-mail was one of the first uses of the Internet and is still the most popular.

An e-mail can be sent to an individual or a list of people. Each e-mail user has his or her

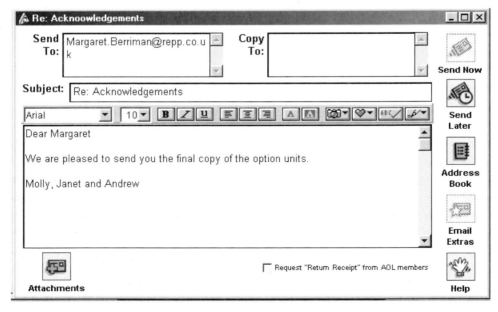

Figure 3.22 An e-mail message ready to be sent

own e-mail address. This is usually a short code, often made up of the user's name. For example, Sally Jones might be known as 'joness' and David Thorndyke as 'thornd' followed by the network provider's code.

It is very easy to send an e-mail. The recipient's e-mail address must be inserted against 'Send To' and the message typed in the space provided (see Figure 3.22).

Almost as quickly as you click on Send Now the message will be delivered. It is very much quicker than using the telephone or Royal Mail and saves paper! You can attach data files to your e-mail, such as word processed documents, spreadsheets and even presentations. The recipient can read the e-mail, delete it or save it, forward it or reply to you immediately. Attached data files can be opened, read, printed or amended and e-mailed back to you. You can even be informed that your message has been delivered and read.

? Did you know?

E-mails are legal documents. You can be prosecuted if you write something that could be construed as libellous.

ACTIVITY

What is your e-mail address at school or college?

You might find that it includes your school/college name (possibly abbreviated) followed by .ac.uk. The 'ac' indicates that you are using an **ac**ademic network that links all colleges and universities in the UK.

What other e-mail addresses have you come across? Create an address book within your e-mail software to record the e-mail addresses of some

of your friends. Create suitably named mail folders so that you can file your e-mails when you have read them.

Utilities

Utility programs provide diagnostic and measurement routines that check the performance of the system. They are programs built into the memory which continually monitor the executable files (the main applications) for any damage or change. If any change is detected the file is prevented from being run and a user message is given.

The increasing use of the Internet and e-mail has greatly added to the risk of picking up a virus. Anti-virus software is a utility program that can scan files, detect and remove viruses from hard and floppy disks. The process of removing a virus is known as 'disinfecting'.

You might have seen reports on the television news from time to time about problems caused by computer viruses: for example, letters that have visibly 'dropped off' the screen, data that have been deleted or whole systems that have become unusable.

Some web sites have been infected so that anyone visiting them will automatically transfer the virus to their computer. E-mails that infect the system as soon as they are read have been sent to large numbers of people.

Programming languages

All computer software is written in a programming language. Some are very complex and require experts to use them. These languages include C++ and Java. Languages that were widely used in the past include Cobal and Fortran.

Later in this unit we will look at some very simple programming languages – for example, those that are automatically produced for you by the computer when writing macros. The computer language used in writing macros in Microsoft Word, Excel and Access is called Visual Basic. Pages on the Internet are written in Hypertext Markup Language (HTML).

Before a computer program can be written there are various stages of development that must be undertaken. These are known as the software cycle and include the following:

- Analysis of the requirement – what does the computer program need to achieve?

- Design of a solution.

- Development of the program – probably broken down into small subprograms.

- Implementation and testing of the program, including training of the eventual users of the program.

- Preparation of documentation, which will include documentation relating to the actual program and documentation for the users (i.e. a users' guide or manual).

- Ongoing maintenance and development of the program.

In Chapter 3.3 we will look at simple programs written in Visual Basic and HTML. If you want to learn more about programming, Optional Unit 11 will give you the opportunity to explore it in more detail.

CHAPTER 3.3 COMPUTER PROGRAMMING

To use a computer you do not need to be able to write computer programs. Somebody else has already done the hard work for you. As we have already seen on page 123, there are several different programming languages in use today.

The software you use everyday for word processing, spreadsheets, etc., is known as 'off-the shelf' software and has evolved over many years. It has been developed as a commercial enterprise and is quite affordable to most people, who can buy it, install it on their computer and use it straightaway. For example, Microsoft's original word processing software for the windows environment was Word 1. This was developed and subsequently we have seen Word 2, Word 6, Word 97 and now 2000. Each release offered the user more facilities and refinements – the development is an ongoing process. Computer programmers at Microsoft are even now looking at ways of developing Word and, in due course, another version will be released offering even more capabilities.

Large organisations (such as banks and building societies) have software written especially to meet their needs. This is sometimes referred to as 'bespoke' software. It is extremely time-consuming to develop complex 'one-off' programs and, as a result, they are very, very expensive. These programs, too, need to be constantly updated to cope with the changing needs of the organisation.

Most computer programs are written by teams of programmers who each work on a small part or subprogram. The subprograms are then combined – a bit like a jigsaw puzzle – to form the whole or complete program. In this way it is much easier to revise programs at a later date.

Before any computer program can be developed you must know:

- what you want to achieve
- if it is already available off-the-shelf (or can off-the-shelf software be adapted to meet the need?)
- what programming language you can use.

In other words, you need to analyse the problem in detail before you can design the solution. This applies equally to complex programming languages and to simple, easy-to-use languages.

In this chapter we are going to look at some simple languages that are available in your existing applications software, namely:

- macros programming language
- HTML (Hypertext Markup Language).

Macros

What is a macro?

Have you ever used a cassette recorder to record a favourite song from the radio, or a video recorder to record a football match or film? The purpose of recording it was so that you could play it back whenever you wanted to.

A macro is very similar – only this time you are recording a series of actions you regularly perform so you can play them back automatically. It is a sequence of commands that is activated by a special key combination, a click of the mouse on an icon or through the drop-down menus.

For example, when you finish using a software application, instead of selecting File and then Exit with the mouse, using ALT + F4 will automatically take you through the actions.

Everytime you click on you are activating a macro that automatically goes through the process of selecting File, Print, OK – one click instead of three.

Purpose

The general purpose of macros is to make using software applications convenient, easier and more effective. They do this in three specific ways. By:

- reducing input errors
- speeding up processing
- standardising routine procedures.

All three save time by replacing often-used, sometimes lengthy series of keystrokes with shorter versions. This eliminates frequent retyping and reduces keying-in errors. It also enables users who are unfamiliar with a program to play back sets of instructions prerecorded by someone more adept with the application.

For example, a secretary using a word processing package might always use the same signature block for his or her boss:

Yours sincerely

Chris Huntley
Systems Engineer

This takes almost 50 keystrokes. Assign the block to a macro and it could be run with only one keystroke each time it was needed. Try it for yourself.

ACTIVITY

Creating macros in most applications software is easy. You start the macro recorder then record a sequence of actions. You can then run the macro

whenever you need to perform that same sequence. Although the way that macros are recorded in different applications varies, the general procedure is the same. Here is a typical outline for recording a macro to insert the signature block described above:

1 Open the application's Record Macro dialogue box (Tools, Macro/Record New Macro).

2 Type a name for the macro (in this case call the macro 'example') (Figure 3.23).

Figure 3.23 Record Macro dialogue box

3 Type a brief description of the macro – **Signature block for Chris Huntley**. This is useful for future reference, particularly if somebody else wants to know what the macro is for.

4 When you run or use the macro it can be activated in three different ways:

   a by using the pull-down menu and selecting 'example' from the macro list

   b assigning an icon to the toolbar

   c assigning keystrokes using the keyboard.

   This is the time to decide how you want to access it in future. For this exercise we will assign keystrokes to the macro. Click on the Keyboard button shown in Figure 3.23. The Customize Keyboard dialogue box appears (Figure 3.24).

Figure 3.24 Customize Keyboard dialogue box

You can assign keystrokes in the 'Press new shortcut key' box. Try Ctrl + S. Did you notice the message 'Currently assigned to FileSave'? It is better not to use a combination that already exists so try Alt + S instead. This time the message is 'unassigned' so it is available for this macro. Click Assign and Close and start to record your macro.

5 Perform the actions you want to include in your macro – type in the text below:

Yours sincerely

Chris Huntley
Systems Engineer

6 Finish the recording process.

7 Save your macro.

The computer has created simple code for you that enables you automatically to enter this text every time you use Alt + S . Open a new document and try it for yourself to see if it works.

You can view the code that has been created by selecting Tools, Macro from the menu. Click once on the macro called 'example' and then select edit. The code will look similar to Figure 3.25 if it was created in Word 6 or Figure 3.26 if it was created in Word 97.

The code is written in Visual Basic and is simple to understand. You should be able to see the code that represents every action you performed. For example, when you pressed your Enter/Return key to move on to a new line it is represented by **InsertPara** or **TypeParagraph**. In each case text is displayed between quotation marks.

If you want to amend the signature block, for example, to insert three additional clear lines beneath **Yours sincerely** and to put **Chris Huntley** and **Systems Engineer** into bold, it is very easy to do.

With the code on display on the screen, add the lines of text shown in italics and bold in Figures 3.27 and 3.28 into the coding of your macro.

```
Sub MAIN
Insert "Yours sincerely"
InsertPara
InsertPara
Insert
"Chris Huntley"
InsertPara
Insert "Systems Engineer"
InsertPara
End Sub
```

Figure 3.25 Macro created in Word 6

```
Sub example()
'
'example Macro
'Signature block for Chris Huntley
'
Selection.TypeText Text:="Yours sincerely"
Selection.TypeParagraph
Selection.TypeParagraph
Selection.TypeText Text:="Chris Huntley"
Selection.TypeParagraph
Selection.TypeText Text:="Systems Engineer"
Selection.TypeParagraph
End Sub
```

Figure 3.26 Macro created in Word 97

```
Sub MAIN
Insert
"Yours sincerely"
InsertPara
InsertPara
InsertPara
InsertPara
InsertPara
Bold 1
Insert
"Chris Huntley"
InsertPara
Insert "Systems Engineer"
Bold 0
End Sub
```

Figure 3.27 Amended macro: Word 6. Have you noticed how the 1 and 0 switch the bold on and off?

```
Sub example()
'
'example Macro
'Signature block for Chris Huntley
'
Selection.TypeText Text:="Yours sincerely"
Selection.TypeParagraph
Selection.TypeParagraph
Selection.TypeParagraph
Selection.TypeParagraph
Selection.TypeParagraph
Selection.Font.Bold=wdToggle
Selection.TypeText Text:="Chris Huntley"
Selection.TypeParagraph
Selection.TypeText Text:="Systems Engineer"
Selection.Font.Bold=wdToggle
Selection.TypeParagraph
End Sub
```

Figure 3.28 Amended macro: Word 97

Run the macro for a second time and it should look like the example below:

Yours sincerely

**Chris Huntley
Systems Engineer**

You have now created a simple macro and edited the coding. However, this macro was only created for practice and so you can delete it straightaway by selecting Tools, Macro from the menu. Click once again on the macro called 'example' and this time select Delete.

Imagine you were preparing some tourist information for the Welsh Tourist Office about the train station in Wales with the famous long name, **Llanfairpwllgwyngyllgogerychwyrndrobwllllantysiliogogogoch.** Try copying it – isn't it difficult to get it right? It comprises **58** keystrokes and is a perfect example of how the use of a macro could reduce input error and save time.

These are both very simple examples of macros using a word processing application but, macros exist in spreadsheets and databases too. Whenever you click the AutoSum button to add up a column of numbers in a spreadsheet, you are using a calculation macro.

When you use to create a chart you are using a macro called a wizard. Wizards take you step by step through a sequence of actions and help you to carry out automated routines (see Figure 3.29).

You might also have come across wizards in your database software which help you produce forms and reports. You have the opportunity of choosing various options in the design of the form or report and the wizard quickly creates it for you (see Figure 3.30).

All these examples demonstrate how the use of macros can save time and make everyday tasks easier.

Figure 3.29 Chart Wizard dialogue boxes in Microsoft Excel

Figure 3.30 Report Wizard dialogue boxes in Microsoft Access

Macros can help organisations to process enquiries efficiently and to collect valuable research by standardising enquiry procedures. For example, if you want a quote for car insurance you might telephone the insurance company and talk to an operator in the call centre. The operator will ask you a series of questions. He or she will be following screen prompts to ask for information which will then be entered into a form on the screen.

This is to ensure all relevant information is gathered. When all the data have been entered, a macro will automatically calculate an insurance premium based on the information you have given. At the same time the company can collect useful information to help them monitor their service and, again, macros can be used to total the number of times specific requests have been made.

ACTIVITY

In your word processing software, create a macro to insert automatically a footer displaying the filename and path of your document, the page number and date (all of which you can do through the Header and Footer dialogue box illustrated in Figure 3.31).

Filename and path   Page number   Date

Figure 3.31 Creating the footer

Add your name and a line to separate the footer from the page above. Figure 3.32 shows you how your finished macro will look.

Figure 3.32 Your finished macro

Figure 3.33 Assigning a button to the macro

Assign a button to the toolbar so that you can run it by selecting an icon (Figure 3.33).

Every time you click

on your toolbar the macro will run and will insert your footer automatically.

When you have created the macro print the code and try to identify the separate processes to:

- open the Header, switch to Footer

- insert AutoText for filename and path

- insert the date

- insert the page number

- change line style and insert top border

- close Footer.

Compare your code with a friend's. Can you account for any differences you can see? Amend your code in some way (for example, try to put your name in bold), run the macro again and see if you have been successful.

A macro is created in spreadsheet software in a very similar way. You are going to create a macro that will open a file, copy data into a new worksheet, create and print a chart. The data file you will use is the one you created for Select Sandwiches in Unit 2.

ACTIVITY

1 Open your spreadsheet software.

2 Select Tools, Macro, Record New Macro from the menu bar and then name your macro or assign keystrokes.

   The macro will now record every action you perform.

Type of Sandwich	Price per Unit	Jan	Feb	Mar
Egg Mayonnaise	1.60	200	198	234
Corned Beef & Salad	1.70	120	110	130
Ham & Tomato	1.75	212	208	178
Cheese & Pickle	1.75	167	189	175
Chicken Salad	1.80	234	223	278
Bacon Lettuce & Tomato	1.80	189	237	196
Chicken Tikka	1.80	203	234	286

Figure 3.34 Select Sandwiches macro

3 Start by opening the Select Sandwiches spreadsheet you created in Unit 2.

4 Select the Types of Sandwich and the data for Jan, Feb and March. (You highlight the range A2:A9, release the mouse button, hold down the Control key and then highlight the range C2:E9.) It will look like Figure 3.34.

5 Select Copy and open a new workbook.

6 Click on Paste and the highlighted text will be inserted in the workbook (without the Price per Unit column).

7 Use Chart Wizard to produce a suitable chart on a new sheet.

8 Print a copy of the chart.

9 Stop Recording.

10 Save the macro.

Once again, print the code and see if you can identify the stages that you went through when you created it.

Default macros

A default macro is the choice made by a program if the user does not specify an alternative. For example, a computer's start-up program might default to the hard disk if it does not find the operating system in a CD-ROM or floppy disk drive.

Default macros are built into programs. Each time you open a new document or worksheet you are presented with default values. For example, a word processing program might default to normal page style, regular 12 point Times New Roman font, single spaced paragraphs with left alignment, margins set at 3.17 cm and tab stops every 1.27 cm. It does this to present a recognisable format, a starting point, until the user specifies otherwise. This default style is sometimes referred to as a style sheet, and we look at these in more detail on page 152.

If your user wants to adopt a different style regularly, he or she could record a macro to change the default settings. For example, changing the font to Arial 11 point, justified paragraphs in one and a half line spacing and margins set at 3.5 cm.

However, rather than recording a macro there is an alternative solution. You might decide to create a template.

Templates

One of the most commonly used types of macro is a template. Templates are standardised document types, such as letters, fax cover sheets or invoices (Figure 3.35). Selecting a specific template activates the sequence of layout and formatting commands that results in the saved document type.

A template is a blueprint for the text, graphics and formatting in a document. A fax template, for example, contains the company name, a date field and placeholders to indicate where to type the recipient's name, address, fax and phone numbers, the number of pages and the message text.

The benefit of a template is that you can use it time and time again. When you create a template you save it specifically as a template rather than as a word processed document or a spreadsheet worksheet. Each time you open the template and use it, the file type automatically changes from template to

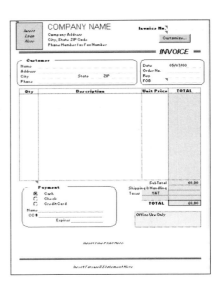

Figure 3.35 A letter template, fax template and invoice template

document or worksheet, which removes any risk of saving data in the original template. In this way the template is always ready for you to use again.

 ACTIVITY

Templates in a word processing application may include letters, memos, faxes and reports. In a spreadsheet you may find examples of invoices, expense statements and timesheets. Look to see what examples are available in your software. You will find templates through File, New. Do you like the look of some more than others? What is it about these designs that you particularly like or dislike? Make a note of the features that appeal to you and save them in your Layout Reference log. Try to incorporate them into your own designs.

Template macros have become the foundation of many organisations' house styles or printed images. A standardised company image creates an impression of consistency and reliability. Consequently, most organisations are careful to use the same style on all their documents. If you have received different letters from the same organisation, compare the layout. You will notice that, although they may be written by different people and on different machines, they all have the addresses, dates and references in the same position and all use the same font.

A printing company might regularly produce a price list of services for photocopying, binding, etc., which is in the form of a two-sided A4 sheet folded to form an A5 leaflet. A template could be set up which has landscape page layout, columns and holds all constant data – i.e. company logo, address, telephone number, opening times, list of services, etc. It could be used to produce new price lists as required. A template of this nature would save considerable time when a new price list was needed.

 ACTIVITY

You have already designed macros in both word processing and spreadsheet software applications. Now create templates in the same software.

In your word processing software, set up a template to be used as a letter heading showing your home address.

This is how you create a template in word processing:

1 Create a new document and insert your address in a size and style of font you like, either in the centre or right aligned. Leave two or three clear line spaces and then insert the date using Insert, Date and Time. Return two or three more lines (this is ready to insert the name and address of the recipient of the letter).

2 Select Save As. Choose the appropriate folder/directory, type a name for the new template and change 'save as type' to a Document Template (see Figure 3.36).

Figure 3.36 Save As: Document Template

3 Select Save.

4 Close your template and reopen it through File, New.

5 When you open and use the template and select Save, you will see that 'Save as type' has automatically reverted to Word Document. Save in the usual way.

In your spreadsheet software, create a template to show the footer area of a spreadsheet with the filename and path, your name and the date.

A template in a spreadsheet is created in a similar way to word processing:

1 Open your workbook.

2 Select File, Page Setup, Header/Footer, Custom Footer.

3 Insert the filename and date using the buttons in the Footer dialogue box (Figure 3.37).

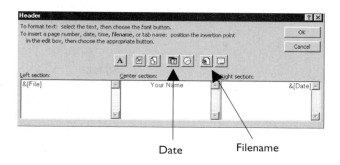

Figure 3.37 Footer dialogue box

4 Close the Header/Footer and Page Setup dialogue boxes.

5 Save as a spreadsheet template in the same way as you saved your word processing template.

6 Close your template and reopen it through File, New.

7 When you open and use the template and select Save, you will see that 'save as type' has automatically reverted to an Excel worksheet. Save in the usual way

HTML (Hypertext Markup Language)

HyperText Markup Language is the code used to write pages for the web. This code is in the form of *tags* which surround blocks of text to indicate how the text should appear on the screen so that it looks the same when viewed through any web browser.

To explain it simply, the author of a web page designs the page and links all the material together using HTML. When the page is viewed (either by the author or someone viewing a published web page), the web browser software interprets the HTML language and displays the text exactly as the author intended.

It enables you to create *hyperlinks* within the text so that, when you click on a hyperlink, you automatically jump to another part of the page or another page on the web. A hyperlink might be a word, a button or a picture.

 ACTIVITY

Find a page on the Internet that interests you – preferably one that does not have too many pictures on it. Read the page to familiarise yourself with its contents. Is there a hyperlink? What happens when you click on it?

You can see how the page has been put together with HTML code by viewing the source code through View/Source or Document Source from the menu of your web browser. (This facility might not be available through all Internet service providers – if not, try clicking the right mouse button or ask your tutor or teacher.) The source code is what the author used to enable you to see the finished page as he or she intended when it was designed.

It probably looks *very* complicated because it will have been written by an expert in HTML and will have been designed to include many advanced concepts. Can you pick out some of the text you read amongst the coding?

Copy some of the coding, paste it into a Word document and print it out. As you read through this section see if you can identify the HTML codes in the printout. It is better to copy and paste the code rather than print it direct from your web browser so that you don't end up with pages and pages of code.

Most word processing software today enables you to produce programs in HTML without the need to understand the coding, and we will look at this method and web page wizards later in this section. However, in order to gain a better understanding of the coding, we are going to look at HTML program code in some detail and then produce a simple web page using code.

What do you need to create a web page?

To create a simple web page there are four things you will need:

- A simple text editor (like Notepad) to create the page or a dedicated HTML editor or converter that is now standard with a great many word processing applications or Web Page Wizards.

- A web browser which is a dedicated software application that will enable you to browse the web and view your own web pages (e.g. Internet Explorer or Netscape).

- You will need to learn the codes (or tags) used to format and structure the text.

- Finally, and perhaps most importantly, the design and presentation skills you learnt in Unit 1.

Tags

Did you notice words or letters inside the < and > marks in the document code you viewed? These are known as *tags* and are the way the web browser knows how we want the document to appear. For example, they tell the web browser where to start a new paragraph or print a line of text. They usually come in pairs with the second tag of the pair beginning with a slash symbol /. As an example the <p> and </p> tags indicate where a paragraph begins and ends.

The first tag of any document is <html>, which tells the web browser that you are beginning a page of information written in

HTML. The closing tag **</html>** is put at the end of the document.

If you look on page 140 you will see a list of the most common codes used, and we will be using some of these tags when we create a web page later in this chapter.

The simplest HTML document might be made up of the following tags and text:

```
<html>
This is my first example of HTML.
</html>
```

What it would look like in your text editor is shown in Figure 3.38.

It must be saved with the file extension .htm and can then be viewed in a web browser. It would look like Figure 3.39.

Figure 3.38 Simple HTML code in a text editor

Figure 3.39 Simple HTML code viewed in a web browser

Hypertext links

The World Wide Web is like a giant electronic book that you can read through a computer. It consists of millions of documents stored on computers throughout the world, which are all joined through hypertext links or hot spots – which is what HTML is all about. When you move your mouse pointer over a hyperlink the arrow changes to a pointing hand, and clicking on the mouse button connects you to the link. You might click on text, a button or a picture. You can create a hyperlink to one of your own documents or to a page on a different web site altogether. HTML *anchor tags* enable you to do this. An anchor tag might look like this:

<a href="destination">text of hyperlink</a>

To simplify this: the first letter **a** indicates it is an anchor and **href** tells us it is a hypertext reference. The "**destination**" denotes the place you will go to when you click on the hyperlink. On your own web page it may be the file reference of a second document you have created or it may be the URL of a different web site. The **text of hyperlink** will be the word(s) you display on your page to indicate the link – you might merely want to indicate 'click here'. Finally the </a> shows the end of the anchor.

You can also insert hyperlinks in a document that enable you to jump to a different place on the same page. The place in the page you jump to is called the **target**. The anchor tag is slightly different:

<a name="target">target text </a>

The word "**target**" is the name of the target text that will actually appear in the web page at the location of the target. In other words, the tag above is inserted at the point

you want to jump to. To jump to this target you insert another hyperlink that looks like this:

<a href="#target">hyperlink text</a>

The destination of this hyperlink is the name of the anchor with a hash sign # (or number sign) in front of it.

For example, if you wanted to say 'I come from a very large family. If you want to read more about my family click here' the HTML code would look like this (at this stage don't worry about codes you haven't been introduced to):

<p>I come from a very large family. If you want to read more about my family click <a href="#family"> here</a>.</p>

Further down the page you might have text that reads 'My family consists of my Mum, Dad, Sister, 2 dogs, 1 cat, 1 rabbit and 2 goldfish.' And the code for this would be:

<p>My <a name="family">family>/a> consists of my Mum, Dad, Sister, 2 dogs, 1 cat, 1 rabbit and 2 goldfish.</p>

Graphics

You might have heard the phrase 'a picture paints a thousand words' and, indeed, pictures included in a web page can create more interest, add impact and help get your message across. They may come from ClipArt, be something you have drawn or scanned yourself or something you have downloaded from the web. A graphic feature might be flashing text, a moving image or animated clip.

The BBC have a web site specifically designed for the hearing impaired – www.bbc.co.uk/see_hear. If you look at this site you might be able to see the moving image of a signer using sign language.

Non-moving images can be added to web pages by using the *image tag*. An image tag might look like this:

<img src="picture.jpg">

This tag does not need to be closed, so there is no </img src> at the end of it. The **img src** means <u>im</u>age <u>so</u>u<u>rc</u>e and **"picture.jpg"** is the name of the graphic file.

Any picture to be stored on your web page must be stored on your hard drive in a graphics file format. The two formats that can be used with a web browser are GIF (pronounced 'giff' or 'jiff') and JPEG (pronounced 'jay peg'). A GIF (graphics interchange format) image is similar to a bitmap image and is made up of pixels (or dots). A JPEG (joint photographics experts group) file format is ideal for displaying photographic images because it can use over

16 million colours compared to 256 for GIF images.

Special software, called Shockwave, is available for producing animated graphics, video and sound sequences. This software is designed to download quickly because a visitor to a web page does not want to wait a long time to see the full page. However, it is a very expensive and complex program that takes a long time to learn. At this stage you will find it interesting just to view examples. If your system has a Shockwave plug-in installed you should be able to view Shockwave files. (A plug-in is a mini-program attached to your web browser that allows it to handle unusual file formats.)

The BBC education web pages have examples of Shockwave activities. For instance the page in Figure 3.40 has Shockwave games for very young children to play.

A visit to the web page www.macromedia.com will give you some more examples.

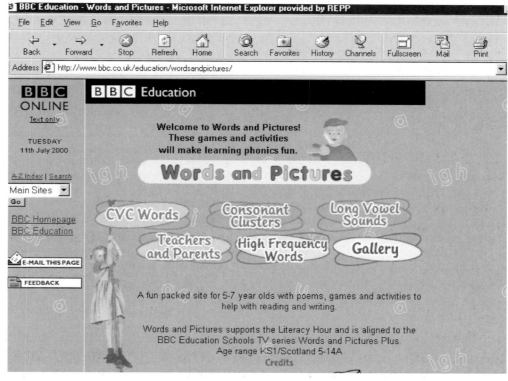

Figure 3.40 www.bbc.co.uk/education/wordsandpictures/

Including background sounds

Adding sound to a web page can bring it to life (see Figure 3.41).

Imagine how a page promoting travel to Scotland would be if sounds of the bagpipes accompanied it! A recording of crowds cheering at a football match might be inspiring on a football web page. On a serious note, sound is as beneficial to the visually impaired as a visual image is to the hearing impaired.

Most PCs today come with sound facilities built in and a sound card is an essential piece of software. The most popular sound formats for short extracts are:

- WAV$_e$ format in Windows with the **.wav** filename extension

- AIFF format in Apple Macs with the **.aiff** filename extension.

WAV$_e$ files can be created using the Windows Sound Recorder found in the Accessories Multimedia command and they can be set up using the **<BGSOUND>** tag.

Figure 3.41 Sound can bring a web page to life

Creating your first web page

To ensure all your files are kept together it would be a good idea to create a new directory or folder with a suitable name, like 'Web Pages'. This will help you find everything quickly and easily (e.g. files you may want to link, graphics files, sound files, etc.).

What to type	Why
<html>	This indicates the start of an HTML page
<head>	This indicates some header information
<title>My demonstration Web Page</title>	This indicates the text that will appear in the title bar at the top of your web page
</head>	This indicates the end of the header information
<body>	Indicates the start of the main part of the web page
<h1>This is the largest size heading</h1>	A heading in the largest size. We will look at other sizes later
<p>Anything that I type now will be part of my web page. This is an example.</p>	The <p> tag tells the browser to start a new paragraph
</body>	I have now finished entering the main part of my web page
</html>	The end of my HTML page

Figure 3.42 Creating a web page: initial text

There are three ways of creating a web page. One way is to use a text editor, another is to produce your page in Microsoft Word and save it as an HTML file or, thirdly, to use a Web Page Wizard. In order to introduce you to HTML code you are going to use the text editor first. Once you understand the basic coding you'll find it fun to do and you'll be on your way to becoming an expert! Then you can try the other two methods.

Your text editor is probably Notepad, which you will find with the Accessories in Program Manager if you are using Windows 3.11 or by clicking on Start, Programs, Accessories in Windows '98 or NT.

Let's get started. Check in your text editor to see that Word wrap is switched on (Edit/Word wrap). Now key in the text shown in Figure 3.42 exactly as it appears on the left. Start new lines at each new tag. Remember the closing tags have an additional / inserted. (The notes on the right are to help you understand what you are doing.)

It should look like Figure 3.43.

Figure 3.43 Initial text

You must save your file as a text file in your new web page folder/directory and insert the extension **.htm** to the filename (Figure 3.44).

Figure 3.44 Saving the initial text

To view your page, open your web browser and select File/Open. Type in the drive, folder and the name of the file in full – e.g. f:unit3/web pages/demonstration file.htm. It should look something like Figure 3.45.

This is the largest size heading

Anything that I type now will be part of my web page. This is an example

Figure 3.45 The text viewed in the web browser

Comment tags

If you want to write something in your HTML page that you don't want to appear on your web page you use a *comment tag*. The tag that turns the comment on is `<!--` and the tag that turns the comment off is `-->`.

Why do you need to write comments the browser will ignore? An HTML comment is like a note to yourself (or someone else who might later need to look at your program) to remind you about something important that you don't want to forget.

Add this comment to your text editor between the two sentences of your body text in your demonstration page (see Figure 3.46):

<!--This is just a comment -->

```
Untitled - Notepad
File  Edit  Search  Help
<html>

<head>

<title> My demonstration Web
Page </title>

</head>

<body>

<h1>This is the largest size
heading</h1>

<p>Anything that I type now will be part of my web page.
<!--This is just a comment-->This is an example.</p>

</body>

</html>
```

Figure 3.46 Adding a comment tag

Save the changes and open the file again in your web browser. It should look exactly the same as before. Just to check it's the new version, view your code through View/Source. Can you see the comment tags? Remember that, if you can, so can anyone else who wants to view your document source so don't write anything you wouldn't want them to see!

Well done! You've successfully created your first web page.

ACTIVITY

Now that you have been successful in creating your own web page and have been introduced to some of the code, look at another web page to see what you can understand. Print the code as you did

before by copying and pasting into Word, then draw a circle round all the code you now recognise.

Table 3.2 acts as a reminder of some of the tags we have already looked at and includes some others that will enable you to be a little more adventurous and to improve the look of your web page designs.

In addition to these tags, don't forget the hyperlink anchors, picture and comment tags.

Tag		What it does
<html>	</html>	Indicates the beginning and end of an HTML page
<body>	</body>	All the text in the document is between these tags
<head>	</head>	The head section of the web page
<title>	</title>	The text that will appear on the title bar
<h1>	</h1>	Inserts a heading in the largest font. Sizes go down h2, h3, h4, h5 and h6, which is the smallest
<b>	</b>	Displays characters in **bold**
<i>	</i>	Displays characters in *italics*
<blink>	</blink>	Causes the enclosed text to blink or flash
<a>	</a>	Anchors used to mark the beginning and end of hypertext. Read the earlier paragraphs on page 136
<center>	</center>	Everything between these tags is centred
<hr>	</hr>	Places a horizontal line across the document

Table 3.2 Tags

Using Word to create a web page

We have looked in detail at the programming code that enables you to create a web page. However, as mentioned previously, there are alternative ways to do it. The first is by using your word processing software.

Type the following heading and the three paragraphs as shown below. The text is Arial, the heading is in 14 pt bold and the body is 12 pt.

HTML PROGRAMMING

This is an example of simple text prepared in MS Word and saved as an HTML file. By opening the file in Notepad you can see the coding that has been applied.

If you are not using a version of Word that enables you to save as an HTML file you can prepare your text in Notepad and save as a .htm file.

When you open the file in a web browser it looks like this!

You need to save your text using the special **Save as HTML** option illustrated in Figure 3.47. Remember to save it in your web page directory.

Figure 3.47 Saving the text

Go to your web browser and open your file. You will need to specify the drive and folders/directories as well as the full filename. It should look like Figure 3.48.

If you view the source code you will recognise the tags you have already used, plus some additional codes the computer has inserted:

```
<HTML>

<HEAD>

<META HTTP-EQUIV="Content-Type" CONTENT="text/html; charset=windows-1252">

<META NAME="Generator" CONTENT="Microsoft Word 97">

<TITLE>HTML PROGRAMMING</TITLE>

</HEAD>

<BODY>

<B><FONT FACE="Arial" SIZE=4><P>HTML PROGRAMMING</P>

</B></FONT><FONT FACE="Arial" SIZE=3>

<P>This is an example of simple text prepared in MS Word and saved as an HTML file. By opening the file in Notepad you can see the coding that has been applied.</P>

<P>If you are not using a version of Word that enables you to save as an HTML file you can prepare your text in Notepad and save as a .htm file.</P>

<P>When you open the file in a web browser it looks like this!</P></FONT></BODY>

</HTML>
```

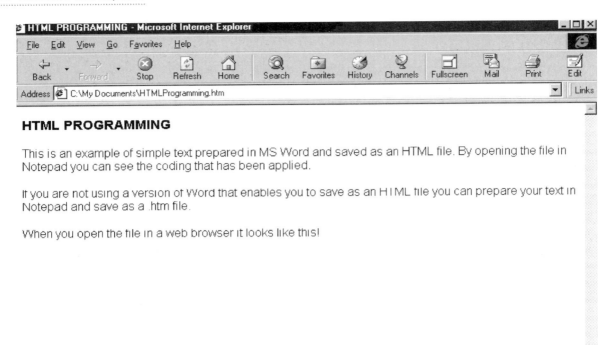

Figure 3.48 The text as it appears in the web browser

Using Web Page Wizard

You can also access Web Page Wizards to help you create web pages. You will find these through File, New under the Web Page tab (Figure 3.49).

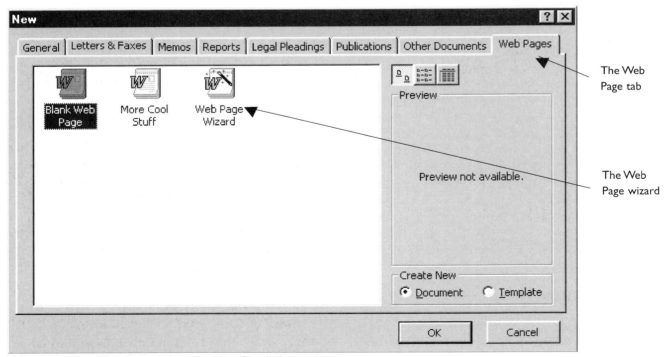

Figure 3.49 The Web Page tab in the New file dialogue box

The Web Page Wizard offers you a choice of page layouts (Figure 3.50).

Figure 3.50 The Web Page Wizard

The Simple Layout is illustrated in Figure 3.51 and is ready for you to enter your text and create hyperlinks. You can do this using the Insert menu on your web browser.

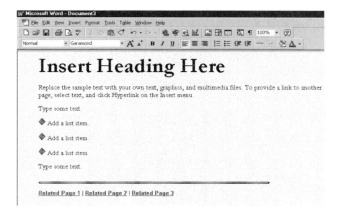

Figure 3.51 Simple Layout

You can also choose from a variety of styles (see Figure 3.52).

You are now a computer programmer! You have used a simple language to produce a

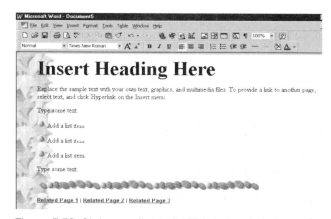

Figure 3.52 Styles available in Simple Layout

web page and have looked at the tools that are available to help you produce more complex programs. You should now be able to combine all three to produce some interesting work.

Before you start producing your own web pages, think back to Unit 1 and the techniques for presenting information. Apply these techniques to your web page design so that you design something suitable for your target audience. Think about the structure of your page and, if you intend to use hyperlinks, consider where you will place them on the page. Your web pages can include images created by you, ClipArt or scanned pictures and, if you have the facility, sound clips too. Remember to save *all* your work in your web page folder.

Use your web browser to view your page(s) as you create them and in that way you can edit regularly as you go along. Finally . . . good luck!

ACTIVITY

At this point it might be useful to create a template of your own containing the standard HTML codes so that you don't have to type them everytime you want to design a web page. You can use comments to remind you of what goes where.

Open Notepad and type in the following:

```
<!--This is a sample template I
can use for web pages-->

<html>
<head>

<!--This is where I can put a
title to appear on the tool bar of
my web page-->

<title>Type the title here</title>

</head>

<!--Anything from here onwards
will appear on the page as the
main body of text-->

<body>

<!--The heading that follows will
be in the largest size font-->

<h1>Type the main heading
here</h1>

<!--Remember to start and end
paragraphs with the p tag-->

<p>Start typing the text here.</p>

</body>

</html>
```

Now save in your text editor as **template.htm**. Each time you use the template you must save it with a different filename. Unlike the templates we looked at before on page 131, Notepad will not automatically give your files different names so you must do it yourself by selecting File, Save As.

There are of course many, many more things you can do on a web page. This chapter is just an introduction and you will learn more complicated coding if you proceed to an advanced course at a later date.

CHAPTER 3.4 CHOOSING AND SETTING UP A SYSTEM

What would your reply be if a friend asked you the question in Figure 3.53? Would you say:

1 'I think you should buy the Celcius 700 MHz. It's got fantastic speakers, a 19 inch screen and a DVD-ROM. It will be great for watching movies.'

2 'There are some really cheap reconditioned computers in that shop in the High Street.'

3 'It all depends what you want it for and how much you want to spend.'

To give good advice it would have to be 3 because before you can answer the question you must know exactly what your friend requires from the computer. To know this you need to consider the following:

• What does he or she want the system for?

• What type of processing does he or she want to carry out on the computer – e.g. letter writing, financial calculations?

• What does he or she want the computer to produce?

In the previous three chapters in this unit we have looked in detail at the hardware and software that make up a computer system and have also looked at simple programming that can make everyday computer tasks easier and quicker.

To fulfil the requirements for Unit 3, you must show you can select an ICT system and configure it to meet the needs of users. This means choosing the appropriate hardware and software, setting up the system and making modifications to the default settings to help the user get the most benefit from the system.

Selecting an ICT system

Consider the case of Ian Duncan who runs a small catering business. This is what he has told us about his business.

'I started the business accidentally – a friend asked me to do a couple of business lunches. It was a very informal arrangement – he would phone me the day before a lunch, we'd agree the menu and I'd deliver it the following day.

Figure 3.53

I gave him a hand-written invoice and he sent me a cheque. Then all of a sudden the business seemed to take off and I started getting calls from other local businesses. Now I'm thinking of expanding the business from just business lunches to cater for weddings at the weekend. At the moment my Mum types out the menus and then gets them photocopied and she also works out the bills with a calculator, then types out the invoices although, sometimes, she gets it wrong and I have to check them. Everyone says I should get a computer for the office but I really don't know much about them. Can you help?'

From what Ian has told you so far, do you think you know enough to offer him the right advice? It certainly sounds as if he needs some help but, perhaps, you need to find out some more information first. Think back to the three questions at the start of this chapter and imagine the answers you might get if you asked him some direct questions:

Question: What do you want the system for?

Answer: I am a caterer and know that people who taste my food are impressed. However, I have also got to impress people who don't know me and I think that the standard of our menus and letters, etc., lets my business down. I need to raise the image of the company and I need to find ways to help my Mum cope with the extra work that has been generated as the business has expanded. At the moment we don't have time to follow up enquiries and I think we must lose quite a lot of business through this.

Question: What type of processing do you want to carry out on the computer? How do you think it can help you?

Answer: I need to produce menus for the business lunches and I would like to include photographs of some of my dishes. I also offer several different wedding menus and I need to be able to send these out with covering letters. I'd quite like a logo of some sort on our letters, etc. It would be great if I could find a way of helping Mum work out the invoices correctly first time!

Question: What do you want the computer to produce?

Answer: Naturally, I want everything to look professional and neat and I want all documentation – letters, invoices and menus – to have a standard style. Advertising leaflets will be useful and we certainly need to improve our invoicing system.

By asking some simple questions we have found out quite a lot more about Ian's needs and you should now be able to identify the hardware and software that will help him.

 ACTIVITY

To help you it will be useful to prepare a checklist that incorporates details of the hardware and software that make up an ICT system. Prepare a three-column table similar to Figure 3.54. The middle column can be used to tick (✓) the components that you consider essential or to question (?) those that might be useful. The last column can record the reasons for putting a ✓ or ? in the middle column.

Save your checklist as a template – refer to page 133 if you don't remember how to do it – so you can use it again if you need to.

When you have finished compare your list with your friend's. How similar are they? Why do you think you might have made different selections? A suggested system is in the TRF.

We have looked at choosing a system for Ian. Whomever the system is for – yourself or somebody else – there are several stages to go through before you can actually sit down and use it to its full potential.

Component/software	✓/?	Justification for use
Input devices		
Keyboard		
Mouse		
Rollerball		
Scanner		
Digital camera		
Microphone		
Joystick		
Main processing unit		
Describe the type of processor, memory, hard drive size, disk drives, etc., you would recommend		
Backup system		
Modem		
Network card		
Output devices		
VDU		
Printer		
Speakers		
Software		
Operating system		
Word processing		
Spreadsheet		
Database		
Desktop publishing		
Graphics		
E-mail		
Personal organiser		
Utilities		
Programming languages		
Cables and connectors		
Describe briefly		

Figure 3.54 Selecting an ICT system: checklist

Setting up the system

Perhaps this warning is basic common sense but, nevertheless, it is something you must always remember when connecting/testing a computer or if something appears to have come loose when you are using it.

Connecting it all together

Connect up your cables for the keyboard, mouse, VDU, etc., then plug into the main

? Did you know?

Electrical surges and voltage spikes can cause serious damage to computer systems. Surges and spikes are momentary over-voltages of up to several thousand volts that last a few millionths of a second. They may be caused by the switching of large loads, such as air conditioning or lifts, hydro-power adjustments or lightning storms.

If any device is not connected to a surge protector, a surge can enter and damage the whole system through that one unprotected device.

No surge protectors are much help against lightning. If the weather is severe or if there is any threat of an electrical storm, disconnect the entire system from the power supply. If you are working with a system that has a modem, lightning can ride in on the phone line connected to the modem, destroy it and then the system connected to it. So, always disconnect systems from telephone lines before a storm starts – and perhaps this is also a good reason to keep backup copies of your software and data files.

electricity supply to make sure the system powers up and runs properly before connecting any accessories such as printers or scanners and so on. This keeps things simple so, if there are any problems, they will be easier to isolate and deal with.

Installation

Once you have the basic system connected, powered up and running smoothly, you are ready to install the software and prepare the system for use. Almost all systems come with the operating system preinstalled and configured. From this point, you may have to install drivers for the display, the printer and any other peripherals, as well as the applications software.

Device drivers are programs that enable a computer system to communicate with a device. A printer driver, for example, translates computer data into a form that is understood by the specific type of printer you have connected. In most cases, device drivers also manipulate the hardware involved in sending data to the device.

The installation procedure for device drivers and for applications software under most operating systems is very similar. Once activated the software walks you through the rest of the process.

Most computers today come complete with a CD-ROM drive and, therefore, software is usually loaded from a CD-ROM. Before the advent of the CD-ROM, software came on floppy disks and you had to load several disks before the application was complete!

When you are installing new applications software, the program setup usually asks if you would like it to create a new directory (or folder) to store the new program in. It also suggests a name and shows the path. For example, if the program is called Gamer, it might suggest C:\Gamer. We will look in more detail at data directories and folders on page 150.

Testing

Your installation and setup is only successful once you have tested it thoroughly. Testing means being able to perform each of the following actions without any problems:

- powering up

- accessing applications software

- entering, saving, retrieving and printing data.

Powering up

When you power up you should hear the hard disk beginning to spin and see the

monitor flicker into life. If nothing happens, switch off the computer and check the power cables to make sure they are still plugged in securely. If you are using a surge protector, make sure it is switched on. If you can hear the power supply fan whirring, but nothing shows up on the monitor, make sure the monitor is turned on. You may also need to check and adjust the monitor brightness control.

Accessing the applications

If your software has been loaded successfully you should be able to open it from Start, Programs and by selecting the program you want or by clicking on the appropriate icon on the computer desktop.

To ensure that each application is functioning correctly, you need to test it. The following procedure will be adequate:

1 Open the application.

2 Type <Test1> with your initials and the date.

3 Save the file as <Test1> with an appropriate extension.

4 Exit the application.

5 Reopen the application.

6 Open the file.

7 Select Print.

8 Save and close the file.

9 Exit the application.

Your computer is now set up but, before you start using it, make sure any cables are safely tucked away and do not cause a trip hazard. Remember the health and safety aspects you learnt about in the Preparatory Unit – Standard Ways of Working.

? Did you know?

Keeping a system in good shape has a lot to do with the way you power up and down. Here's the advice of top systems suppliers:

- Power up the monitor first, then each of the accessories before you switch the system on – this causes fewer devices to pull on the same power source simultaneously.

- Avoid turning the system on and off frequently.

- Never turn the system off when the hard drive indicator light is on.

- Once you have shut the system down, do not turn it back on again until the hard drive has come to a complete halt.

- Whenever you restart the system, use the reset button rather than the power button.

- Always close whatever programs you are using and shut down the system before switching off.

- If you use an extension lead, never turn the system on and off from the extension lead switch.

System configuration

The system will be set up with standard settings which, for most people, will be quite acceptable. However, some people will find the system much easier to use if some small adjustments are made. This is called configuring the system. For example, the left-handed user will find the mouse more comfortable to use if the button functions are reversed. Someone who is colour blind might find certain desktop colours difficult to distinguish. Experienced typists might like to assign more functions to the keyboard to avoid interrupting their work to use the mouse. Some may like to work with the ruler in inches and others in centimetres.

Changes to system configuration can be made in several ways:

- by creating data directories or folders

- through the Control Panel

- through the pull-down menus

- through style sheets.

Additionally, the creation of templates and macros will make the system easier to use but, remember, to test them to make sure they work as you intended.

Creating data directories or folders

When software is installed on a computer, the operating system ensures that directories/folders are created to keep all the relevant program files together. It is equally as important to create directories/folders to separate data files from program files. If we didn't do this we would end up with a very long, muddled list of data files.

Imagine a filing cabinet with everything thrown in – how difficult it would be to find

anything (Figure 3.55). A computer without directories/folders is similar to a disorganised filing cabinet. A tidy filing cabinet will have drawers labelled and, inside the drawers, files are used to separate the papers into subjects (Figure 3.56).

In computer terms, think of the drawer as a directory (or folder) and the hanging files as subdirectories. The use of directories/folders results in data files being in the right place

Figure 3.55 A disorganised filing system

Figure 3.56 A well-oragnised filing system

and therefore easy to locate, edit, view and manage. There is also less likelihood of accidental deletion of program files.

You can create directories/folders in Explore or My Computer. If you are using Windows 3.11 you create them in File Manager.

ACTIVITY

Create a directory/folder for each of the three Mandatory Units 1, 2 and 3. Create subdirectories in Unit 1 called 'classwork' and 'assessments'. In Unit 2 create subdirectories called 'assessments' 'spreadsheet' and 'database' and, in Unit 3, create subdirectories called 'classwork', 'assessments' and 'web pages'.

You can now move your data files into the appropriate directories by dragging and dropping.

If you have started any Optional Units create directories for those too.

Your list should look something like Figure 3.57 when you have finished.

Figure 3.57 Explorer showing folders created to organise data files

Control Panel

The settings in the Control Panel (Figure 3.58) enable you to personalise your computer by making changes to operating system software. For example, you can change the mouse settings, the desktop appearance, etc. The easiest way for you to investigate Control Panel is to look at each item in turn.

Figure 3.58 Control Panel window

ACTIVITY

Open your Control Panel by selecting Start, Settings, Control Panel and look at the icons on screen. Click on each item in turn and list everything you can find that will help you configure a computer system.

 ACTIVITY

Just as you investigated the Control Panel, look through the different items available in the Tools menu. In particular, check out Options and Customise. Again, note all the opportunities you can find to configure the system.

Tools pull-down menu

Modifications to your applications software are made through the Tools menu on the menu bar at the top of the screen (Figure 3.59). For example, you can set the language of your computer dictionary to take account of regional variations in the use of English.

Figure 3.59 Tools pull-down menu

Style sheets

The default settings in your word processing software are recorded in the Normal Style Sheet which you will find within the Format menu (Figure 3.60).

We have already considered the use of macros and templates as a way of changing default settings. They are useful if you do not need these different settings all the time. If, for example, you wanted to ensure your font was *always* Arial 11 point rather than the default setting of Times New Roman 10 point it would become irritating to open the template or run the macro each time you wanted to do some work. By making changes to the Normal Style Sheet your default settings will change too, and every time you open your application the new settings will operate.

Figure 3.60 Style Sheet

ACTIVITY

You will find Style Sheets under the pull-down menu Format, Style.

See if the settings shown on your style sheet match the settings shown on your computer screen. There are several different style sheets stored on your computer. Make a list of them and note the different styles that apply to each sheet. Think of occasions when you might be able to apply these styles.

 ACTIVITY

Now you have had an opportunity to investigate different ways to configure a computer system, write down how you can carry out the procedures listed in Figure 3.61. Check your answers by following the instructions you have suggested to see if you were right!

The answers are in the Tutor Resource File.

Earlier in this chapter we considered a suitable ICT system for Ian Duncan. He has now bought a Pentium III 600 MHz computer with 64 MB RAM and 10 GB hard drive. In addition he has a DVD-ROM, CD

Change the ruler from inches to centimetres	
Remove the Status Bar	
Change the desktop colours	
Ensure backup copies are always created	
Remove vertical and horizontal scroll bars	
Set keyboard control keys	
Save a template	
Add a tail to the mouse	
Change file locations	
Display the vertical ruler	
Use a template	
Turn off drag and drop editing	
Set a password	
Remove the option that underlines spelling errors	
Create a macro	
Change backup timing	
Change the toolbar display	
Change the computer time and date	
Ensure days of the week are automatically given capital letters	

Figure 3.61 How would you carry out these procedures?

writer, colour printer and scanner. This system runs through Windows 2000 and the following software has been installed:

- word processing
- spreadsheet
- database
- graphics
- personal organiser
- e-mail
- Internet access.

Imagine he has asked you to come in and help set up his system. How might you configure the system?

Just to remind you, his specific requirements included the following:

- Producing business menus incorporating photos of a selection of dishes.
- Producing a selection of wedding menus.
- Producing covering letters enclosing menus to people who enquire.
- Producing a logo to go on his stationery.
- Producing an invoice that he won't have to keep checking.
- Producing advertising leaflets.
- Following up enquiries.

When you have made your suggestions, check with the list in the TRF.

This unit gives you an opportunity to work on an ICT activity you are interested in, or to extend work you have already carried out for another unit.

After studying this unit you should be able to:

- identify an ICT design project you would like to carry out
- define the purpose of the project and plan how you will undertake the work
- use software to produce the required facilities or product
- test and evaluate your work
- understand and develop good practice in your use of ICT.

In order to do this you will need to:

- identify an ICT design project
- produce a project proposal
- obtain permission to proceed
- plan the design
- monitor the production and progress
- test the product and produce documentation
- evaluate the product.

You might choose to undertake this project alone or with fellow students. You will have the opportunity to discuss ideas for projects with your fellow students and your tutor.

You will be assessed through your portfolio work and your project will enable you to help other users of ICT to be more effective in their work or to improve the quality of their work.

Stages of a design project

To help you understand the different stages that embrace any project, we are going to look at the story of George. George has just acquired a plot of land and has decided he wants to build a house on it. Unfortunately, he cannot expect to telephone his builder one day and for the work to start the next. Obviously, there is a lot of preparatory work George must do before the builder can even dig the first trench for the foundations.

First of all George would need to persuade a building society or bank to lend him the money to build the house. He would then

Figure 4.1 'Where do you want this house, then, Guv?'

have to discuss his thoughts with an architect, who would turn his ideas into a plan. He would then need permission to build the house, and this might take several weeks to obtain.

In the meantime, the builder would need to know where to dig the first trench and how deep to dig it. He also needs to know how much concrete, cement and timber to order, how many bricks, tiles, window frames, etc. He will need to employ a roofer to tile the roof, a plasterer to finish the walls and ceilings, a carpenter to fit the kitchen and a plumber to fit the bathroom . . . and so it goes on.

You will readily see from the above that a great deal of thought and preparation are needed before the building project could even begin, irrespective of all the work required to see it through to completion.

This situation is very similar to an ICT design project. In order to complete an ICT project you have to:

- identify what is required

- produce a project proposal

- obtain permission to proceed

- plan the design

- monitor production and progress

- test the product and produce documentation about it

- evaluate the product.

Standard ways of working

By the time you are ready to start this unit you will probably have been working towards your GNVQ Intermediate award in ICT for several months and will, by now, be fully aware of what constitutes good practice in your use of ICT. If you haven't read the Preparatory Unit recently, go back and look at it *now*! It is especially important you comply with these guidelines whilst working on a large project such as this. You are going to spend a long time working on it and may find it impossible (especially in the later stages) to redo tasks you have already completed.

The following notes are given to remind you of the simple things you can do to ensure you complete the project without unnecessary problems and delays:

- Use folders/directories to keep all your project work together – perhaps one main folder with other folders nested within it for the different stages of your project.

- It is a good idea to save updates of your work regularly with a different filename. In that way, in the unlikely event you find yourself with a corrupt file, you can revert to the previous version and you will not have too much work to repeat.

- Make sure you back up your work *regularly* on floppy disk – carry one copy with you to and from school or college and keep a second copy safely at home. If you have a computer at home, save your work on the hard drive and make sure it is also saved on the hard drive at school or college. You would be amazed at the number of students who work with a floppy disk only, and then lose the disk or spill a drink over it and have to start all over again. Learn from their mistakes!

- Delete any data files you don't need any more – it will free up disk space and help you to find the right file quickly.

- Don't rely solely on spelling and grammar checks before submitting your project to your tutor. Remember, the computer does not understand what it is checking so you must proofread your work to ensure it makes sense.

- Check the layout using Print Preview before you print. Is your style of presentation consistent? Are your headings all the same size? Does the size or style of your font change without reason? Are your page breaks in sensible places? Are your pages numbered? Do you have unnecessary amounts of white or empty space? Does your margin allow for your project to be bound? If you think about things like this before you print, you will not only save yourself a lot of time but also paper.

- If you discover a virus, ask your school or college technician to clear it for you. You need to be particularly watchful if you download from the Internet or use your disk in different computers. If you do have a serious problem but have taken the precaution to back up regularly, you won't waste too much time.

- If you are working with information that is confidential or subject to copyright, make sure you do not breach the regulations.

- Continue to log any ICT problems you encounter and make a note of how you solved them. You may need to include details in your project documentation if the problem concerns your product.

NB: Throughout this unit we refer to the outcome of your project as the *product*. This might be the creation of a database or spreadsheet, or the setting up of macros. Your product might be one large task or comprise several smaller tasks.

NB: To illustrate the development process you will follow, we have included an example of a hypothetical project that takes you through the different stages involved – the Steam Locomotives Enthusiasts Club. We have used a series of prompt sheets to do this and these are included later in the chapter. Your tutor may have blank copies of the prompt sheets in the Tutor Resource File. If not, compile your own using the ones illustrated here as a guide.

Identifying the ICT design project

When we considered Ian Duncan's catering business in Chapter 3.4, it was obvious he knew very little about computers but he did know they could help him in his business. Ian is similar to many people we all know. To help him, we looked at his requirements, suggested a suitable computer system for him and thought about a possible system configuration to help him in his business. This was similar to a mini ICT design project – we identified someone who needed help, discussed his or her requirements and proposed a solution (even though we did not actually implement it).

The end result of any project you undertake for this unit should enable someone to make better use of his or her computer. This might be achieved by making the system easier for him or her to use, by speeding up processes carried out regularly or by improving the quality of the tasks he or she undertakes.

You might already have some ideas for a project following on from work you did in Units 1, 2 and 3 but there are many other possibilities.

Ideas for projects

Some projects might be quite varied and elaborate. For example:

- Producing standard design and layout templates for a magazine. For this you might need to design templates that include logos and page settings plus macros to insert such items as graphic images or advertisements.

- Producing a web site with multiple pages. The site might be to publicise a business, manufacturer or leisure interest and could include hyperlinks to make the site user-friendly. You could include scanned images, digital photos or other graphics, together with sound effects if your system were capable of this.

- Designing a system to keep sports club membership records. This could include the design of an application form to enable you to record relevant details from new members, together with a relational database to record personal details and pictures of each member, their payment details and sports activities. You would also need to design queries (for database interrogation) and reports.

- Producing a database of work contacts, friends and relations. You could set up a facility to merge addresses or to produce lists of telephone numbers, birthday reminders, etc.

Other projects might require a combination of several simple facilities to help someone who is unfamiliar with computers and their possibilities:

- Creating file and folder structures to let users store and retrieve their work easily.

- Setting toolbars in a software application so that users can access a facility more easily.

- Creating macros and templates so that people can work more efficiently.

- Setting the options in a software application to suit particular people's needs.

- Creating files of commonly used text or graphics for others to use as and when required.

- Creating icons or files to let users access an information service more quickly.

- Writing simple instructions to tell people how to use your product.

- Using a scheduler, journal or calendar to take actions or prompt at a given date or time.

- Creating a database or spreadsheet for a specific purpose.

- Using vector or bitmap graphics to design logos, stationery, etc.

- Using a digital camera to produce images for use in a brochure.

Teamworking

Imagine your school or college wanted to produce some new course leaflets for the various GNVQ intermediate awards it offers. This would be too much for one person to complete in a limited time, and so it could be shared amongst two or three students. All the students involved would need to discuss and agree the project outline and decide on individual tasks.

Perhaps one student could create folder and file structures and set up templates so that all the brochures had the same format. Another might collect course information from the

Figure 4.2 'How on earth do I decide?'

different programme teams (e.g. ICT, Business, Leisure and Tourism, Health and Social Care). This student could also prepare brief details for inclusion in the leaflets. A third student might take digital photos of the college and students already at the college and could collect short quotes from them about their courses to include in the leaflets. The team would then put all their work together to produce the final course leaflets.

If you do work on a project of this nature, you must make sure you can finish your part of the project even if someone else in the group does not. You will need to arrange regular meetings of the project group members and should make notes of new ideas that come up at the meetings and of agreements made between members in respect of who is doing what and what deadlines have been agreed on. The notes should be sent to all members so everyone is clear about what is happening and who needs to do what and when.

Choosing and assessing your project

You might be lucky enough to have already identified a 'real' project to work on – perhaps something to help a member of your family

make better use of the computer, or something that will help a club you belong to, or something to help at school or college. If not, talk to people who use computers regularly to see what problems they come across. This might give you ideas you hadn't thought of. Talk to your friends in class or ask your tutor to see if he or she has some suggestions. Then think about the kind of ICT design work each of these projects may need.

As soon as you have an idea for a possible project you think you could carry out successfully, make a note of it (see Figure 4.3). Don't make a note of just *one* project idea – try to include two or three. This will ensure you give yourself the opportunity to choose the one that is the most feasible and the most interesting to do.

Time

Now think about the time you have available to complete the project. This will probably be about 50 hours, but you should check this with your tutor. You should expect to spend about one quarter of this time discussing your ideas and preparing your proposal before you start to plan the project in any detail. Do not embark on a project you know will take you longer than the time you have available. Similarly, make sure the project will give you enough to do!

Pros and cons

Think about the reasons why you should continue to develop the ideas for your project and also about the reasons that might make you abandon it. This will help you to weigh up the merits of your project and to make your final choice. You will probably have more ideas for projects than have been suggested here, but it will soon become obvious which projects are likely to be more suitable for you to develop. You should try to find something that interests you and that you feel confident you can complete.

PROJECT IDENTIFICATION

Your name: ....   Date:...........................

Your project should help someone make better use of a computer in order to be more effective in his or her work or to improve the quality of his or her work.

Whom is the project for?	What is the required product?	How will it improve the user's use of ICT?	How long will it take?	What ICT design is involved?	Reasons to continue with the idea	Reasons to abandon the idea	Continue? Yes/no
My Grandad, who has just retired, wants to develop his hobby of running a club for steam locomotive enthusiasts.	He wants to be able to e-mail club members easily and to set up a web page on the Internet with links to relevant web sites. He has just bought his first computer so doesn't know anything about e-mail or the Internet, although he can word process.	If I prepare distribution lists, address books and folders these will enable him to e-mail everyone in one go and will save time. I can set up his computer with folders to organise his system and produce a web site with relevant hyperlinks of interest to club members.	E-mail – 10 hours. System organisation – 2. Web page design/ research – 20. User docs – 10 hours.	Find out the e-mail addresses to be included. Use e-mail software to create product. Design web page and identify hyperlinks. Produce instruction sheets.	Real user. Software available. Information easy to find out from Grandad. I think the project will interest me.	Will I be able to find relevant web pages easily? I'm not sure if I have estimated time accurately – will I get it all done?	Yes. It will be of real use to someone. I must make sure I can finish each part independently.
Mike, my football team manager.	To set up a spreadsheet to record the results. Produce a database of team members. Design a mail merge letter to remind them about fixtures. Prepare a fixture list for the year and invitations to trophy ceremony.	It will make it much quicker to write to the members, record their subscriptions and their goal averages, etc. If he has a fixture list he won't forget to turn up for the cup matches. He wants to improve the image of the club.	Quite a long time – there is a lot of different things to do. About 50 hours?	Collect all the information about members. Use of word processing, spreadsheet and database. Design templates for fixture list, invitation, produce mail merge letter.	Interesting and varied project will test all my ICT skills. Will benefit Mike and the club.	It may be too much for me to do on my own. It will be hard to contact Mike in the week to discuss ideas. Confidential information about friends.	No. It may be hard to contact Mike and I need to do something that I can work on all the time.

Figure 4.3 Project identification sheet

Be realistic

By this stage you should have an idea of what you are going to need to do to complete your project. You must think about the different stages involved and estimate the time you think it will take to complete each one: there's no point in embarking on a project that is too large for you to complete!

Resources

In addition, you must identify the resources you will need for each of the projects on your list. Again, you must question your ideas: what is the point in spending time developing a project if you don't have the resources available to complete it? For example, you will find it difficult to undertake a project involving web page design if you have access to Notepad but no web browser.

Resources will vary from one project to another but will probably include the following:

- people (and their time) to tell you what they require

- instruction manuals

- textbooks

- input or output hardware

- application or operating systems software

- data files, Clip Art, CD-ROMs

- consumable materials, such as paper, disks, ink, toner

- access to the Internet.

Producing a project proposal

Obtaining approval

If we think back to George for a moment, we will realise that he may need to borrow money from a bank or building society to

Figure 4.4 Fingers crossed!

finance his project, and he would need to convince them his idea was sound and achievable before they would agree to loan him the money.

Similarly, you will need to get approval from your tutor before you do any more work on your project. You don't want to be in a situation where you have spent time developing your project only to be told that, for some reason, it isn't suitable.

You should therefore produce a *project proposal* to outline the work you want to carry out and in which you describe what you want to achieve. The proposal will include:

- a description of your user's needs

- an outline of how you intend to meet these needs

- a description of the tasks you will carry out

- a list of any new skills you need to learn

- a list of the resources needed to create the product

PROJECT PROPOSAL

Your name: ....   **Date:** ....

Project title: *Steam Locomotives Enthusiasts Club* ....

Use this sheet to make notes to help you put your project proposal together.

A description of what the user wants
My Grandad has just retired and bought a new computer. He runs a Steam Locomotive Enthusiasts Club and hopes he can use his computer to help him. The use of e-mail will make it easy for him to communicate with club members. He thinks I can help him organise his computer system so that he can find his files easily. He is thinking about having a web page for the club that has links to web sites that will be of interest to club members.

What do I need to find out before I can start this project?
Exactly how does my Grandad want to use his computer in connection with his club? He has indicated he wants to be able to e-mail members and set up a web page but I need to know the e-mail addresses of members. I also need to know how folders can help him store e-mails he sends and receives. I need to find out how I can reorganise his computer system with folders. I need to find out about web pages of interest to the club and discuss ideas for the design of his web page.

Brief but clear description of the tasks you will carry out and the expected results
Set up a distribution list within e-mail so that he can e-mail members in one go — also address books so that he can easily find individual members. *Create folders to sort out e-mails sent and received.* *Create suitable folders on his main system to enable him to find data files easily.* *Design a web page for the club and find a selection of hyperlinks to other sites of interest to members.* *Produce user documentation for all these tasks and for attaching files to e-mails.*

How will I collect this information?	
Speaking to people? *Speak to my Grandad to find out his user requirements in detail and to get the information I will need to create distribution lists for his e-mail system. Discuss web page design.*	*Books/manuals, etc.?* *Find out about Grandad's e-mail system* *Look on the Internet for existing sites about steam locomotives.* *Look at examples of web pages on the Internet to get some ideas.* *Use library books for information on steam trains.*

What resources will I need?

People	Books/manuals	Consumables
My tutor at school/college to help me if I get stuck.	*Library books on steam locomotives.* *Manual for Grandad's e-mail system.*	*Paper for printer.* *Disks for back up.*
Hardware – input devices *Keyboard.* *Mouse.* *Scanner (for train pictures).*	**Hardware – output devices** *VDU.* *Colour printer.*	**Software** *E-mail software.* *Word processing.* *Notepad/Web Page Wizards.* *Web browser.*

Description of the output or results expected (attach sketches to support your ideas)
E-mail – produce distribution list and set up address books of members. Create series of folders within e-mail to sort out e-mails (diagram attached). *Set up folders on hard drive (diagram attached).* *Produce web page(s) with suitable hyperlinks (possible page designs attached).* *Produce user documentation, including screen dumps for using e-mail, saving work in folders on system and using the Internet.*

Figure 4.5 Project proposal sheet

- a brief outline and sketches to illustrate the output or results you expect to achieve

- a time schedule showing how long you expect it will take to produce each item.

Presenting your ideas

Before you write your proposal in detail, it is useful to make notes of the points you want to include in it (see Figure 4.5). You will have already considered some of these points during the process of identifying your project, but you now need to expand your ideas and give more detail. Unlike your initial ideas, the project proposal will form part of your final project documentation and should therefore be written and presented in an appropriate style, as you learnt in Unit 1.

Sometimes it will be easier to sketch what you are hoping to achieve rather than trying to put it into words. For example, if you want to produce a template for a magazine page, a sketch would illustrate the layout you have in mind much more clearly than a description in words (Figure 4.6). Remember, you should annotate (or label) your sketches in order to explain your ideas more fully.

If you are designing a database (for example, to record details of sports club members), you will need to find out exactly what information the club needs to collect from members. You could then design a data capture (application) form new members could complete to gather this information (Figure 4.7a). New members would not appreciate it if the club kept

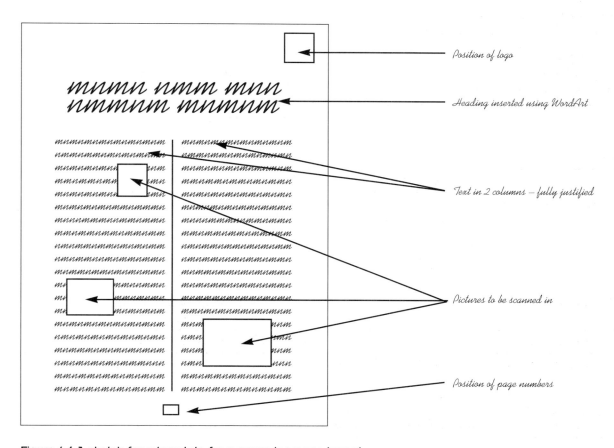

Figure 4.6 A sketch for a template for a magazine page layout

ANYTOWN SPORTS CLUB
MEMBERSHIP APPLICATION FORM

Could put the club's logo here

Last name: ....
First name: ....
....
Address: ....
....
....
.... Post code: ....
Title: (Mr, Mrs, Miss, etc.) ....
Tel. no. (home): .... (work): ....
Date of birth: _ _ / _ _ / _ _ _ _

Type of membership required (delete as appropriate):
Family / Full / Senior Citizen / Junior
Notes: mnmn mnmnmnmm mnmnm mnmnm mnm
mnmnmn mnmnmnm mnmnmnmn mn nmnmnm
Fee payable (please see current list of char
Method of payment (delete as approp
Visa / Switch / Solo / Cash / Chequ
To be paid (please delete as appr
Annually / Monthly
Credit card detail
Expir

Make sure I leave enough space for all the details to be entered

The photo could be scanned + pasted on the membership card

Need to check these details with the club

(a)

Name of field	Data type	If text – length required If number – type required. Decimal places needed?	Choice fields – if yes, list the choices (You use a combo box in Access to create this)	Would an 'input mask' help? (An input mask allows a set layout, e.g. for national insurance number, post code, phone field)	Is it a required field? Yes or no?	Should it be indexed? Yes or no?
Last name	Text	20			Yes	Yes
First Name	Text	15			Yes	
Title	Choice		Mr/Mrs/Miss			
Road	Text	25				
Town	Text	15				
Post code	Text	8				
Tel no.	Text					
Date of birth						

(b)

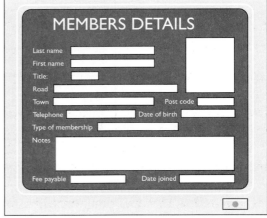

MEMBERS DETAILS

Last name
First name
Title:
Road
Town   Post code
Telephone   Date of birth
Type of membership
Notes

Fee payable   Date joined

(c)

Figure 4.7 Sketches for: (a) a data capture (application) form; (b) planning database (form available in TRF); (c) a data input computer screen contacting them asking for more details once they had joined! In order to create the database into which this information could be entered, you would need to think about the field names and data types (see Figure 4.7b). Do you have fields into which all the information you are gathering from the data capture form can be entered? Will you need to create more than one table? How will you relate the different tables? How will you enter the data into the computer – through a table or form? If you are going to use a form, plan your data entry screen so that it is straightforward to read details from the form and to input the data into the computer (Figure 4.7c). It can be very frustrating if you have to keep looking up and down the application form or screen to find the right information and the right place to enter it.

Time plan

To convince your tutor you have thought your project through thoroughly and that you can complete it in the time available, you will need to include a time plan. This will list the order of the tasks and will show how long you anticipate each will take (Figure 4.8). You will need to allow time to test your product to make sure it is working as you intended, and you will need to allow time to overcome any unforeseen problems that may arise as a result of testing your product.

Obtaining permission to proceed

Your tutor will need to approve your project proposal before you can continue. He or she may simply read your proposal and agree to it or might suggest some changes before you go ahead. Alternatively, you may be asked to meet with your tutor to present or discuss your proposals. This means you must be able to convince your tutor your project proposal is achievable and worth while. To do this you need to be well prepared and able to answer any questions that might be put to you:

- Can you explain exactly what you want to do and why?

- Can you demonstrate how you will do it, using the resources available?

- Can you state clearly how you plan to manage your time?

To be well prepared, it always helps to run through a presentation with someone else first – a fellow student or parent/guardian, perhaps – who might be able to identify any potential problems so that you are ready for your meeting with your tutor.

Once you are given the go-ahead you can start work on your project immediately. Remember, everything you have done so far will have accounted for about 25% of the time allocated to this project, so be sure to use your time plan to help you keep on target.

Planning the design

Now that George has the go-ahead for his new house he can engage an architect to draw

Figure 4.9 Drawing up the plans

TIME PLAN

Your name: .... Date: ....

Project title: *Steam Locomotives Enthusiasts Club*

Start date: *1st May*   Finish date: *28th May*

List all the steps from design to completion of the project, indicating how long you anticipate each step will take. Remember to include time to test your product and to produce any user documentation.

List each task you will have to complete	Hours allocated	Duration of Project (in days) 1–29
Interview Grandad to establish what he needs	2	days 1–2
Look at web pages for ideas and possible links	2	days 3–4
Find out how his e-mail system works	2	days 4–5
Create distribution lists, address books and a number of folders within e-mail	3	days 7–9
Test system and make modifications if necessary	2	days 10–11
Produce user documentation including how to attach data files to e-mails	2	days 12–13
Set up folders on main system to handle data files	2	days 13–14
Test system and make modification if necessary	2	days 15–17
Produce user documentation	1	day 16–17
Design web page and discuss designs with user	7	days 3–4, 19–21
Set up web page(s) and create hyperlinks	5	days 22–23
Test system and make modifications if necessary	3	days 24–25
Produce user documentation	2	days 26–28
Evaluate project and compile full project documentation	4	days 7–29
Total anticipated hours	**39**	

> The hours allocated for each task should take place at some point during the period indicated by the shaded days.

Figure 4.8 Time plan sheet

up the plans and to produce the building specifications. Similarly, you have an outline of your project but must now plan each stage in full detail. Your plans may take the form of notes and/or sketches but must include such details as the following:

- Any information you will need and the sources of this information.

- The people who will help you in your planning (users, fellow students, tutors, etc.).

- The layout of any screens, reports, templates or documents.

- Descriptions of computer programs or macros needed.

- Lists and perhaps simple sketches of graphic images.

- Examples of records, data types and relationships you intend to use.

- Examples of calculations or formulae to be used.

- Specifications for any search or sort requirements your project may require.

- The layout of any toolbars or menus you may need to create.

- A description of software applications to be used.

- Ideas about how you can test each part of the project.

Your project will probably not include everything in this list, and there will almost certainly be other things to add. However, whatever your project involves, you must check your list matches the tasks in your project.

Steps in the planning process

To help you plan your project, you might find the following steps helpful:

1 *Consider each task in turn* Look again at your time plan, which shows each of the tasks you have identified. Next, think about each task in turn and write down exactly what you want to achieve. Then think about what you need to do or find out before you can go any further:

- Do you need to talk to your user to clarify his or her requirements?

- Do you need to go to the library to find out some information, or ask your club leader what information he or she needs to hold on the database?

- Will you need to use the Internet to get some information/ideas?

- Do you need to ask your tutor how to do anything on the computer?

Careful thought now will save you a lot of time later!

2 *Check the resources you will need* Do you have access to all the resources you have identified (hardware, software, paper, etc.)? How will you make backup copies of your data files – do you have spare disks? Are all the resources available all the time, or can you use some at certain times only? For example, can you use the colour printer on Thursdays only and the scanner on Tuesdays only? If so, check your time plan to make sure you have taken this into account.

3 *Go into detail* You are now ready to think about the detailed design of each task. Some tasks will inevitably overlap but, wherever possible, try to concentrate on one task at a time. You produced some initial sketch designs in support of your project proposal:

- Do you need more designs and more detail?

- What filenames will you use?

- Where will you save your files?

If your project involves creating a macro:

- What is it designed to do?

- How will your user access it – through keystrokes, a pull-down menu or an icon on the toolbar?

- What will you call it?

If your project is to produce a web site:

- How many pages will your site require?

- How will you link one page with another?

- How will you get back to the first page?

- How will you get from the top to the bottom of the page, and vice versa?

- Can you include colour in your logo designs, or should you use only grey tones?

- Do you need to find images to scan?

- Do you need to get permission to use an image that is covered by copyright?

Your project may involve creating a database:

- What data types and field sizes will you need?

- What queries will you need to design?

- Do you need to set up reports?

It might involve a spreadsheet:

- What formulae will you need?

- Which cells need to be reformatted (e.g. currency, date)?

- Do you need to add borders and shading?

These lists can give you only a few ideas to help you get started. The more planning you do now, the easier it will be to create your product.

4 *Check for accuracy* How will you check your work for accuracy? Obviously, you can test your macros, use your templates and click on icons to see if they work. At the same time, however, you also need to consider the accuracy of any written work you produce to support your product. For example, you may need to ask a fellow student or friend to try out your user instructions to make sure they are clear and unambiguous.

As you can see, there is a lot to think about. It would be a good idea to make separate notes on each task so that you are well prepared to move on to the next task (see Figure 4.10).

When you have reached this stage you have completed the preliminary work that has to be done before you can start to produce the final product. If the preparatory work has been done thoroughly, the production stage should be relatively straightforward.

Production and progress monitoring

Once building starts on George's house, the architect will *monitor* progress closely to make sure the work is up to standard and that the house will be finished on time. Monitoring means keeping a careful check on each stage:

- Is one stage taking too long?

- Is another stage using up more resources than the architect planned for?

- Has yet another stage hit problems the architect did not foresee in the planning phase, despite every effort to think through all eventualities?

If one stage is held up for some reason, the architect will have to reschedule the job to compensate for the delay.

Similarly, you will have to monitor your project, and it would be useful here to use a monitoring sheet (Figure 4.11). This sheet will also act as a reminder of the order you plan to carry out your project. Every task should be included on your monitoring sheet and, as each task is completed, check it off the list. Note the time it has taken. Was your estimate about right? Did you have to change your plans? If so, make sure you give the reasons why and include a revised end-date, if necessary.

It is important you finish the *whole* project. If you spend more time than you planned on one item, you might need to revise the time you can spend on something else. Remember, you don't want to rush at the end or find you run out of time before your project is finished.

Testing and documentation

Just as the builder will run the central heating system, check the lights are working, etc., before finally handing the house over to George, so you must check your product is ready and working as you intended. You should *log* (make careful notes of) the tests you carry out on your product and record the results (Figure 4.12).

Some tests will check that things work as they should and will be straightforward to execute – running your macros or entering data, etc. Other tests will be more involved.

Spreadsheets

You must check your spreadsheet *formulae*. You can do this by designing and entering test data and checking the answers with a calculator.

What will happen if you change the contents of specific cells? Will the formulae recalculate totals? Which cells must you change to see the effect? Is data displayed in the correct format, e.g. is all currency displayed as £0.00 or is some displayed 0.00? Do you need to reformat data to two decimal places so that data is displayed as 28.34 rather than 28.33763?

Databases

You must design test data for each field type in your database – data that you think should be accepted and data you think should be rejected (this is covered in detail in Unit 10, page 233).

How will you test your data capture (application) form? Perhaps you could ask two or three friends to fill it in to make sure they understand it. It is quite usual for someone to misinterpret a question, so you might need to modify the wording to make it clearer. Have you left enough space so that there is enough room to enter all the information legibly? Have you have included clear instructions for capital letters to be used so that you can read the handwriting?

When you have set up your database, ask a friend to try entering data from the data capture (application) form. In this way you will see if they are synchronised – i.e. can you work in a logical order, or do you have to jump about on screen to find the right 'box'? Design test data that will enable you to use queries to test the database – e.g. produce a report of all girls under 18 or of all boys who live in a particular town. Make sure the test data will give you the results you are looking for.

Web sites

How will you test your web pages are working as you intended? Can you design some questions that can be answered from within your pages? Ask a fellow student or

PROJECT DESIGN

Your name: ....   **Date:**..

Task No: ...*4*..   **Description:** ....*Create distribution lists, etc.*......

Use this sheet to plan each stage of your project in detail.

What is the objective of this task – what do you want to achieve?

Create distribution lists, address books and a number of folders within e-mail.

What information do you need to collect? Where will you collect it from?

Information	Source
E-mail addresses of members.	*Grandad*
Names for distribution list(s).	*"*
Names for address books.	*"*
What folders do I need to create?	*"*

What resources do you need to complete this task?

Hardware – input devices	Hardware – output devices
Keyboard.	*Monitor.*
Mouse.	*VDU.*
	My computer at home to receive, test e-mail and send back to my Grandad.

Software	Other
E-mail.	*E-mail operating instructions.*

Describe your design and attach detailed illustrations to show layout, formulae, images, records/data types, relationships, search or sort requirements, etc. (as applicable)

See attached diagrams.

Where will you save your documents? State paths/folders/filenames

Everything will be created within the e-mail software. There is no need to create additional folders on the system.

How will you check the accuracy of your work?

Proofread e-mail addresses with a friend to make sure they are correct.

How will you test your product?

E-mail to my computer with/without attachment and vice versa. Send a test e-mail to users on the list and ask them to reply so that I can check they all received their copy. Try to move e-mails into folders. Check copies of e-mails sent are in 'Copy to Self' folder. Follow instructions in user documentation to check accuracy.

Figure 4.10 Project design sheet

PROJECT MONITORING

Your name: .... **Date:**...

Project title: *Steam Locomotives Enthusiasts Club* ....

List all the tasks in the order you will do them to enable you to complete your project. (Remember to include the time to produce user instructions and full project documentation.) Indicate the time you think each stage will take you to complete. Use this sheet to monitor your progress throughout your project. Tick each item when you complete it.

	Task	Start date/ hours	End-date	Changes to plan. Give reasons	Revised end-date	✓
1	Interview Grandad to establish what he needs	1/5 2	2/5			✔
2	Look at web pages for ideas and possible links	1/5 2	4/5	Unable to start this because my computer is down	6/5	
3	Find out how his e-mail system works	3/5 2	6/5	This took me longer than anticipated	9/5	✔
4	Create distribution lists, address books and a number of folders within e-mail	7/5 3	9/5			✔
5	Test system and make modifications if necessary	9/5 2	12/5	3 e-mails did not arrive. Data was incorrect. Had to re-test	14/5	✔
6	Produce user documentation including how to attach data files to e-mails	10/5 2	13/5			
7	Set up folders on main system to handle data files	13/5 2	15/5			
8	Test system and make modifications if necessary	16/5 2	17/5			
9	Produce user documentation	17/5 1	18/5			
10	Design web page and discuss designs with user	3/5 7	17/5			
11	Set up web page(s) and create hyperlinks	18/5 5	23/5			
12	Test system and make modifications if necessary	24/5 3	26/5			
13	Produce user documentation	25/5 2	28/5			
14	Evaluate project and compile full project documentation	8/5 4	29/5			
15						

Figure 4.11 Project monitoring sheet

TEST LOG

Your name: ....   **Date:**..

Task No: *4* ....   **Description:** *Create distribution lists, etc.* ....

Use this sheet to plan and record the tests you carry out on each part of your product.

Describe the tests you will carry out to ensure your product works
E-mail to my computer at home with and without attachments. E-mail attachment back to Grandad's computer. E-mail test message to distribution list and check replies. Move e-mails to appropriate folder and check.

What non-computing test will you apply to your product?
Follow user instructions to check their accuracy.

Enter details of tests carried out	Result
E-mail attachment to my computer	Successful
E-mail plus attachment to Grandad	Successful
Send test e-mail to distribution list	7 out of 10 replied
Move messages to folders and switch off system. Re-boot and check	E-mails all in correct locations
Try to follow instructions in user documentation	Instruction on deleting unwanted messages left out

What modifications were carried out?
E-mail addresses in distribution list rechecked. Three errors identified. Errors corrected and test e-mails sent. User instructions amended.

What happened when you re-ran the tests?
Replies received to three e-mails. A friend tried to follow user instructions – correct this time.

How did you try to stop your design working?	What was the result?
Left .uk off one address Left 'Subject' blank	Message generated 'Delivery unsuccessful' Computer asked for verification

Figure 4.12 Test log sheet

friend to try to find out the answers. This will tell you if your hyperlinks work and if your messages come across clearly.

Testing for when things go wrong

Other tests should be designed to see what happens if things don't go to plan, or if users make mistakes. For example, you could design tests to see what happens if the following occur:

- Users press the wrong keys or several keys are pressed at the same time.

- Data is entered incorrectly or entered in the wrong place.

- Macros are used incorrectly.

- Exceptional data values are entered.

When testing a product, you should also look for things that might stop it working. After all, if you accidentally stop your product from working it is feasible your user might do this as well. If this happens you must modify your design so that it cannot happen again.

Recording your tests and their outcomes

Details of *all* the tests you carry out, together with the results, must be fully documented to show the product has been tested thoroughly. This means a written description of the test together with a note of the results. The results may be in the form of a printed copy of the test – e.g. data entered into a database, results of sorting and searching or copies of reports produced. Copies of a spreadsheet will show test data entered and changes to that data to show the formulae are correct.

Hard copy should be annotated wherever possible to show the changes that have been made to the data or to show what is being tested. Include a hard copy of tests that do not work. Annotate these to show what is

wrong, and then include another copy when you have corrected the fault.

Documentation

If we return to George's new house, you will remember that plans and a building specification were produced. In subsequent years, George might sell the house and the new owner might wish to extend it. If the new owner has access to the original plans these will show where, for example, the drains were laid. Without this information the garden might have to be dug up to locate the underground pipes.

The future modification of an ICT product is, therefore, one reason for producing documentation about it. Perhaps the user's needs change and the computer program needs to be adapted accordingly. It is highly probable the designer will have moved on and, without detailed notes, it would be very

? Did you know?

You will remember hearing about the 'millennium bug' when the century changed from 1999 to 2000. Many computer programs in use at that time were over 30 years old and were written when computers were relatively new and computer memory very expensive. In order to reduce the size of programs (and to keep costs as low as possible), years had been recorded by the last two digits only – 69, 75, 99 – leaving out the '19'. Hence it was feared that computers would not recognise '00' (the last two digits of 2000) and would stop working.

To solve the problem, these programs had to be updated but, because programs were not well documented in the 1960s, many of the original programmers were called out of retirement to work on the project! It is estimated that £380 million was spent by the government alone to tackle the problem in government systems.

How will systems cope with 00 again when we move from 2099 to 2100?

difficult, time-consuming and expensive for a new designer to modify the original product.

Full documentation will therefore include details of the proposal, the design, implementation and testing.

You should also include evidence in your documentation that you have organised data files into suitable folders and that you have used the filenames as specified in your design. A screen dump from Windows Explorer or File Manager (depending on the operating system you have used) will provide evidence you have done this and that you have made backup copies of all your files.

User documentation

In addition to all this information, your documentation will also include user instructions, which will tell users how to use the product.

User documentation should be written without jargon so that it can be understood easily. After all, you might not be available to explain how to use your product! It should specify the purpose of the product, and the software and version of that software for which it was designed to be used. Your user will need to know where to find it on the system – the path and file specification – and, if it is a macro, how to run it. It should also show the user what the finished product will look like. If necessary, screen dumps should be included so the user can compare his or her screen with an illustration. This can be very reassuring if you are using unfamiliar software or facilities.

Evaluation

An essential part of any project is the final evaluation. This gives you the opportunity to reflect on the process and the product so that

you can learn from the experience and can improve on it the next time (Figure 4.13).

You must consider the project at all stages of its production and should justify everything you say. For example: 'I ran very short of time towards the end of my design project and had to rush to finish the user documentation because the testing uncovered a fault in my formulae and I had to spend extra time resolving the problem.'

Your evaluation should consider the following:

- Did your finished product meet its original specification?

- Did you achieve your target in the time available?

- What works well, and what works less well, in your product?

- What are the advantages or disadvantages to the user?

- How would you improve the product if you were given more time and better resources?

- Have you used techniques you might use again?

- Can you use your design easily on other computer systems?

- What do the users think of your product?

User evaluation

It is important you involve your user in the evaluation process because it was on his or her behalf that you created the product in the first place. You need to find out if the product is easy to use, whether it speeds up the job and if the quality is as he or she expected. One way to do this is to prepare some questions and to interview the user. You must produce a written copy of the questions and answers. Alternatively, you could produce

EVALUATION

Your name: ....   **Date:**..

Project title: *Steam Locomotives Enthusiasts Club* ....

Use the headings on this sheet to make notes before you compile your final project evaluation.

Does your finished product meet its specification? If not, why?
E-mail distribution list works. Folders created meet user's requirements. Data files on system OK. Web page limited — lack of time — can be improved in due course.

Did you meet the time schedule for the design and creation activities? If not, why?
Problem was web page. Left it too late to start looking for suitable hyperlinks — had to rush to finish it.

What works well and what works less well in your product?
New e-mail system is really useful and it has been used several times by my Grandad. Hyperlinks that work are good but not enough of them — some do not work properly.

What advantages does your product offer the user (speed, quality, ease of use, etc.)?
The e-mail distribution lists mean the user can send a large number of e-mails quickly and easily. The folders keep his e-mails organised and easy to find.

What are the disadvantages of the product (time, cost, failures, poor specification, etc.)?
The web page was not designed in enough detail and there was not enough time left to test it thoroughly.

How could you improve the product with more time or better resources? Could you achieve the same result another way?
I could improve the product with more time. Resources adequate. *Make more use of Web Page Wizards next time, which would be quicker.*

What new techniques have you learnt during this project?
Created a hyperlink to another web site and not just another page. Used scanned image as a hyperlink. Learnt to use another e-mail system.

Could you use your design on another computer or in another project?
The e-mail was designed specifically for my Grandad but I can use the web page design in the future.

What does your product user think? (You must design oral or written questions for the user to answer.) Include any written evaluations from the user in your project documentation.
Very pleased with e-mail and data folders. More work needed on the web pages (see attached completed questionnaire).

Figure 4.13 Evaluation sheet

a written questionnaire for the user to complete.

Why evaluate?

Without evaluation your project is incomplete. Not everything may have gone well: perhaps you ran out of time or the product failed in some way. This is not a problem *providing* you say what went wrong, and why and how you would modify your product if you had more time or better resources. On the other hand, if something was really successful you should try to explain why this was so.

In conclusion . . .

Now you have read this unit you should have a clearer understanding of how a design project should be broken down into small, logical steps in order to plan and implement it successfully. Just like the architect, if you are given clear instructions of what is required and follow the process through step by step, you should end up with a product that meets all the user's requirements.

Good Luck!

Figure 4.14 A job well done

This unit is about the wide range of information sources that are available to both individuals and organisations, and about the dangers of information 'overload'. It will help you to develop the skills you need to navigate your way through the many different sources of information available to you so that you can find out exactly what it is you want to know about.

You have already studied and learnt about many of the skills you need to achieve in the first three mandatory units of this book: Presenting Information, Handling Information and Hardware and Software. However, you will now be expected to demonstrate:

- greater depth and understanding of these topics

- an ability to take a closer look at, and to make more sense of, what you find

- increasing independence and originality in your work

- increasing skills in the effective application of ICT.

To help you meet these expectations, this unit gives you a practical context for presenting information. It also gives you an opportunity to discover and to use efficient techniques for finding information and for making good use of it.

After studying this unit you should be able to:

- use a wide range of sources to track down specific information

- bring together information from a variety of sources

- investigate the types of information sources organisations use

- draw conclusions about the importance and effectiveness of information sources available to organisations

- consider the effects of information overload on both individuals and organisations.

Paper-based sources of information

In Unit 1 we looked at a variety of information sources. Many of these sources are books and other paper-based documents. Although you can sometimes find the same information in electronic format, it is important you can also use paper-based sources to find out what you need to know.

Understanding paper-based sources of information and how to use them will also help you to understand the benefits and problems of using ICT-based sources.

The main paper-based sources of information include the following:

- reference books

- dictionaries

- encyclopaedias
- directories
- card indexes
- paper files.

Most paper-based sources of information are organised in the same way as electronic sources of information (because the electronic forms are often, simply, an electronic form of an original paper version). This means that whatever source you are researching – paper or electronic – you can often use similar techniques.

Two of the most useful search features of *paper-based* information are the contents lists and the index. Contents lists give you a general overview of what you can expect to find from that source, whereas indexes give you a more detailed list and all the relevant references.

Contents lists

Contents lists are a summary of what the document contains. A good contents list will guide you through the information you can expect to find in the document. This book is a good example. Turn back to the contents list and look at the unit headings. These tell you the categories of information in the book. Unit 1, for example, is about 'Presenting information' and Unit 3 is about 'Hardware and software'. The list under the unit headings tells you the topics in that unit. The topics for Unit 1 are 'Styles of writing and presentation', 'Types of information' and 'Document layout and presentation'.

Content lists are a useful way of finding information when you do not know exactly what it is you are looking for. For example, perhaps you need to write a letter to an organisation but you are not sure how to write this type of letter. You might look

through the contents list and see that Unit 1 has something on 'presenting information'. You might then look through the topics covered and notice 'document types'. This sounds as if it might have something to help you, and so you leaf through the pages under that topic. You soon come to 'business letters' and think this is probably what you need. You now take the time to read this section carefully to decide if it really does contain the information you need.

 ACTIVITY

To practise using a contents list, you will need a fairly large catalogue (e.g. a mail-order catalogue, a shop's own catalogue (Argos, etc.) or perhaps something a little more specialised, such as a seed, music CD or book catalogue). The most important thing is that it must have a contents list.

Use the contents list to decide on something you might wish to buy. Now look up those goods using the contents list. If what you are looking for is not where you thought it might be from the contents list, go back to the contents to see if it could have been included elsewhere under a different category.

When you have made your choice, make a note of the details you would have to give the supplier so they could send you the correct item. Make sure you include a note of which page in the catalogue you found the item on. Would it be a good idea to give an alternative if the item you have chosen is out of stock? If so, make sure you record the details of this as well.

Indexes

Indexes are lists of words in alphabetical order. In indexes it is important to realise that it is not just the first letter but *each* letter in a word that is organised alphabetically. For example, 'Singer' comes before 'Singh' because the 'e' in Singer comes before the 'h' in Singh.

Shorter words come before longer words: so Harris comes before Harrison, which comes before Harrumph! Most indexes treat prefixes (such as Mac, or Mc or O') in exactly the same way. For example, 'Macabre' comes before 'MacBeth' which comes before 'Machine'. These might then be followed by 'McDonald', 'McKendry', 'Menzies', 'Metal' etc.

A good technique when using an index is to begin with the first letter then search by vowels (a, e, i, o, u). You will probably need to keep running through the vowels in your head over and over again as you search. Once you have found the word with the correct first letter and the vowel, go to that part of the alphabet that has your next letter. For example, if you're looking for a 't', don't run through the whole alphabet from ABC. Instead, think of letters near 't'. These might be 'p, q, r, s'. This will help you to stay focused and it will help you to move quickly through the words to the one you want.

ACTIVITY

Using the techniques explained above, look in the index of this textbook for the word 'Microprocessor' and see who can find the page reference the quickest. Now look up the following – 'hyperlinks', 'biometric technology', 'pictograms' and finally 'AMD'. Now select three words of your own choice, which relate to ICT and see if they are included in the index.

The Dewey decimal system

When you take a look around your college or local library, you soon notice that the books are organised into subject areas. So if you're looking for a book about your football team for example, you go to the section on Sports. If you're going somewhere interesting for your holidays and want to find out more about that place, you go to the section on Travel.

The most common system for organising and finding books on the subjects you are researching in the library is the Dewey Decimal system. Understanding how the Dewey Decimal system is used to organise a library makes it much easier for you to find the books and other library material you need. From the name Dewey Decimal, you might guess that the system has something to do with someone called Dewey and with decimals (numbers that are based on 10). If that's what you think, you're right.

Melvil Dewey decided that, if each book was given a number depending on what it was about, it would help libraries to organise their books more effectively. All books about the same subject would be close to each other and so would be easier to find. Dewey divided all knowledge into ten main classes and gave each a 100-number range:

Class	Subject
000–099	General works, such as encyclopaedias and newspapers
100–199	Philosophy and psychology
200–299	Religion and mythology
300–399	Social sciences
400–499	Language
500–599	Pure science
600–699	Technology
700–799	Arts (including sports and recreations)
800–899	Literature
900–999	History, geography, biography and travel.

Each of these categories is split into 10 further categories. For example, 790 is 'Recreational and performing arts'. After that,

796 is 'Athletic and outdoor sports and games'.

ACTIVITY

Go to either your college or your local library and use the library's record system (computer, microfiche or card index) to look up:

1 a sports personality

2 a foreign city you would like to visit.

As you look through the system, make a note of the Dewey decimal number and the different categories that led to your book. For example, with the sports personality you begin by writing down who it is, then the Dewey decimal number and the category. Here's how to get started:

(Your sports personality's name)
700 Arts
796 Athletic sports.

Continue with this list until you get to a book with something in it about your chosen personality.

IT-based sources of information

IT-based information sources come in a wide variety of forms, from floppy disks to the World Wide Web. Each has its own purpose, benefits, limitations and access equipment. Table 5.1 is an overview of the main sources you need to understand and to use.

Points to remember

Although Table 5.1 gives you a general overview of IT-based sources of information, you will have to decide which is likely to provide you with the quickest and most accurate route to the information you need. To help you, remember the following:

- From the work you have done for the compulsory units of this course you will already be aware of most of the equipment and software you need to access these different sources of information. These include input (e.g. keyboard, keypad), output (e.g. TV, VDU, printer), storage (e.g. disk, CD-ROM), software (e.g. communications, CD-ROM driver, web browser, search engines) and methods of access (e.g. TV, computer).

- Information can be structured in different ways (e.g. records and fields, hypertext and viewdata). This will affect how you access and use the information. For example, Viewdata systems (such as those used in travel or other booking agencies) provide access by page numbers and codes.

- As with viewdata and specialised bulletin boards, some online databases are public and others are private. Some are accessible only after you have paid a fee, while others (such as web banking) are accessible only after you have provided a detailed and secure identification. Still others, such as confidential records, are accessible only if you have the right security clearance.

- As you will know from the Preparatory Unit, some information must be kept confidential and other information must be kept secure. You will also be familiar with the Data Protection Act and how it works.

ACTIVITY

As a brief review of what you learnt about these topics in the Preparatory Unit, give two examples of information that should be kept confidential and

Table 5.1 IT-based sources of information

Source	Purpose	Benefits	Limitations	Access
Floppy disks	Storing small quantities of information	Easy to carry. Most PCs have floppy drives	Hold up to 1.44 Mb of data. Read by magnetic means so access time is slow	Computer floppy disk drive. Mouse and keyboard
CD-ROMs	Storing large quantities of data – around 650 Mb	Easy to carry. Most PCs have CD-ROM drives. Read by laser optics so access is fast	Less convenient than downloading files from servers	Computer CD-ROM drive. Mouse and keyboard. Any CD player (e.g. for music)
Teletext and Ceefax	Provide access to a huge online database of information via users' TVs. Mainly for general use (e.g. weather, sports, news)	Thousands of pages of regularly updated information	One-way communication system and so not interactive	TV remote control. Enter page numbers
Viewdata	Provides access to another huge database of online information, mainly for business use	Two-way communication system so data can be received and transmitted	Needs telephone line, modem and software	Computer. Select from menu listings via mouse and keyboard
Bulletin boards	Leave messages and information in the format of an electronic noticeboard	Useful way of sharing information (e.g. about a particular product)	Often requires a subscription fee	Computer. Sometimes necessary to download with special software
The Internet	Provides a network connecting many computers	Connects millions of computers throughout the world	Limited only by level of current technology. Information overload	Computer. Telephone line and modem or cable connection
Intranets	Provide a network among related users (e.g. in one organisation)	Share information in medium to large organisations	Current technology. Accessed only by the organisation's staff	Computer. Usually local area network
The World Wide Web	Provides navigation of Internet sites	Simple and easy to use	Information overload	Computer. Telephone line and modem or cable connection

specify three methods of keeping that information secure. Next, write a brief explanation of what the Data Protection Act is designed to do and how it works.

Finding the information you need

As well as being able to identify the sources of the information you need, you must also demonstrate you are able to use these sources to find the information required. The amount of information available in these sources is enormous – beyond imagination! This means you need to plan your search and then carry it out in the quickest and most efficient way possible. You also need to understand the different ways of searching for information, particularly on the web. As you search, remember that the information you find may not be genuine or reliable, so check your sources carefully. When you have your results, from whatever source, you need to draw them together and reach your conclusions.

Planning your search

If you go straight to the first source you think of, you may waste a great deal of time and you may not find what you are looking for. So before you go to your information sources, you need to ask yourself these three questions:

1   What information is required?

2   Where am I most likely to find this information?

3   Which are likely to be the best search techniques in terms of speed, efficiency and accuracy?

The first question is key. You need to be quite specific. Don't just say 'I want to research my favourite football club'. Think about exactly what you want to know, e.g. the transport arrangements for the next away match, information on a particular player or the results of the last match. You must keep reminding yourself exactly what you are looking for so you don't get side-tracked.

The second question is also important. You will find just about anything you can imagine on the Internet as long as you have access to it and so this is probably the best place to start. Bear in mind, though, that different sources (such as CD-ROMs or books) may be faster if you already have some idea of what is contained within them.

Question 3 depends on how the information in your chosen source is organised. Whether the source is the Internet, CD-ROMs, Viewdata systems, Teletext services, or online databases, there is usually a starting point. This may, like a paper-based source, be a contents list or index. With one-way systems such as Teletext, you simply have to wait as the system turns its information screens for you. With Viewdata systems, you can usually enter numbers or codes to get straight to the information screen you need.

Carrying out your search

Although IT-based sources do a great deal of the searching for you, because of the way information is organised, they use similar methods to paper-based sources. As we have already seen above, the most useful and important of these are the contents list and indexes. In IT-based sources, you access the contents list through what is often called a category browser and the index through key word searches. CD-ROM-based encyclopaedias are a good example. Once you have entered the encyclopaedia, your main search approaches are usually the category browser or the key word search.

Using web search tools is a little more complicated, but a general understanding of how these work will make your searches faster and more accurate. The first thing to understand is that search tools are produced by businesses in competition with each other. So ignore those blinking adverts and banners and focus on the search box and any hints or tips provided.

There is a variety of different search tools. The main types are search engines, subject directories, meta-searches and name directories. The following is an overview of each type (with examples), how they work and when to use them:

- *Search engines*   Search engines (such as AltaVista or Google) use a program called a spider, robot or crawler to index huge, random collections of Internet files. Use search engines when you want to find a large number of related documents or specific types of document such as image files, MP3s (music files) or discussion lists.

- *Subject directories*   Subject directories (such as Yahoo! or BUBL) are smaller collections of Internet files. These files are categorised by subject heading and rated for relevancy by humans rather than by software. Most subject directories allow you to browse by subject category (similar to a contents list), or by key words (similar to indexes). Use subject directories to research general topics and to avoid all those irrelevant documents you get when you use search engines.

- *Meta-searches* Meta-searches (such as Savvy) send your request to several different search tools at the same time. Each search tool, however, returns only a limited number of results. Use meta-searches when you want to get an overall picture of what the web has on your topic and to check whether the web is really the best place for you to search.

- *Name directories* Name directories (such as www.bt.com/phonenetuk) are the white and the yellow pages of the Internet. Use name directories when you want to search for people by name, telephone number, e-mail address, post code and so on.

You might well be thinking that not only is there a huge amount of information to search but also many different ways of searching, and you would be right! There are even web sites designed to help you choose a search tool! But do not be put off. Choose one search tool and just use that one for a while. If you are not sure which one to choose, ask your friends or your tutor. When you are comfortable with how it works and what sort of results you get, then try another.

Search tips

Once you have decided which sort of search tool to use and when, there are various techniques you can use to make your search more accurate and efficient. These sometimes depend on the individual search tool, so it is always worth your while to read the search tips or help page for the tool you are using. The following are some of the most useful techniques:

1 Use lower case letters (that is, do *not* use capital letters). Lower case letters find results in both lower and upper cases, whereas upper case letters find results that are in capitals only.

2 You will get more accurate results by putting quotation marks around an exact phrase. For example, to find information on man-eating sharks, type "man-eating sharks". This will get you information that is only about man-eating sharks rather than any sharks, anything to do with 'man' or anything to do with 'eating'.

3 Ask direct questions. Some search engines (such as Ask Jeeves or AltaVista) let you type in a search question, just as you would ask a person. For example, 'Which shark is the most dangerous?'.

4 Use what are called operators (and, or, not, +, -). For example, key in 'shark(space)+dangerous(space)-whale', or 'shark(space)and(space)dangerous(space)not(whale). Note that in most search engines, you must use spacing – denoted by the word 'space' in brackets in the above examples.

 ACTIVITY

Choose a search engine you have heard is a good one, or ask your tutor to recommend one. Then:

- Look through the help feature and/or the search tips and make a note of one other tip that is different from those above.

- Looking up either dangerous sharks or any other dangerous creature, try out your new search tip and each of the four search tips above.

A note of caution

Because no single individual or organisation controls the information that is published on the web, you should not always trust the information you find. It may appear convincing and correct but, in fact, be completely wrong or at least misleading. The following are three ways to help protect yourself from inaccurate web data:

- Check whether there is a date on the site and when it was last updated.

- Look to see if it's possible to contact the site's developer. Is there an e-mail address to contact?

- Try to work out (or at least be aware of) whether the site was developed by someone or some organisation that wants to put its message across – for example, a political (sometimes, an extreme political) view.

Gathering your findings and drawing conclusions

Sometimes the information you are looking for is quite straightforward – for example, you may only need to find out how your team did in their latest match. At other times, and especially when you are studying or at work, there is not one straightforward or correct answer. You will have to search a number of different resources, record the information in each, bring all your findings together and draw your conclusions.

For example, you may be asked to recommend a digital camera. After asking what it is wanted for, the next big question is 'What sort of budget are you working with?' or 'How much would you like to spend?'. By asking further questions you should get a reasonably clear idea of what to look for.

The next step is to select the most likely sources. As you go through them, make sure you:

- get copies (e.g. of brochures or pamphlets)

- print out your findings

- save the information on disk

- take notes if the information is brief or you cannot print or save it.

You will probably have a great deal of information, so you will need to assemble the important details into one easily readable overview. From the work you did for Unit 1, you will know that a good choice is to prepare a chart showing the names, prices and features of the cameras you found in the price range. As you put your findings into the chart, you will begin to think that one or two of the cameras are better value than the others – perhaps they have more, or more advanced, features. When you ask yourself why you think one camera is better than another, you are in fact drawing a conclusion. Write it down.

 ACTIVITY

Research and recommend a digital camera in the £400–500 price range. Use at least two paper-based and two IT-based sources. While you are carrying out this research, keep a log of the steps you take. Use the three questions given earlier (page 182) to get you started.

Methods of communicating information

Once you have found the information you were looking for, you will need to use it in some way. Most of the time you will need to use ICT to help communicate information to others. To do so, it is useful to have a good general understanding of the main communication technologies and how they work. These technologies are as follows:

- radio
- television
- telephone
- fax
- e-mail
- networks.

Radio

Radio is a system of communication that sends waves through space. Radio waves are used not only in radio broadcasting but also in wireless telegraphy, telephone transmission, television, radar, navigational systems and space communication.

Conventional radio signals (e.g. using FM, AM and short, medium and long wave bands) are limited by the number of frequencies available in these bands. Digital satellite broadcasting, on the other hand, is the probable future for radio transmission as it opens up the possibility of hundreds of different radio stations. This could mean, for example, that a radio station might be devoted exclusively to a type of music enjoyed by only a small, minority audience. In the past, each radio station tried to attract as many listeners as possible but, nowadays, broadcasters look for what are known as 'niche' or specialised markets.

? Did you know?

Wireless headphones use radio waves to transmit sounds from your hi-fi system to your ears. Because radio waves travel through most walls (except metal), you can wander from room to room, go upstairs or downstairs or even out in the garden, depending on the capabilities of the headphone set's range.

Cellular radio

Mobile telephones and cell broadcast networks use cellular radio – a technique that was developed to enable the use of mobile telephones. As it would be impossible to provide each phone with an individual radio frequency, the country is divided into geographical areas called 'cells'. These cells vary in size depending on the number of mobile phone users in a particular area. In cities cells are small whereas in the country they are much larger. Cells use a set of frequencies that are different from the cells next to it but that can be the same as another cell as long as that other cell is further away. Figure 5.1 illustrates this.

Cell A	Cell B	Cell C	Cell D
using frequencies 1–100	using frequencies 101–200	using frequencies 201–300	using frequencies 101–200

Figure 5.1 Radio cells and frequency distribution (NB The numbers do not represent the actual frequencies; they are simply a reference for the purpose of clarification.)

Each phone within a cell uses a different frequency to maintain privacy. The system also keeps track of which cell a phone is in so that calls are routed to the right cell. Just as with the conventional phone system, the cellular system can transmit voice or any other data.

Television

Television is the transmission of audio and video signals to a mass audience. Its main use is for popular entertainment, news and educational programming transmitted directly into people's homes.

You may have noticed that miles of suburban roads have been dug up to lay cables for cable TV. Cable companies are linking homes over wide areas to the services they provide.

Subscribers pay a monthly line rental for the use of the cable, which allows the user to receive satellite and terrestrial TV broadcasts and/or standard telephone services, including e-mail and Internet services.

Telephone

Telephone communication was originally designed for speech but it is now also possible to send digital data via the telephone system. This ability to send words, files and pictures along telephone lines has led to an increase in electronic communication networks, which provide facilities such as viewdata.

The ability to transmit digital data has also resulted in the videophone which, although quite rare at the present, may become commonplace. Videophones enable you to see

as well as hear the person on the other end of a telephone. You can choose whether to let the other caller see you or not! To activate the video link, you just press one button and, if the person at the other end wishes to accept the link, a full-colour image appears on a small screen attached to the telephone unit. If you wish to *show* the other person a still picture, the quality is even better.

ACTIVITY

Earlier in this unit you looked through the contents list of a large catalogue. Now imagine you want to order two items from the catalogue by telephone.

In your class, split into pairs to role-play the telephone conversation. One of you will be the customer making the call and the other will be receiving the call.

When you finish the call, ask yourself how you think it went.

- Did you plan it well?
- Was it an effective and pleasant call?
- Did the other person understand you and did he or she find out exactly what you wanted?

Now switch roles and try again. Was it better this time? Did you learn from your mistakes?

The telephone is an essential part of our social and business relationships. A good telephone manner is a highly valuable skill, especially in the world of ICT. Figure 5.2 gives a few simple tips that can make your telephone calls a lot more effective.

Faxes

Faxes (i.e. facsimiles) are used to send the contents of a document (including text and/or pictures) via a telephone line. The image is

- Plan your call in advance. Be clear about why you are making the call and what you want to happen as a result of the call. For example, if you are calling to make a complaint, ask yourself whether you just want to complain because that will make you feel better, or whether you want the person or company to do something about your problem. If you want action, help the other person to help you – what sort of action do you want? Be ready to make a suggestion or two.

too fast is a common problem in telephone calls. For example, when we are asked to spell our names or give our telephone numbers, because we all know very well how to spell our names and what our phone numbers are, we tend to say them very quickly. Quite often the listener cannot catch what we're saying.

- Begin with a greeting – 'hello', 'good morning', etc. – then announce your name clearly.

- Try to speak at a comfortable and relaxed pace. This will help the other person to understand you easily and to feel comfortable speaking to you. Speaking

- When you are answering the phone, begin with your name – first name then family name. The caller then knows who you are and that he or she has dialled the right number (or not).

- If you dial a wrong number, be sure to say something such as 'I'm sorry to have bothered you'. If you receive a call directed to the wrong number, tell the caller you think he or she has dialled the wrong number.

Figure 5.2 Tips for making a telephone call easier

converted into electronic form so it can be transmitted and an exact copy of the document is printed by the receiving fax machine.

PC fax software does not even need the document to be fed into the machine as hard copy. The fax software creates your header sheet for you and you just type in your

message. The computer communicates directly with the receiving fax machine. Similarly, a fax received by a computer will be stored *electronically* and printed as hard copy only if desired.

As with other office equipment, when you are using a fax machine for the first time, make sure you get someone to show you how. Fax machines may all seem the same but they each have their peculiarities. If you put the paper face up and head in first on machine A, the chances are it should go face down and foot first on machine B!

E-mail

As we have already learnt in Unit 1, e-mail is like an electronic letter sent via a computer. E-mail is a sophisticated method of electronic data transfer through which messages and attachments are sent from one computer to another via a modem and telephone line.

 ACTIVITY

If your college provides you with access to e-mail or if you have e-mail at home, ask your classmates about their e-mail habits. How often do you check your mailbox? Do you have a system for filing e-mails once you've read them? Do you copy yourself on all the e-mails you send? How many e-mails do you get per week?

Although most e-mail messages are sent in a matter of seconds, if your e-mail or attached file contains large amounts of data (especially graphics and sound files), these may take a few minutes to send. When sending an e-mail, make sure you watch the screen to check your transfer is not interrupted or does not go through for some other reason (for example, you have keyed in the address incorrectly, or the recipient's address has changed). You can also 'tick' the confirm delivery box to ensure the e-mail has arrived.

Networks

Networks are systems whereby as few as two computers or as many as millions of computers are connected to each other

electronically. Two of the most important types of networks are LANs and WANs. LAN stands for 'local area network' and WAN stands for 'wide area network'.

LAN

A LAN is located in a building or where there are several buildings on the same site, such as a college. A LAN can be set up anywhere it is practical to link the system together with direct cabling. The purpose of a LAN is to link a number of PCs together so they can share the same software and hardware. The LAN can be as small as two PCs or may consist of a large number of computers housed in several buildings. There are a number of ways in which the members of a LAN can be linked, and each different network configuration (layout) is known as its *topology*.

The advantages of a LAN (compared to having several standalone PCs) include the following:

- The sharing of hardware (such as a file server, printer or other peripherals).

- The sharing of software.

- The ability to access files stored on the network by *any* PC, without the need to pass disks from one user to another.

- The ability to communicate with other PCs on the network, which is especially useful if the PCs are not all in the same room.

The basic function of the network is to allow the user to send and receive messages:

- From one PC to another (e.g. e-mail sent to other users on the network).

- Between a PC and the file server (see below) (e.g. a request to run a program, such as Word).

- Between a PC and the print server (see below) (e.g. a request to print a file).

Through the use of a LAN, the PCs are connected to one computer known as the *file server*. The file server is not used by any one person but contains a large hard drive that stores data which can be accessed very quickly by all the other PCs in the network. The network will probably also include a *print server* (sometimes the file server and print server will be the same), which is a PC connected to a printer (or printers), that allows everyone using the network to print his or her work. If you are familiar with using a network, you will know that the print server in effect controls the requests for printing. As each print request is received, it is placed in a print queue and, once the previous request has been completed, it is printed out.

Refer back to Figure 3.13 on page 112 which illustrates a LAN. The arrows represent the flow of information between the network components of a LAN.

 ACTIVITY

It is highly likely that the computers you use at school or college are linked together in a LAN. Find out the following:

- Whether the PCs you use are connected in a LAN.

- If so, what method is used to connect the LAN.

- How many computers are linked.

- Whether they are they linked to a mainframe, minicomputer or powerful PC.

- Whether the college uses any other LAN or WAN (possibly the administrative office?).

Now list as many organisations as you can that will almost certainly use a LAN.

WAN

A WAN (wide area network) is spread over a very large geographical area – even across the entire world. Communication is made possible not by a physical cable between the computers but by ordinary telephone lines (supplied by companies such as British Telecom or Cable & Wireless), or by microwave or satellite link.

The original telephone link (the Public Switched Telephone Network, PSTN), which was designed to carry voice messages, operated at fairly low speeds but, nowadays, high-speed networks are used instead. Public data networks (PDNs) have been designed specifically for *data* transmission, whereas the Integrated Services Digital Network (ISDN), carries voice, data, images and video through a single digital line. With the PDN and ISDN systems, it is no longer necessary to convert the signal into analogue form for transmission.

ASDL (Asymmetric Subscriber Digital Line) is the very latest technology for bringing the Internet into our homes. It is faster than the fastest modem currently available.

There are two types of WANs – public and private. Public WANs are available to most of the public, usually through telephone and cable TV networks, whereas private WANs use privately owned or rented lines.

The best known examples of public WANs are the Internet and cable television. The Internet is an international web of interconnected commercial, educational and government networks. It began life in the USA when a number of government bodies linked their computer systems together so they could exchange information.

The Internet now enables the subscriber to receive information from (or send information to) anywhere in the world. In March 2000, there were an estimated 300 million users, the majority of whom live in North America and Europe. Any digital data, including sound, can be transmitted via the Internet. Indeed, it is possible to obtain the details of units, assessment evidence, etc., for this course from the Internet, and Heinemann Educational (the publisher of this book) puts out some worksheets over the Internet.

 ACTIVITY

Look up the site of your awarding body (http://www.edexcel.org.uk for the GNVQ in Intermediate ICT). Find the GNVQ Intermediate specifications and study the assessment details for this unit.

Communicating information

You might be thinking that the communication technologies we have just looked at are very complicated. This is just a general overview of how such communication technologies work. To understand them more fully requires a great deal of study and practical, hands-on experience. However, for now, our main concern is how we can use these technologies to communicate information. It may seem strange, but one of the reasons the technologies become more complicated is in order to make actual communication easier!

Information in organisations

Just like individuals, organisations make use of a wide range of information sources and means of communication. The success of a business may well depend on how it communicates with its customers, suppliers and, even, how well the departments within that organisation communicate.

Using the following case study, consider the 6 points below.

1 The role each individual department within an organisation is expected to fulfil.

2 The types of information each department deals with and where this information comes from.

3 The means each department uses to communicate this information *internally,* and the advantages/disadvantages of each of these methods of communication.

4 The means each department uses to communicate this information *externally,* and the advantages/disadvantages of each of these methods of communication.

5 Other possible methods of communication a business might have and the advantages and disadvantages of these other means of communication.

6 How the Data Protection Act affects the way an organisation manages information.

Case study – scenario

You might have come across Southern Activity Holidays during the induction to your GNVQ Intermediate ICT course. To remind you, it is based at Sandleigh and offers activity holidays throughout the year. Accommodation is in a converted stable block on a working farm and the activities include swimming, sailing, diving, ten-pin bowling, horse riding, tennis, skating and cycling.

Southern Activity Holidays has recently been taken over by Leisure Breaks plc – a national group, specialising in activity breaks, who own several holiday companies.

Leisure Breaks have a sound reputation in the leisure industry and this has been built up over the last 25 years. They are committed to providing a first-class service and putting their customers first at all times. They are determined to offer the highest standards in customer care and aim to improve efficiency throughout their operation by using the latest technology. The group maintains good human relations with customers and staff and ensures that the staff and shareholders profit from its success.

Task 1

In small groups, make a list of all the business activities you think Leisure Breaks might be involved in during the year. Some may be constant (e.g. paying salaries to their staff) and some might be seasonal (e.g. taking photographs one year for inclusion in the advertising material the following year).

Don't forget, the main purpose of the business is to sell holidays.

Create your list on the computer so that you can each have a copy of the finished list.
To get you started your list might look like this:

All year	Activity	Occasionally
✓	Paying salaries to staff	
	Taking photographs for advertising	✓
	Working with printer to produce advertising material	✓

Task 2

Next, think about each of the activities in turn and try to decide which area of the business it fits into, e.g. finance/accounting, human resources/personnel, marketing, IT services, production, sales, other.

Again, create your list on the computer. To start you off, look at the examples below – finance/accounting and marketing would

seem to fit the bill but notice how human resources/personnel fits in too.

Finance/ Accounting	Marketing	Human Resources/ Personnel
Paying staff salaries		Recording hours worked
Paying photographer	Taking photographs for advertising	

When you have finished your lists you should begin to have a good idea of the function of each of the different departments.

Task 3

Combine with another group and compare your lists. Add anything you might not have included.

Now think about the type of information each department deals with and where it comes from. Remember, some information will come from outside the organisation, e.g. customer details.

For example, **Finance/Accounting** need to know from **Human Resources/Personnel** what hours staff work, the rate of pay for the job and bank account details to arrange payment. **Human Resources/Personnel** in turn need to be advised by each department of staff absences through sickness or holiday so that they can give **Finance** the correct information.

Your lists will probably get quite long now, so it might be a good idea for each of you to record the information for different departments. Make sure you all have a copy of the lists when you have finished.

Task 4

Still in groups, think about the methods of communicating this information internally from one department to another and the advantages or disadvantages.

For example:

Information	Method	Advantages	Disadvantages
Hours worked and rates of pay	Telephone Memo E-mail	Immediate Written record Immediate and written record	No record Delay in receipt

Task 5

Next, think about the methods of passing information between Leisure Breaks and external contacts, e.g. customers, the bank, the photographer, etc., and the advantages or disadvantages. (Don't forget e-commerce and teleconferencing.)

Information	Method	Advantages	Disadvantages
Paying salaries	Producing cheques		Security Time consuming Cheque clearance
	Automatic transfer (BACS)	Instant	

Task 6

In this area you need to consider how the Data Protection Act may affect the way the organisation manages information. To begin, return to the section on the Data Protection Act at the beginning of this book (Preparatory Unit – Standard Ways of Working, page 11). You will remember from this section that 'Any organisation holding personal data in a computer system must register with the Data Protection Registrar, stating clearly what details are to be included and for what purpose.'

This is your starting point: Think about the different departments you have included in your chart so far, and ask yourselves whether each department might hold personal data in its computer systems, what detail is included and why.

Department	Hold personal data? (Yes/No)	Details	Purpose
Finance/ Accounts	Yes	Staff information (names, salaries etc.)	Paying salaries

To refresh your memory, it is a good idea to read through each of the Data Protection Act principles again.

Information overload

Data is like food – when we eat reasonable quantities of good food at regular intervals, we feel healthy and well. When we eat too much or the wrong types of food, we may feel sick. Just as we need to eat properly, so we need to manage information properly.

The information culture

Organisations and individuals feed on information but, sometimes, there is so much information there are problems. Sometimes people feel left out if an organisation keeps information to itself. Other people feel bloated by the masses of information coming in from the Internet, the dozens of cable and satellite TV channels, Teletext, e-mail, voicemail, faxes, pagers, cellular phones, advertising boards, newspapers, magazines and books. Most of this information is simply irrelevant to our studies or our other needs.

? Did you know?

The number of pages on the web at the start of the year 2000 was estimated at one billion and growing.

One edition of *The Sunday Times* carries more information than the average nineteenth-century citizen accessed in his or her entire life.

In North America, advertising is even stuck to the sides of police vehicles.

Think about trying to find the cheapest way to go on holiday – sometimes we're faced with so much information we don't know which way to turn. We end up just choosing the first rather than making an informed choice.

Symptoms of overload

Information overload has become a problem in our private lives, our studies and our work.

Too much information causes stress and makes it difficult for us to think clearly. One way we deal with so many messages and information bites is to spend very little time on each. This can lead us into having a reduced attention span and an inability to pay attention to anything that isn't dramatic and outstanding. Psychological studies of the symptoms of information overload have suggested we might experience the following:

- Prioritise what you need and reject anything you don't really need.

- When information comes in, either read and use it or delete it quickly. If information is not worth dealing with now, it probably won't be worth dealing with later.

- Be strict with your phone time. Don't sit on hold, listening to music or advertising. A recent Reuters survey found that 20% of all voicemail time is spent fumbling through menus. So, when in doubt, press 0 for the operator.

- You can usually tell which e-mail messages are worth opening just by scanning the header. Try not to reply to non-important messages unless you really have to, and delete anything you do not need.

- Be wary of unusual e-mails – they may contain a virus – so delete, don't open.

- Don't get caught in the web: use the advice given earlier in this unit about carrying out searches.

- Don't give out your e-mail address unless you have to because software robots will see it and will automatically add your address to mailing lists.

Figure 5.3 Managing information overload

- Increased cardiovascular (heart) stress, due to a rise in blood pressure.

- Weakened vision (a recent Japanese study predicts that most people will be near-sighted in the future).

- Confusion and frustration.

- Poor judgement.

Managing information

The problem of information overload lies in the limited ability of our minds to process information. It is not that there is too much information, it is that we cannot process all that information into useful knowledge. Although we have advanced search engines, 'smart' filters and gigantic hard drives to store data, the speed of the most important processor – our brains – has not changed.

The most important way to deal with information overload is, generally, to decrease quantity and increase quality. Figure 5.3 gives some useful techniques for managing information overload.

 ACTIVITY

As a review of what you have just learnt, you are going to work in small groups to prepare some essential tips to avoid information overload. Over the course of the next week gather together all the information you come across in your normal day to day routines that you **do not** want from the following areas:

- The Internet.
  Make a note of the number of different web sites you navigate in order to find what you are looking for and note any advertisements that appear along the way.

- Other communications technologies (including e-mail).
  Maybe you could ask a member of your family or one of your friends who uses e-mail at work to keep a brief note of the number of unwanted messages they receive.

- Advertising (paper-based and electronic).
  Collect all the 'junk mail' and inserts from magazines and advertising flyers that come into your household during the week.

In your groups discuss and agree on the three best ways to avoid information overload for each of these areas. Decide how you would best present your findings to someone who feels he or she is suffering from information overload but does not know what to do about this. For example, you might decide you could put your ideas into a simple leaflet or present them as a poster for display in your classroom. But remember, your objective is to help with information overload, not to add to it! Keep your messages short and to the point!

To fulfil the requirements necessary to achieve this unit, you will produce a portfolio demonstrating your skills in, and understanding of, solving graphic problems.

After studying this unit you should be able to:

- use graphics software to create original pictures and diagrams

- make drawings and plans using suitable software

- compare different methods of producing graphics

- examine commercial graphics critically

- design graphical solutions to problems.

The evidence required for Unit 6 includes a minimum of two vector-type graphic images and two bitmap-type graphic images. It will also include records of you designing, producing and evaluating graphic solutions to one or more problems that are solved by a combination of plans, words and pictures. Computer graphics were introduced in Unit 1, where you created a Graphics Reference Log and experimented with the graphics tools. To undertake the preparatory work necessary for this unit you will look at graphics in more detail and continue the reference log you have already started.

Why use graphics?

Sometimes it is very easy to describe or explain something in words. If your friend said he or she had just seen a bus painted like a zebra, you would have no difficulty in imagining what it might look like.

Sometimes, however, words are not the clearest way of explaining something and, in these situations, graphics (with or without text) can prove a better option. If you look at many everyday items in your life you will probably find that most of them include graphics in some form.

For example, if I am thinking of buying a new car I will probably visit a dealer to look at the models and then take a glossy brochure home to study in more detail. The car brochure will almost certainly contain photographs of the cars and drawings

showing dimensions, together with written descriptions of the vehicles' features.

Figure 6.1 Sometimes we can picture things simply through the use of words

Most electrical equipment – kettles, refrigerators, TVs or hi-fis – will have an instruction book with diagrams that identify the different parts of the equipment. Advertising material that drops through your letterbox at home usually includes graphics – sometimes photographs, sometimes sketches. Many diaries contain a copy of the London Underground map – which is essential for anyone trying to find his or her way round the capital.

These are just a few examples – all different – of the uses made of graphics in everyday life, but the graphics as we see them didn't just appear: considerable time and thought will have been given to the graphics and to

- their purpose

- their design

- the tools and techniques available for creating drawings

- the tools and techniques available for creating pictures

- evaluating the finished graphic.

Purpose

We have already seen that there are many different types of graphic images, but what might be a good choice of graphic in one situation might be totally unsuitable in another. The graphic chosen, therefore, must be suitable for its purpose. The different purposes graphics can have are summarised below.

Making explanations easier to understand

The diagram in Figure 6.2 is used to simplify a very complicated component within a computer – the microprocessor. The diagram identifies the different parts and makes the whole system much easier to understand.

Apart from textbooks (where diagrams are often used to explain complex topics), diagrams are also used in many everyday situations to illustrate things – for example, instructions for assembling your flat-pack computer desk, for putting your computer together or for wiring an electrical plug, etc.

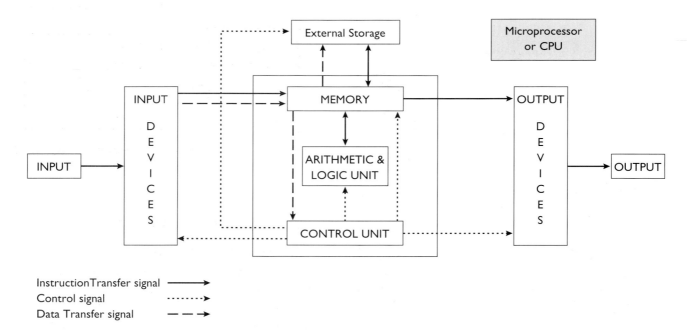

Figure 6.2 The components of a microprocessor system

If you produce user documentation (instructions to help a user perform a task or to use a product more efficiently), you will probably include graphical illustrations of the software to help the user recognise and understand a sequence of actions he or she might need to undertake.

Presenting information briefly

Using signs and symbols means a message can be put across briefly and in a recognisable form. For example, when we use roads as either pedestrians, cyclists or drivers, we see road signs we recognise and can act on instantly (Figure 6.3).

If graphics were not used, in some cases (e.g. the Give Way sign) words might be adequate to get the message across on their own, but there might be occasions when so many words would be needed we would have driven past the sign before we had time to read it (e.g. 'No motor vehicles except solo-motorcycles, scooters or mopeds' in Figure 6.3). Graphics are once again used to simplify information and, of course, the use of internationally recognised signs helps

visitors to foreign countries to be safe on the roads.

ACTIVITY

There are many instances when signs are used to present information briefly and clearly. To test their effectiveness, how many signs do you recognise from the selection in Figure 6.4?

Figure 6.4 Common signs we encounter in everyday life

Figure 6.3 Road signs

Showing relationships

The organisational chart in Figure 6.5 is perhaps the most effective way of showing how each job in a department is related to the other jobs. Try describing these relationships out loud – anyone listening to you will soon lose the substance of what you

Data Processing Department

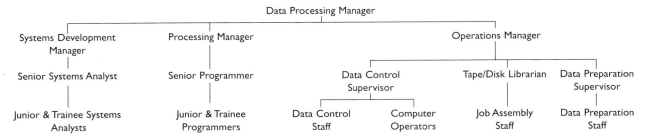

Figure 6.5 An organisational chart

are trying to say! Look back at the other examples of charts and diagrams given in Unit 1 on pages 39–42. Do they make it easier to understand the relationships?

Capturing attention

The graphic illustrated in Figure 6.6 has been designed to capture your attention with its combination of words and teddy bears hiding their eyes. Do you think it succeeded?

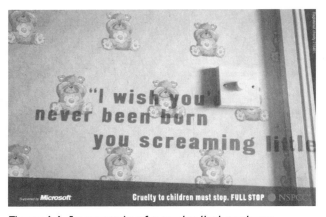

Figure 6.6 An example of a poster that captures attention (© NSPCC)

However, this is not the only way an image can get your attention. The example in Figure 6.7 is very different – it uses *association*. The advertisement was designed to introduce a new bank that is available only through the Internet. It uses computer symbols to capture the attention of computer

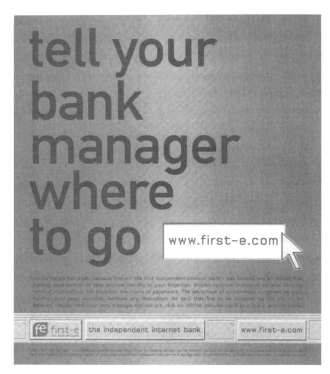

Figure 6.7 An advertisement that uses association to capture attention (© First-E, the Internet Bank)

users (who are, of course, the bank's potential customers!).

Simplifying complex information

When you have to visit a new place for the first time, it is very useful to have a map to help you find it. The map in Figure 6.8 is included in Croydon College's prospectus. This amusing illustration serves two purposes: it shows how to get to the college and it also advertises the fact that the college

Figure 6.8 Croydon College

is situated in the centre of town, easily accessible and near the main shops.

Showing plans for development

Showing plans for development

An architect uses plans and elevations to illustrate the design of a building (see Figure 6.9). He or she measures the site, discusses the proposal with the client and designs the building according to the client's requirements. The architect's drawings show the layout of the rooms on each floor of the building, and include such details as the size of the rooms and the positions of the doors, windows, staircases, etc. The elevations show what the finished building will look like, and give an indication of the materials that will be used to build it. The drawings combine graphics and text.

Establishing an identity

In Unit 1 you learnt that many organisations specify a 'house style' all employees must

Figure 6.9 An architect's plans for the design of a house

follow, which often includes a company logo. This is part of the 'corporate image' an organisation is easily recognised by.

 ACTIVITY

Figure 6.10 Company logos

Companies spend many thousands of pounds to have their logo designed. They want something that is clear, simple and immediately recognisable. As soon as you see the logo, you know the company: the logo has been used to establish the company's identity. Figure 6.11 shows how one well-known company uses its logo on all its products. The logo has become synonymous with the company.

Figure 6.11 A corporate image

Designing a graphic

Before you can start work on any ICT project, it is necessary to establish precisely what is required. If you are producing a graphic design, the questions that need to be considered are as follows:

- What is the purpose of the graphic product?

- Is it for a particular client?

- Is there a tight budget?

- How long do you have to complete the work?

- What tools are available?

- Is it part of a larger presentation (such as a diagram in a book)?

- Is it complete in itself (such as an advertisement for a lipstick)?

If you look through this book, you will see we have used a variety of graphic styles – including photographs, freehand sketches and diagrams. All have been included for a *purpose* – to make explanations easier to understand, to capture attention or to simplify complex information.

Audience

If we had published the book with no illustrations you might not have been inclined to read it. If you had read it, you would probably have found it quite difficult to understand some of the topics. All the graphics we have used illustrate something we are saying in the text – and some of the graphics are serious and some humorous. Our purpose in including graphics was to make sure the book was suitable for our target audience – you!

Had we been writing a book for very young children, we would have designed something very simple with many more colourful graphics and much less text. An ICT textbook written to accompany a degree course would have contained far fewer illustrations, and those that were included would probably be complex and highly technical.

Figure 6.12 shows how the same topic – road safety – has been treated differently for different people. The first poster is targeted at children and the second poster is designed to capture the attention of adults.

It is important you choose a style of graphic that will meet your client's requirements. If you were commissioned to design a new college logo, your style would be very different from the one you might use to design the logo for a local children's nursery school.

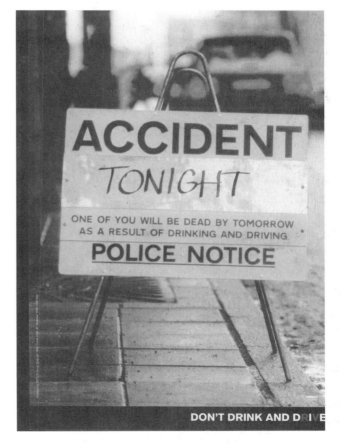

Figure 6.12 Posters targeted at different audiences (Crown Copyright)

Budget

Because this is a black-and-white textbook we had to design graphics that would be clear in black and white. We might have chosen different graphics if we had been able to use colour. However, the production of the book had to be kept within a strict budget, and colour would have been too expensive. The budget (or cost limitation) is another important consideration in the design of any graphic.

Time

Another consideration must be the time available to produce the graphic. If you take a digital photograph it can be incorporated within a document very quickly. However, an existing photograph taken by someone else might be protected by copyright (see later in this unit, page 212, for more details) and, therefore, you would need to get permission to use it, which could take several weeks to obtain. If you have only a few days in which to complete your design project, it might be quicker to use a graphic from a source such as a CD-ROM, which does not have copyright restrictions. We had to get permission to use some of the illustrations in this book from the owners of the graphics because they were protected by copyright, and you will see we have included acknowledgements to this effect.

Tools

In producing the illustrations for this chapter, we made use of the standard tools, for example, Clip Art, line and fill tools and the cropping tool. Many of the graphics were produced using vector and bitmap software – Paint, CorelDraw, Corel Photo-Paint. Some were produced by other people and, with their permission, scanned in – for example, photographs, signs, cartoons and sketches.

Our graphics are combined with text to produce a book. They are part of a large

project. If you were to take any illustration out of the book and present it on its own without the text, it probably wouldn't have much meaning.

However, sometimes a graphic has to stand alone without supporting text. A picture like the one shown in Figure 6.13 doesn't need words!

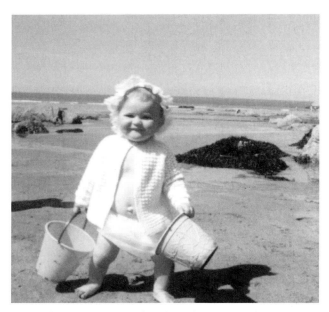

Figure 6.13 Some graphics do not need words

 ACTIVITY

Collect a selection of commercially produced graphics, such as advertisements from magazines or newspapers, flyers, instruction leaflets, signs, posters, etc. Examine the images critically to consider:

- their purpose

- how effective they are

- any improvements/changes you might suggest.

In small groups, discuss your selections and find out whether the images provoke different responses. Keep a record of people's different reactions.

Tools and techniques for drawing

No doubt you are already familiar with cutting, copying and moving items, but you will also need to show your ability to use specialist software for drawing plans or similar artwork. This software is known as 'vector' based (or sometimes 'object' based). As you will have already seen in Unit 1, this type of software typically provides tools that enable you easily and quickly to create the following.

Lines

- You can vary the thickness of your drawing lines:

- You can use broken lines and arrows:

- You can join two points with a straight line. Programs such as CorelDraw provide guidelines (see Figure 6.14) that can be placed anywhere in the drawing window. The toolbar shows the distance between the lines.

  If you use the line tool and click on the guideline, then click on the second guideline, your line will be straight.

  Objects you move or draw near a guideline automatically snap to that guideline. This helps to align objects precisely, and is particularly useful if you wish to draw lines or rectangles that have precise measurements.

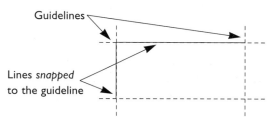

Figure 6.14 Guidelines

Shapes

- You can draw circles:

- You can create curves:

- You can draw regular and irregular shapes:

Colours

You can set colours. Obviously, colours don't show in a black-and-white textbook, but the first shape could be red, the second in customised shades of blue.

Fill

You can fill areas with patterns or shading:

Enlarge or reduce

You can magnify or reduce the scale of shapes. The magnifier allows you to see an enlarged view of the item, which is often useful whilst working (Figure 6.15). You can revert to the normal size when the image is complete.

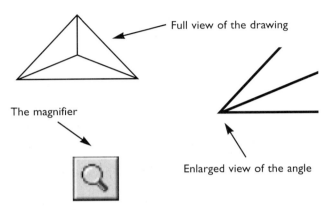

Figure 6.15 Use of the magnifier

Co-ordinates

You can use co-ordinates to specify positions. You are familiar in your word processing software with the ruler. The position at which you can start entering text is set to zero, but that does not represent the corner of the page – i.e. space for margins has been allowed.

Figure 6.16 Co-ordinates

In a drawing package such as CorelDraw, the default setting puts the zero for the horizontal setting at the top corner of the page and the vertical setting at the bottom corner (see Figure 6.16). However, you can easily change this so the zero point starts at any position of your choice. This is very helpful when you are drawing to scale, as illustrated in the example for grids.

Grids

Grids are rather like graph paper, but you can decide the distance you would like between the dots in the grid. A grid is very useful if you wish to draw a plan to scale and, just as with guidelines, objects can be set to snap automatically to the grid.

The ground floor of the house in Figure 6.17 is 8 metres by 6 metres. The scale for the plan is set to 1 cm on screen (which equals 1 metre on the ground). The markers on screen are shown in millimetres. Therefore, the plan is 800 mm wide by 600 mm deep.

Figure 6.17 A grid

Measurements and units

These days, if you wish to refit your kitchen, the kitchen planner will probably use a software package specifically designed for this purpose to create the plan. Initially, the design can be created in a two-dimensional format, using a scale to represent the precise measurements of your kitchen. The program will have ready-prepared shapes for cookers, fridges, dishwashers, cupboards, etc., which can then be positioned into your room layout (see Figure 6.18. *By permission Europress*).

Figure 6.18 A two-dimensional plan of a kitchen, showing the measurements of the walls and the grid that has been used to draw the plan to scale

The software allows you to switch between the plan, with or without the gridlines and measurements (see Figure 6.19).

Figure 6.19 The plan of the same kitchen, but without the grid and the measurements

Once the plan is complete, you can switch to the view in three dimensions and take a 'look' at your new kitchen. You can really *look* into the room and, if you don't care for the design, the plan can easily be changed (see Figure 6.20. *By permission Europress*). Similar software is available for designing gardens (with shapes for plants and shrubs), whereas a design program for architects would include shapes for doors and windows.

Figure 6.20 Three-dimensional views of the same kitchen

ACTIVITY

Now you have been introduced to the different facilities available for drawing, try out the following techniques for yourself and save them in your

Graphics Reference Log. Make a note of how you achieved the effects (to remind yourself if you want to try them again at a later date) and of anything you particularly liked about each technique. Later on you can refer to this when you are designing your own graphics.

Use a *vector drawing package* to design the following:

1 Draw a box approximately 8 cm × 8 cm but **do not use the guidelines**.

- Divide it into four equal squares.

- In each of the four squares, draw a different type of line – vary the thickness, colour and style.

2 Now draw the same box again (and divide into 4) but this time, **use the guidelines** to help size it accurately. You will find it easier to draw the correct size if you set the co-ordinates for the top-left corner to zero.

- Duplicate the box (i.e. copy it so you have two the same).

- Using one of the boxes, fill each square with a different pattern or shading effect.

3 Using the other box:

- Put a star in one square, a circle in another, an irregular shape in the third and choose a ready-made symbol to go in the fourth (e.g. from Wingdings).

- Colour the star red, the circle yellow and shades of blue for the irregular shape. Choose your own colour for the symbol but watch out – you may find it necessary to ungroup or break apart the image in order to be able to fill sections separately.

4 Measure the size of your ICT room (you could work in small groups to find the dimensions of various parts of the room or objects in it and share the data). Use a suitable vector graphics application to draw the plan to scale. Include windows, doors, work benches, chairs and any other furniture in the room (also drawn to

scale). If the room is 15 metres by 20 metres you could use a scale of 1 cm:1 m, i.e. 1 centimetre on screen will represent 1 metre of the room.

Tools and techniques for pictures

Painting packages allow you more flexibility and freedom when creating graphical illustrations. These tend to be bitmap based, and you have already been introduced to them in Unit 1. There are many different applications on the market – some very sophisticated and others quite basic. For the purposes of illustration in this unit, we have used two paint applications – Paint and Corel Photo-Paint – both of which will probably be available to you. If you are fortunate enough to have access to something more complex, you will no doubt be able to find many additional facilities to enhance your graphics.

The skills you need to practise are described below.

Creating freehand designs

Using a combination of tools – freehand line, ellipse, text, fill, etc. – will enable you to create simple freehand designs (Figure 6.21) you can edit pixel by pixel using zoom (see below).

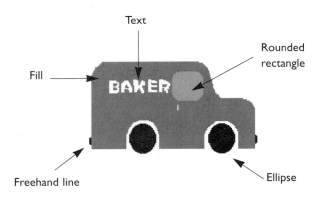

Figure 6.21 A freehand design

Rotating/flipping images

Images can be imported (for example, from Clip Art) and manipulated in various ways (Figure 6.22).

Horizontal flip   Rotated by 270°

Figure 6.22 Flipped and rotated images

Distorting images creatively

A variety of tools are available that enable you to stretch and distort images (Figure 6.23).

Figure 6.23 Distorted images

Controlling brush size and shape

You can choose square or round brushes of varying thickness, and can combine them to make interesting graphics (Figure 6.24).

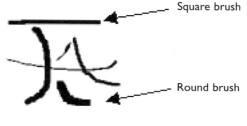

Square brush

Round brush

Figure 6.24 Brush strokes

Sprays, rollers and airbrushes

This facility enables you to fill areas of your graphic with different densities of colour or shade (Figure 6.25).

Figure 6.25 An image created using sprays, rollers and airbrushes

Smearing and smudging

Smearing and smudging are facilities found in some paint applications (but not Paint) that enable you to enhance an image by selectively brushing over colours. Smearing is rather like dragging your finger through wet paint to create a 'spider's web' effect. Smudging is like blending chalks or pastels to soften the edges.

The illustrations in Figure 6.26 show the before and after effects of smearing and

Original picture   Centre enlarged   Smearing and smudging

Figure 6.26 Smearing and smudging

smudging as applied to a flower. This technique combined with cloning (see below) would be useful if you were working on a repeated image.

Making tile patterns

If the image you are printing is too big for the paper on which it is being printed, you can choose to print your image as tiles. Portions of the image are printed on separate sheets of paper, which you can assemble into one large image. This might be useful if you wanted to make a poster (see Figure 6.27).

Figure 6.27 A poster created using tiling

Editing shapes after enlarging them

Enlarging shapes is useful for tidying up or editing a freehand drawing. You can see the pixels clearly and have more control over your freehand designs (Figure 6.28).

Figure 6.28 A shape that has been enlarged to make editing easier

Working on individual pixels

Zooming to 800% and displaying the gridline identifies the individual pixels very clearly (Figure 6.29).

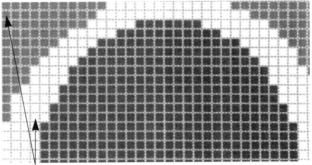

Individual pixels

Figure 6.29 Working on a graphic pixel by pixel

Converting colours to greyscale

Some applications let you convert colour to black and white, while others give you the option of converting to greyscale (Figure 6.30). This can be a better option if you are printing in black and white.

Figure 6.30 A palette showing greyscale

Colour palettes

Colour palettes provide a wide variety of shades. They use matching systems, such as Pantone or Trumatch. Variations in shades of colour are referenced numerically, just like font styles are given names. If you are designing a graphic for a company that has a fixed corporate colour, you can match the colour exactly by the colour reference (Figure 6.31). For example, if you were making a slide presentation, you might match the logo's colour and use this colour as a border on the master slide.

One referencing system mixes red, green and blue to achieve very subtle changes in colour. The example here uses:

R – 215
G – 145
B – 232

This results in a deep lilac colour

Figure 6.31 Customising a colour using the Edit Colors dialogue box

Stitching images together

Programs such as Adobe PhotoShop have the facility to 'stitch' together pictures taken from different angles, to create a three-dimensional image. This technique is used to create holograms and is also used in computer games such as Dungeons & Dragons.

Image stitching can also be used to join photographs. For example, if you stood at the top of a mountain and took several overlapping still photos of the view around you, they could also be 'stitched' together to form one panoramic photograph. The examples in Figure 6.32 show two holiday snaps, which have then been stitched together to show the complete picture.

Figure 6.32 Stitching images together

Cloning

This is another way of copying an image. However, if you clone the image rather than copy or duplicate it, any changes you make to the original image will also take effect on the cloned image. The first example in Figure 6.33 shows the Crest for London. In the second example, the sword has been removed from the left-hand image and it has also disappeared from the cloned image (on the right). This technique might be useful if you were designing fabric or wallpaper with a repeating pattern.

Cloned image before editing

Cloned image after editing

Figure 6.33 Cloning

Scanning and editing images

Scanners allow you to add pictures from other sources into your documents. The scanned image can be used intact or edited as required (Figure 6.34).

Original image   Edited image

Figure 6.34 A scanned and edited image

Digital cameras

As mentioned in Unit 3, photographs taken on a digital camera are processed through the computer, not from film. Again, the image can be edited if desired (Figure 6.35).

Figure 6.35 Photographs taken by a digital camera are processed through a computer

Saving files in different formats

Unlike word processing files which usually end with the extension .doc, graphics files adopt different bitmap formats depending on the application they are created in, such as .bmp (the standard Windows Bitmap format), .tif (Tagged Image File) and .pcx (Paintbrush format). Tif files are compressed, which minimises size without degrading quality. The most user-friendly format is

.bmp, as most Windows programs will load these files (Figure 6.36).

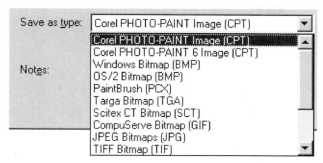

Figure 6.36 Save as type drop-down menu

Two additional bitmap formats are .gif (Graphic Interchange Format) or .jpeg (Joint Photographic Experts Group), which enable drawings and graphics to be viewed on the Internet. As we saw in Unit 3, .gif formats use only 256 colours and are therefore better for diagrams or drawings, whereas .jpeg format uses the full 16 million colours and are therefore more suitable for photographs.

 ACTIVITY

Now you have been introduced to the different facilities available for pictures, try out the following techniques for yourself and save them in your Graphics Reference Log. Make a note of how you achieved the effects (to remind yourself if you want to try them again at a later date), and of anything you particularly liked about each technique. Later on you can refer to this when you are designing your own graphics.

Use a *paint package* to design the following:

1   Try copying the baker's van shown in Figure 6.21:

   • Draw the van shape freehand.

   • Zoom in to tidy up the edges of the picture, pixel by pixel.

   • Fill the shape with a colour.

   • Use the rounded rectangle for the window and the ellipse for the wheels, and fill these with a different colour.

   • Add the text choosing a suitable font size and style.

2   Make seven copies of your baker's van and:

   • Flip one image horizontally.

   • Flip one image vertically.

   • Rotate one image by 90°.

   • Skew one image horizontally by 30°.

   • Skew one image vertically by 60°.

   • Use one copy to edit the van colour to match the RGB colour reference as follows – R 215, G 145, B 232 – it should be a deep lilac colour!

   • Change the colour of the last van by experimenting with the RGB reference until you find one you like. Note the reference underneath the van.

3   Copy the baker's van image into a new file:

   • Make two copies of the baker's van.

   • Convert the colours to greyscale (make sure the colour palette has changed to greyscale).

   • Experiment by using different shades of grey.

4   Recreate the boat in Figure 6.25 to practise using sprays, rollers and airbrushes.

5   Use a drawing package, select an image from Clip Art. Experiment with stretching and distorting the image to create several variations.

6   Select another suitable image from Clip Art, *duplicate* two copies and *clone* two more copies. Experiment with the smearing and smudging tools on the **original** image, and notice what happens to the others.

7 Bring in a photograph of yourself with your family or some friends to scan. Save the complete image and also another copy where you have edited around the outline of the people (like the example in Figure 6.34).

8 Use the digital images your tutor has in the Resource File and try stitching them together.

Copyright

You should already know from the Preparatory Unit about the law of copyright. It gives the creators of certain kinds of material – including literary, dramatic, musical or artistic work as well as photographs – certain rights. You cannot use copyright material without the owner's permission. Sometimes this permission will be sought directly from the copyright owner (the creator of the graphic) or sometimes through an organisation that represents him or her. The Patents Office at the Department for Trade and Industry and the British Copyright Council can provide further details about copyright. It can take quite a long time to obtain permission to use someone else's work, so sometimes it might not be feasible to use such a graphic.

Earlier in this unit we saw that some graphics (e.g. Clip Art) can be reproduced freely because there is no copyright on them. *You hold the copyright on any graphics you produce*, and your work is automatically protected until you have been dead for 70 years. What is particularly important to remember about copyright pictures is that, although you may have permission to use the graphic, you should not alter it! You might be tempted to use your new skills to stretch it, flip it, crop it or change the colours. Don't!

Evaluation

It is very important you evaluate the work you produce on the computer. Part of evaluating your work involves finding out what other people think of it. You need to obtain other people's opinions of your work to be sure your work is successful. This applies equally to setting up a computer system as it does to producing a graphic image.

We have looked at examples of different graphic styles throughout this unit – some you might have liked and others you may not have liked. This will also happen with images you produce. No matter how skilled you are technically in producing graphics, it is essential to 'test' your design before you can be fully satisfied with it. You must always ask the following questions:

- Do clients, users, other students, etc., respond to the graphic as you intended?

- Do your graphics support any overall message?

- Have your graphics made understanding easier?

- Did you keep to your deadlines?

- Did you stay within your budget?

If the answer to any of these questions is 'No', you will need to amend your design. However, the best form of evaluation is to ask your client, user or friends to be critical of your work.

In addition to judging your graphics you must also consider the hardware and software you have used to produce the graphic. Ask yourself:

- What particular tools were most useful?

- Which tools were difficult to use?

- What features of the hardware caused problems?

If you had a choice of hardware and software:

- What did you select, and *why*?

And perhaps most importantly you should ask:

- If you were doing the project again, would you use the same tools/techniques?

Unit 10 extends the knowledge of designing relational databases required for compulsory Unit 2. In addition to the skills you need to achieve Unit 2, you will be expected to demonstrate greater knowledge and understanding.

After studying this unit you will be able to:

- use databases efficiently
- set up databases for others to use
- apply database techniques to solve problems.

You will need to learn about:

- purposes of databases
- social effects
- techniques
- creating the user interface
- documentation.

As with all your other units, to complete your evidence effectively, you will need to follow the standard ways of working, which have been covered in detail in the Preparatory Unit. These will probably be quite familiar by this stage, but keep checking you are using the correct procedures.

Unit 10 will be assessed through your portfolio work. You will have to produce a more complex relational database than that required for Unit 2, to include three related tables. You will probably prepare the evidence for the database aspect of Unit 2 jointly with the evidence required for Unit 10. It may seem a great deal of work at first, but do remember you are completing almost two units at the same time.

In addition to the evidence required for Unit 2, you will also need to produce:

- a selection of user-friendly screens
- more detailed notes of user and technical documentation
- test data and a test schedule.

You may find it helpful to read the section on 'Evaluation' (at the end of this unit) <u>now</u>. It suggests you keep a diary whilst you are creating the database to keep track of any relevant points. You may also find it helpful to refer to Unit 4 – Design Project – which gives hints on tackling a large project.

Purposes of databases

The main purpose of databases is to store information and to make information easier to find. Look back at page 72, where we considered the advantages of a computerised system over a card index box. The employment agency we discussed in Unit 2 might have hundreds or thousands of clients on their books wanting temporary or permanent jobs. Of course, CVs could be stored in filing cabinets but, if the CVs were stored electronically, it would be much easier, quicker and more efficient to search for suitable applicants for a particular job. For example, if you needed to find an applicant with GNVQ Intermediate experience of working with databases and two years' experience doing general office administration, an electronic database could identify suitable

applicants immediately by searching for these *attributes* (explained later in this unit). To find the same applicants in a paper-based system, you would first have to search for ones with the right educational qualification and then sift through them again to identify those with two years' office experience.

We have already looked at the facilities provided by a computerised database. These enable us to:

- Organise information into tables that can be linked together, reducing the need to duplicate data (page 78).

- Index fields to speed up searching (page 82).

- Sort information alphabetically or numerically, in ascending or descending order (page 81).

- Search for specific information (pages 80 and 82).

- Produce answers or reports to standard queries (page 80).

- Examine different *views* of the same information, e.g.:

    - Table view, where all records are shown (Figure 10.1).

    - Form view, where only one record is visible (Figure 10.2).

    - A query – explained in more detail later – which shows *selected* fields from one or more tables (Figures 10.3 and 10.4).

It is not so long ago that most offices used stand-alone PCs and therefore database programs could be designed only as flat files – i.e. you could not link the tables in the databases together. Although computerised database files were very useful to businesses problems often arose. Imagine an office with three stand-alone PCs with the customer

Applicant : Table								
Applicant Ref	**Title**	**First Name**	**Surname**	**Address**	**Town**	**Postal Code**	**Telephone**	**Date of Birth**
123	Mr	Chirag	Patel	12 Ivy Close	Anytown	AN2 7SF	(0111) 289 6734	04/12/84
636	Mrs	Sarah	Fitzgerald	25 Oak Avenue	Anytown	AN4 2CS	(0166) 650 2341	24/02/65
734	Mr	Joseph	Williams	6 Pine Crescent	Anytown	AN4 6CT	(0166) 289 1365	11/06/78

Figure 10.1 Table view showing all records

Figure 10.2 Form view showing one record only

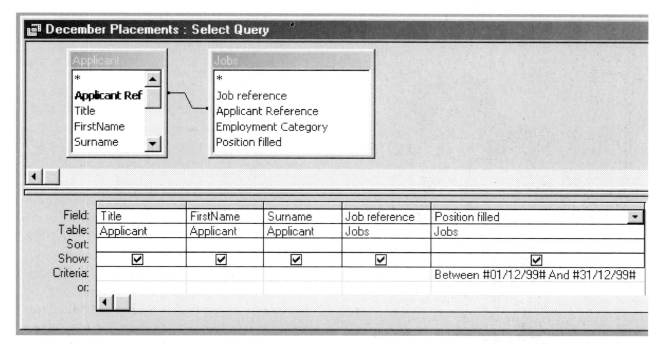

Figure 10.3 Design view of a query to find which applicants were placed during December. Notice the search criteria under 'Positions filled' is limited to dates between 1 and 31 December 1999

Title	First Name	Surname	Job reference	Position filled
Mr	Chirag	Patel	DI235	01/12/99
Mr	Joseph	Williams	DI312	19/12/99

Figure 10.4 The result of the query in Figure 10.3

database stored on each one. A customer's address changes. One of the clerks amends the record. He or she has to remember to copy the file to disk, take the disk to the other two machines and copy the file on to those machines. Alternatively, the clerk could go to each machine in turn and make the changes. You can imagine how easy it was either to forget to change the files on all three machines or to mistype the changes on one of them.

One way of overcoming this problem was to maintain the database on one machine only. This, however, created other difficulties. Different members of staff often needed to

use the database at the same time. You can imagine the irritation this kind of situation created, and the difficulty in deciding whose work should have priority! For example:

- A sales clerk is receiving customer orders by telephone and wants to access the database to process the order.

- An accounts clerk needs to send out monthly invoices.

- The marketing department is planning a promotion soon in a particular area and wants to search the database for customers located in that area.

The sophisticated facilities of networked PCs and relational database have overcome these kinds of problems. There is only one database file, which can be accessed by any PC on the network. If a record is changed, the new information is available to everyone without the need to copy files on to different machines. Different departments can access the database at the same time. Therefore, the sales clerk could be producing orders whilst the accounts department is preparing invoices, and the marketing department can be obtaining a list of customers for the promotion.

Another important feature of a modern database is the ability to access data from different software applications, which also reduces the need to duplicate data and so reduces the risk of error. For example, the marketing department might want labels for envelopes and a letter to send with the promotion details. Using the mail merge facility in a word processor and linking this with the names and addresses in the database file could produce both these. It is also possible to import data from a spreadsheet (such as Excel) into a database (such as Access) or to export data from the database into the spreadsheet. You might prepare invoices in the spreadsheet by importing customer details from the database.

Prior to the development of integrated software such as Microsoft Office, many large organisations had systems designed specially for their own specific needs. Unfortunately these customised systems are often inflexible and do not provide the facility to import and export data between the different sections. As a result, data already available in one part of the system has to be manually updated in another.

Social effects

The versatility of the modern database has vastly increased the number of databases in use. Whilst this has its advantages in business, individuals may well feel less enthusiastic! These days we are bombarded with *junk mail* from all kinds of organisations, and we have no idea how these organisations obtained our name or address.

Undoubtedly, at some time we have completed a form with a disclaimer 'If you do *not* wish to receive further information on our products or related products, please tick the box'. Companies cleverly leave the onus of responsibility on us to indicate we do *not* want further information. Often this disclaimer is in very small print and we don't even notice it. In effect, by *not* ticking the box, we are giving permission for our name and address to be passed on to other organisations. Some companies exist just to collect together lists of names and addresses to provide mailing lists for other organisations.

The data held on an organisation's computer is one of its most valuable assets. Therefore, when designing a database, it is important to consider the security, reliability and privacy of information. Is the data confidential because it contains vital information about the organisation or because the data contains personal information? If it is the latter, the database is subject to the Data Protection Act, which you learnt about on page 11. For whatever reason, the database must be protected as much as possible against unauthorised access.

Security

Database security can be maintained by:

- using login names and passwords to access the computer network

- changing passwords regularly

- using additional passwords to access the database

- setting access rights and privileges.

Giving staff different privileges or security levels that limit their access to certain files only or some tables only within a file is a common method of protecting data and maintaining confidentiality. The most senior staff would have greater privileges and therefore a high security level with access to all or most of the data, whereas more junior staff would have fewer privileges, low security and be allowed access to less important data only. Some staff may also be allowed to read or extract information from the file, but not to write to the file (i.e. make changes).

 ACTIVITY

Your school or college network probably has a P:\ drive available for staff to save files, which they wish students to access. The students are able to open the files but, if changes are made, the student has to save the file in his or her own user account. Staff have different privileges from students.

Find out if the network is partitioned into other drives. If so, who has access to them?

Figure 10.5 Setting a database password

It is also possible to *encrypt* data (i.e. transpose data in plain text into a coded text). A typical example is a password changed into a series of asterisks. Figure 10.5 shows a screen dump setting a password to open or modify a file. The password is entered once and then re-entered in the Verify box, to make sure the operator has entered the password correctly. This password to access the file is an additional method of protecting the data.

You will, by now, be well aware of keeping backups of your data. Clearly, it is essential to have a backup of a database, but this backup must also be kept securely. In a business environment it is quite likely that backup tapes or disks are kept in a fire-proof safe. Frequently, backup tapes are also stored at a different location. If you are keeping confidential information in a database, you must think carefully about where to store your backup copy.

? Did you know?

Another method used to check security is to program the system to track exactly which user has logged on, to which files and for how long. This is known as an *audit trail* and its purpose is to check whether someone has accessed information to which he or she is not authorised.

Reliability

How can you be sure the data in your database is reliable (i.e. accurate)? As we have already discovered, a modern networked database has a much greater chance of being reliable and accurate than databases stored on stand-alone machines. In addition, the actual design of the database helps to make it reliable.

If you just use text for all the fields, the database will be less reliable than if you think about the data and select the appropriate type of field (e.g. date, time, number, choice fields). These fields limit the type of data that can be entered. The computer can then make a *type check*, comparing the data entered into the field with the type of field stipulated (e.g. letters will not be accepted in a field designed for numbers; a choice field of male/female will not accept child as it is not included in the list). It is not possible to enter the wrong type of data in fields designed this way. Therefore you are reducing, although not eliminating, the possibility of errors in the data entry (Table 10.1).

Table 10.1 A type check

Data to be entered	Data actually entered	Data correct?
125	125	✓
125	12w	✗ – the computer immediately signals an error because it is the wrong type
male	male	✓
male	child	✗ – the computer will not accept child because it is not in the list

A number field can be further limited within a particular range (i.e. by setting minimum or maximum values or both – a *range check*). For example, if items are priced in a range of £20–50, the computer will not accept an entry below 20 or above 50 (Table 10.2).

Table 10.2 A range check

Data to be entered	Data actually entered	Data correct?
20	20	✓
29	19	✗ – the computer immediately signals an error because it is below the *mimimum* level – below the range
35	35	✓
35	36	✗ – but it is *accepted* because it is the right *type* of data, and within the correct *range*
50	50	✓
50	51	✗ – the computer immediately signals an error because it is above the *maximum* level – above the range

A date field will have an automatic range included so that 13 will not be accepted as a month in a date field, and 31 will not be accepted as a date for the months of February, April, June, September and November (Table 10.3).

Table 10.3 A date field check

Data to be entered	Data actually entered	Data correct?
12/02/68	12/02/68	✓
12/02/68	12/13/68	✗ – the computer immediately signals an error because 13 is above the *maximum* level for month
29/02/80	29/02/80	✓ – 29 is accepted because 1980 was a leap year
29/02/80	29/02/81	✗ – the computer immediately signals an error because 1981 was not a leap year and therefore 29 is above the *maximum* level for the month

Another way of ensuring reliability is by limiting the number of people who are allowed to edit or delete data. For example, I am able to look up data in the college student database but, if a student moves, the new address has to be written on to a form the student must sign to confirm its accuracy. I do not have the access rights to alter records, so the form is passed to the management information unit to modify the record. Remember, records are up-to-date only if the staff responsible for making amendments, such as the change of address, actually enter the new data into the system.

Privacy

You have already considered the Data Protection Act and are aware of the laws relating to personal data. In addition, confidential data will almost certainly be stored that is not personal – company financial accounts, for example. Measures to ensure security have already been mentioned, but it is also important to prevent casual passers-by observing what is on screen. Most computer systems would be set up so that, if the keyboard has not been touched for a short period – say 5 minutes – a screen saver is activated. Often it is necessary to enter another password to access the program again.

Consideration should also be given to preventing the screen being observed accidentally. For example, a PC at a library or doctor's reception desk should be positioned in such a way that someone standing at or approaching the desk cannot see personal information about someone else. It might not seem to matter very much if someone discovers you are a member of a library, but your address and telephone number are likely to be listed, which you may not want this other person to know. Certainly, you are not likely to want other patients to discover personal information about you that is held by your doctor.

Care should also be taken in an office environment, where visitors passing by (or even other members of staff) may be able to see the screen. You might be working on confidential material, so it is important to close files when you are not working on them, or hide the screen if someone lingers near your desk.

Techniques

You should already have acquired much of the knowledge and understanding required for this unit when you studied Unit 2. You will have learnt about the technical terms:

- files
- records
- fields
- data types
- key fields – primary and foreign
- data structure
- relationships.

All the above should be familiar to you, but refer back to Unit 2 to remind yourself before proceeding with any assessment for Unit 10.

We are now going to consider additional technical terms you should be aware of.

Database management system

A database consists of the entire collection of data required by all the departments of a business, and access to the database is controlled by software known as the database management system (DBMS). The role of the DBMS software (Figure 10.6) is to:

- Allow a department to have available *only* the database relevant to that department's operation.
- Ensure that changes to data need to be made only once, so that all departments have access to up-to-date information at all times.
- Prevent accidental or deliberate corruption of data by other application programs.

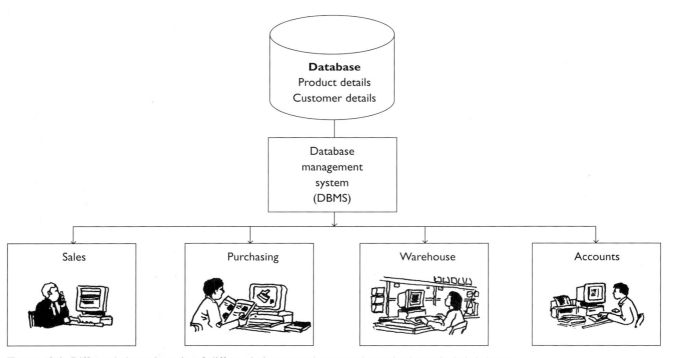

Figure 10.6 Different departments of different sizes need access to a stock control database

Physical and logical view of data

A complex business database must therefore satisfy the different needs of the various departments. Inevitably, each department will require access to many of the same data items, which is the *logical view* of the records. Let's look again at the estate agency database studied in Unit 2:

The sales clerk needs to know which

- properties are for sale
- clients are looking for properties.

The accounts clerk needs to know which

- properties have been sold
- vendors have paid the commission fee.

Clearly, both clerks will need to use much of the same data, but not *exactly* the same.

The important point to bear in mind is that the *physical view* of the database (i.e. the way it is actually built) must satisfy the requirements of all users with the *minimum* of duplicated data (see the section below on normalisation).

Entities

You are an individual, independent and different from any other individual, but every individual has relatives: mother, father, aunts, etc. The relationship between these relatives can be described like this:

- One individual has one birth mother.
- One individual has one birth father.
- One individual can have many brothers or sisters.
- One individual can have many aunts.
- One individual can have many uncles.
- One individual can have many cousins.

In database terms, an *entity* is rather like an individual: it is an object about which we want to store information. It is independent of every other entity, but entities may well be related. The entity is in effect the table, which we looked at in Unit 2. The way the tables are linked is known as the relationship and can be the same as those illustrated above (i.e. one-to-one or one-to-many). Let's think about the entities for a stock control database and the relationships between them.

The entities or tables are:

- product
- manufacturer
- customer.

One manufacturer makes many items of stock, which can be purchased by many customers.

The relationships between them can be expressed like this:

A *One* product is made by *one manufacturer*.

B *One manufacturer* can make *many* products.

C *One* customer can purchase *many* products.

D *One* product is purchased by *many* customers.

These relationships can be represented by diagrams A, B, C and D, as shown in Figure 10.7.

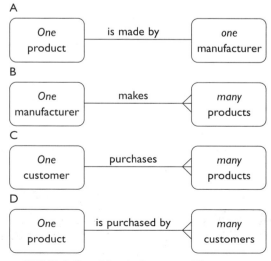

Figure 10.7 Relationships between entities

Figure 10.7 illustrates two types of relationships between entities (as shown in Figure 10.8).

Figure 10.8 Types of relationships

Diagrams A, B, C and D in Figure 10.7 can be simplified into just one entity relationship diagram, as shown in Figure 10.9.

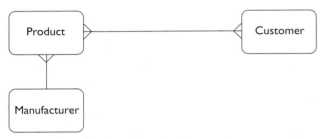

Figure 10.9 Entity relationship diagram for a manufacturer's database

Figure 10.9 illustrates the relationship model for a manufacturer's stock control database, and also introduces a third type of relationship (Figure 10.10).

Figure 10.10 Many-to-many relationship

In a many-to-many relationship, there will be many matching records between the two entities (tables). Clearly, one customer can

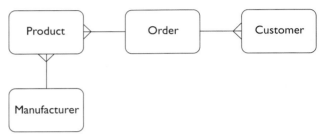

Figure 10.11 An entity relationship diagram after removing any many-to-many relationships

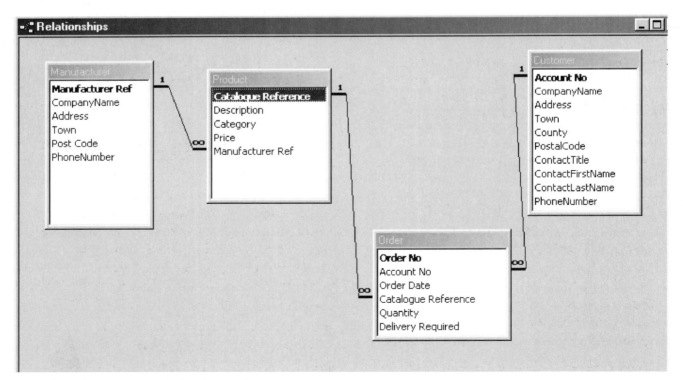

Figure 10.12 One-to-many relationships in Access

order more than one product, and one product can be purchased by more than one customer. However, a relational database will not actually allow you to create a many-to-many relationship – it is, in effect, a faulty design. Therefore to overcome the problem, you have to define another intermediary relationship. In the stock control database this new entity will be an order table (Figure 10.11). The order table can list one or more products ordered by the customer on this particular occasion. The unique order number will prevent any confusion between other orders made by the same customer, or the same products ordered by different customers. The order table makes it possible for businesses to keep track of exactly what a particular customer orders on a given date. It is very important for companies to have records of this information. (Figure 10.12 illustrates one-to-many relationships in Access.)

 ACTIVITY

Think about a library database as having three entities, Book, Borrower and Publisher. A borrower can borrow whichever book or books he or she wants, but each book has only one publisher. Another way of saying this is:

A *One* book title can be borrowed by *many* borrowers.

B *One* borrower can borrow *many book titles*.

C *One* book title is published by only *one* publisher.

D *One* publisher publishes *many* book titles.

1 Draw a diagram similar to the one in Figure 10.7 to represent the relationships between these entities.

2 Simplify the diagram as we have done in Figure 10.9.

3 Check whether any many-to-many relationships exist and, if necessary, amend the diagram as illustrated in Figure 10.11.

Attributes

Imagine a conversation between two friends about an acquaintance called Lyndsey. One person can't recall this girl, and the friend says something like 'You know, she's about 5´4", has long, dark hair, brown eyes. She's really pretty'. These descriptions would be her *attributes*.

Similarly, the entities or tables in a database have attributes. The attributes are, in effect, the fields. The formal style of listing entities and attributes is illustrated below, with the entity in capitals, the attributes in brackets, the primary key underlined and a # sign to denote a numerical field. (Account No and Order No are not numeric fields because they do not have a value and they often include letters as part of the reference.)

CUSTOMER (<u>Account No</u>, Company Name, Address, etc.)

ORDER (<u>Order No</u>, Order Date, Account No, Catalogue Reference, Description, Price#, etc.)

Key fields: primary, foreign and secondary

In Unit 2 we learnt about primary and foreign keys. To refresh your memory, a *primary* key is the unique field that identifies one record (or row in a table) from every other record/row in the table. When a primary key is included in another table, it is known as a *foreign* key.

The record or table may also have one or more *secondary* keys, which are not necessarily unique but which are placed in an index (i.e. grouped together). The index created allows the user to extract relevant information much more quickly. It is useful to index fields you anticipate using frequently in your searches, such as order date shown in Figure 10.13.

Figure 10.13 shows some of the fields that would be used in the order table of the manufacturer database. The design for the field Order Date is illustrated:

- The format chosen is short date – e.g. 16/01/00.

- The field has been indexed, which means an index will be stored saving all records by date of order.

- Duplicates are allowed because more than one order can be placed on the same day.

- It is required – i.e. data must be included in this field in order to save the record.

- Searching for orders placed on a given date will be much quicker with the index. No order will be omitted because all records will include this data.

The example of the manufacturer database from Unit 2 is shown in Table 10.4 with suitable secondary keys indicated. The tables would automatically be stored by order of the primary keys, but the software will create separate indexes for the secondary keys.

Table 10.4 Manufacturer database

Table	Primary key	Foreign key	Secondary keys
Order	Order No	Account No Catalogue reference	Order Date Description Price
Customer	Account No		Company name

Figure 10.13 Order Date

ACTIVITY

1 Produce a list of attributes for the entities in the library database.

2 Identify the primary, foreign and secondary keys.

Table	Primary key
Applicants	Applicant Reference
Jobs	Job Reference
Applications	Applicant Reference
	Job Reference

Complex key, made from two attributes which, *together*, make a unique reference

Complex key (often referred to as a composite or compound key)

This kind of key is made from two or more attributes (fields) together. The employment agency from Unit 2 would include tables for Applicants and Jobs. One applicant could apply for *many* jobs and one job might attract *many* applicants. Therefore another table – entity – for Applications would be required. This would include the fields (attributes) Job Reference and Applicant Reference, which, together, would be identified as the unique reference – a complex key:

You won't be expected to design a database with a complex key, but you may come across one in a business context.

Data redundancy

At the beginning of this unit we looked at the problems that arose with old-fashioned database systems, whether these were paper-based or a flat file computer system. As we have seen, the modern relational database removes many of these problems, but *only if the design is correct*. In an unstructured system the same attribute is likely to appear in more

Table 10.5 Deciding on entities

Entity	Customer	Order	Product
Attributes	Account No	Order No	Catalogue Reference
	Company Name	Order Date	Description
	Address	Catalogue Reference	Category
	Town	Description	Price
	County	Category	Order No
	Post Code	Price	Order Date
	Telephone No	Quantity	Quantity
	Contact Title	Account No	Account No
	Contact First Name	Company Name	Company Name
	Contact Last Name	Address	Address
	Order No	Town	Town
	Order Date	County	County
	Catalogue Reference	Post Code	Post Code
	Description	Telephone No	Telephone No
	Category	Contact Title	Contact Title
	Price	Contact First Name	Contact First Name
	Quantity	Contact Last Name	Contact Last Name

than one file. These duplicated or *redundant* data are inefficient, as the same information has to be repeated many times.

Let's think about designing a database for a manufacturer. How would you approach designing this database? The first stage would be to decide which entities you require and then to write down all the attributes you think necessary for each of the entities. You would need to know which customers ordered which products, which orders were placed by which customers, and so on. The result might look like Table 10.5.

The problem is that many of the attributes in these lists are not directly related to the entity – Company Name is not a description of the product, Catalogue Reference is not a description of the customer and Contact Title is not a description of the order. In effect, they are three *separate files* rather than three *related tables*. Much of the data is repeated and therefore redundant.

Customer names and addresses, for example, have to be entered three times. Apart from the wasted time and effort involved, the possibility of making a keying-in error is increased. The discrepancies might not be noticed and, if they were noticed, checking to find which version was accurate might not be quick or easy. A busy clerk might think, 'Oh, I'll check it later', but then forget. There is also the risk that amendments, such as a change of address, are not up-to-date in all the files. Therefore, the database becomes inaccurate and unreliable.

The process of normalisation would remove these unrelated attributes.

Normalisation

Normalisation is a step-by-step method of refining/improving the design of a database. Having decided the entities and attributes required, as illustrated in Table 10.5, you can check which attributes are not really relevant to the entity and which attributes are repeated unnecessarily. Table 10.6 shows the same database after duplicate attributes have been removed and the key fields that link the tables.

Table 10.6 After duplicate attributes have been removed and showing the key fields that link the tables

Entity	Customer	Order	Product
Attributes	Account No Company Name Address Town County Post Code Telephone No Contact Title Contact First Name Contact Last Name	Order No Order Date Account No Catalogue Reference Quantity	Catalogue Reference Description Category Price

You can see that the second version of the manufacturer database is much simpler. The normalisation process now results in a database with *one file* containing *three related tables*. Most of the data is entered only once. Data entry has to be repeated only in the key fields that link the tables – Account No and Catalogue Reference. Details of new customers or any changes are entered once only, but are available to all the users of the database.

The formal way of writing this normalisation process is as follows:

Stage one – before the normalisation process has been undertaken:

CUSTOMER (<u>Account No</u>, Company Name, Address, Town, County, Post Code, Telephone No, Contact Title, Contact First Name, Contact Last Name, Order No, Order Date, Catalogue Reference, Description, Category, Price#, Quantity#)

ORDER (<u>Order No</u>, Order Date, Catalogue Reference, Description, Category, Price#, Quantity#, Account No, Company Name, Address, Town, County, Post Code, Telephone No, Contact Title, Contact First Name, Contact Last Name)

PRODUCT (<u>Catalogue Reference</u>, Description, Category, Price#, Order No, Order Date, Quantity#, Account No, Company Name, Address, Town, County, Post Code, Telephone No, Contact Title, Contact First Name, Contact Last Name)

Stage two – after the normalisation process has been undertaken:

CUSTOMER (<u>Account No</u>, Company Name, Address, Town, County, Post Code, Telephone No, Contact Title, Contact First Name, Contact Last Name)

ORDER (<u>Order No</u>, Order Date, Account No, Catalogue Reference, Quantity#)

PRODUCT (<u>Catalogue Reference</u>, Description, Category, Price#)

Field data types

Once you have completed the normalisation procedure and have the list of entities and attributes, you are now ready to plan the most suitable data type for each of the fields. We looked at this in some detail for Unit 2 – see page 77. We now have to consider some additional features, wizards, combo boxes, check boxes and pop-up menus.

Wizards

As you can see, designing a database is a complex procedure. You can design the table yourself, but modern database programs include *wizards* to make it easier. A wizard takes you step by step through the process, giving you choices at each stage. For example, if you are setting up a new database file, the Table Wizard has samples already designed. Figure 10.14 shows a wizard where a form is being created from the Customer table. You can select which fields you want to use by highlighting the relevant one and clicking on the > box. If you click on the >> box, all fields will be selected. Using the wizard does not prevent you customising the

Figure 10.14 Form Wizard dialogue box

form to suit your particular purpose – you can rename fields, alter the format or you can add additional fields, which are not already included in the sample.

Wizards are available for many stages of database design (e.g. creating a form from the table or designing a query or report).

Combo boxes, check boxes and pop-up menus

The importance of database accuracy has been mentioned many times. Clearly, there are no guarantees because data input clerks may make mistakes. However, effective design of the database helps to prevent errors and increases the likelihood the data is accurate. In Unit 2 we looked at the importance of using the right type of field to assist accuracy. Data fields, time fields and using a range check (i.e. setting a lower and/or upper limit for a number field) all help to prevent inaccurate data entry. Often, a well designed field also makes it easier and quicker to enter the data. Combo boxes and check boxes are other facilities provided by the database program to make data entry easier and more accurate.

Combo boxes are used where the data is limited to a particular selection (Figure 10.15). For example:

- male/female
- child/adult
- red/blue/yellow/green
- part time/full time.

Figure 10.15 A drop-down list from a combo box

The data entry clerk does not have to key in the words 'male' or 'female'. He or she either clicks on the correct choice or presses 'm' or 'f' and the relevant selection will be made. This speeds up data entry and reduces the risk of error.

Check boxes (Figure 10.16) are used where there is a yes/no option. The data entry clerk clicks in the box to indicate 'yes' and a ✓ appears, or leaves the box blank to indicate 'no'.

Figure 10.16 A check box

You will be very familiar with pull-down menus where you click on the menu name (e.g. the File menu and a list drops down from which you can select the item you require – New, Open, Close, Save, etc.). *Pop-up menus* are similar but are activated anywhere in the document or by pointing at a specific object and clicking on the right mouse button. The program will activate a relevant menu.

The example in Figure 10.17 'popped up' when the right mouse button was clicked in

Figure 10.17 A pop-up menu

the Design view of a table in Access, giving the opportunity to set a primary key, insert or delete rows, etc. Had some text been highlighted, the cut, copy and paste options would also have been available. This is a shortcut to accessing the menus on the toolbar.

Queries and reports

A well designed database file, with appropriately linked tables, allows the user to search for – to *query* – information by selecting fields from any of the tables. It is important to decide exactly what information you are trying to obtain before you make the query. (Remember we *asked* the employment agency database for a list of applicants who were placed in jobs in December – see Table 10.7.)

Table 10.7 Asking for a list of applicants placed in jobs in December

Entity (table)	Attribute (field)	Criteria
Jobs	Job reference Position filled	Select only applicants placed from 01/12/99–31/12/99
Applicant	Title First name Surname	

The result of a query is presented in table format. If you wish to present the results with a specific layout, you can design a *report*. Figure 10.18 illustrates the difference.

Creating the user interface

One of the benefits of a modern database is the ease with which user-friendly screens can be developed. You need to know how to design and create screens that are user-friendly, both in content and layout, and you will be expected to provide user-friendly data entry screens as well as simple methods of moving from screen to screen.

Layout of screen

Although the Form Wizard makes it very easy to create a Form view from the Table view, the result will probably be in columnar format, where all fields are listed one under the other (as shown in Figure 10.18 – Report view). All the right-hand side of the window is wasted, and the form may not fit in the

Table view

Title	First Name	Surname	Job reference	Position filled
Mr	Chirag	Patel	DI235	01/12/99
Mr	Joseph	Williams	DI312	19/12/99

Report view

December Placements

Position filled	01/12/99
Title	Mr
First Name	Chirag
Surname	Patel
Job reference	DI235
Position filled	19/12/99
Title	Mr
First Name	Joseph
Surname	Williams
Job reference	DI312

Figure 10.18 The difference between Table view and Report view

screen window. Another common ready-prepared format is tabular, where all the field names are listed across the screen with the data in rows underneath. This is not much different from Table view. It might be convenient to use the wizard so that all the fields are transferred from the table into the form, and then move them around as appropriate.

Do try to fit all the fields into the screen window if possible, and do think about the position of the fields – they should be presented in a logical order and follow, where applicable, any data capture form the data entry clerk is following (see Example 1 below). As already explained, the use of combo or check boxes also makes the interface more user-friendly as it is easier to enter the data.

Example 1

Title | Mr   First Name: ....
      | Mrs   Last Name: .... ✓
      | Miss

The data entry follows a logical order and the field for title has been designed as a combo box, with Mr, Mrs, Miss, etc., listed.

Example 2

Address: ....
                 ....
                 .... ✗
Phone No: ....
Town: ....

This time the data entry is inconvenient because the second line of the address is followed by the telephone number, and then moves to the town. It would be better to keep all the sections of the address following on one after the other.

It is also important to consider the following points. In fact, the first three apply to any work you are doing on the computer!

- Font *style:*

Whilst fancy styles may look attractive, they are not necessarily easy to read!

- Font *size*: are main headings in a larger size? Are the field labels big enough to read easily, but not so big they take up too much space?

- Use of *colour*: different colours can improve the appearance, but do not vary the colour too much and make sure it is easy to read (e.g. yellow for the font is not easily visible on a white background, and dark backgrounds do not print well).

- Use of *coded data*: a very large warehouse is often zoned into areas to make finding the product easy (A1, A2, A3, etc.) or a code might be used for categories (K=kettle, T=toaster, I=iron, etc.).

- *Validation of data on entry*: validation (meaning suitable) is an accuracy check. So, is the data valid or suitable for its purpose? If all the fields have been designed as text, any data will be accepted, but if careful consideration has been given to the format of the field (see page 220 and also Table 2.3 on page 75), invalid or unsuitable data will not be accepted. Has a primary key been set? If so, it will not be possible to use the same account number or reference for a new record. If the data entry clerk makes a mistake and tries to enter invalid data in the field, an error message will occur.

Moving between screens

A complex database is likely to include several tables and forms. It is much easier for the user to access the table or form required if an opening screen has been designed with command buttons to open each part of the database (Figure 10.19). It is also possible to include command buttons on a form to switch back to the opening screen.

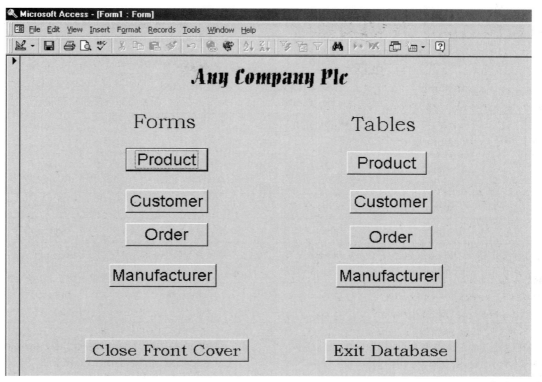

Figure 10.19 An opening screen with command buttons. If you click on the button it will take you to the form or table named, and the 'Exit Database' will close the program

Testing

Once you have designed the database it is important to check it is working as you intended. You will need to consider testing the following:

- Entry of data by type (e.g. will the field accept text when it should only accept number?).

- Entry of minimum and maximum range (e.g. the price range for products is between £10 and £99 – will the field accept £9 or £101?).

- Entry of data out of range (e.g. there are no more than 31 days in a month – will the field accept 32?).

- Is it easy to enter, add, delete or change data? If not, does the layout need changing? Is the field format unsuitable?

- Can you create suitable queries or reports? Decide on the information you require, and check whether it is possible to obtain it.

- Is it easy to progress between different screens in the database you have set up? If not, what can you do to simplify it? Do the command buttons open the right form or table?

Log of testing

You should make a log of testing in which you decide on data to enter into each field, the result you expect and then compare it with what actually happens. Let's look at some examples of test data, which might be used for the manufacturer database (Table 10.8).

Table 10.8 Log of testing

Field name	Field type	Data to enter	Expected result	Actual result
Price	Currency	10.50	Accepted	Accepted
Price	Currency	Ten pounds fifty pence	Rejected	Rejected
Order date	–/–/– (date format)	12/01/00	Accepted	Accepted
Order date	–/–/– (date format)	12/13/00	Rejected	Rejected
Quantity	Integer	5	Accepted	Accepted
Quantity	Integer	five	Rejected	Rejected
Category	Choice of kettle/ iron/toaster	kettle	Accepted	Accepted
Category	Choice of kettle/ iron/toaster	microwave	Rejected	Rejected

In this example you can see the database is working as intended. However, it is very important **not** to assume the database will work as you intend. It is very easy to make a simple error in the design (e.g. you might set the price field as text rather than number, in which case the word 'five' would be accepted). In the example of the category field, you might realise you missed out 'microwave' as a relevant category. A date field set as text would accept 16/13/89, but if you use the date format, the '13' will be rejected as there are only 12 months in a year – 13 is out of the range. Therefore, 13 is unsuitable data for the month.

If the result of your testing is not as expected, you need to revise the design. Once you have tested the database, the data from your information sources can be entered.

ACTIVITY

1 Continue the log of testing for the manufacturer database, taking into account the points made in the list above.

2 Design a log of testing for the employment agency database from Unit 2.

Documentation

Providing documentation to support your database system is a very important part of the work of the ICT professional. There are two aspects to the documentation – user and technical:

1 User documentation exists to help the *data entry clerk* know how to use the database.

2 Technical documentation exists to enable *someone else* to change or improve the design, if necessary.

User documentation should include clear and full instructions on how to *use* the database. The user guide is **not** an instruction manual on how to create a database. **Do not confuse** using it with designing it. Imagine a new clerk in the office who has been told to enter the details of 100 orders received today. This person has never used the database before; all the other staff are too busy to explain. Your user guide should enable him or her to:

1 open the file – so what is the file path and name?

2 find the table or form required

3 enter a new record

4 find an existing record

5 delete an unwanted record

6 change incorrect data in a field

7 produce a report to screen or printer.

The user will find screen dumps very helpful. That way he or she will know exactly what to expect to see on screen. And it's probably easier for you, too, rather than writing long sentences!

Technical documentation should include the following:

1 The data dictionary:

  • Details of the tables (entities) and the fields (attributes) they contain. This can be a word processed table as used in the example for the manufacturer database.

  • Data descriptions (field name, field type, field size, any validation routines). For example, a primary key to prevent duplicate entries, a number field to prevent text entry. Forms to assist you with this are available in the Tutor's Resource File.

2 Diagrams of how your tables are related (i.e. the entity relationship diagrams) and the type of relationship involved (one-to-one or one-to-many).

3 Notes on security aspects:

  • If your database was used in a business context, what security measure would you take?

  • Would the data be subject to the Data Protection Act?

Evaluation

When your database is complete, you will need to evaluate the project as evidence for your portfolio. You should take into account:

• your role in the project (especially if it is a group project)

• what aspects went well

• what aspects needed changing

• any improvements you could make to the database.

It is often difficult to remember at the end exactly what problems you encountered and how you solved them. You will find it much easier to make a comprehensive evaluation if you keep a diary or simple record of your progress, especially those aspects that had to be amended. The record can be as simple as a hole-punched, ruled pad in your file where you note down relevant points. You might use the headings shown in Table 10.9.

Table 10.9 A specimen diary

Date	Problem	Overcome by
12/3/–	Price field accepted 'five'	Changing field type from text to currency
14/3/–	Unique field for account number allowed more than one record with the same data	Set a primary key for account number
3/4/–	Planned to enter the records today, but other members of group had not completed the research	Team discussed the issue and a new deadline was agreed

Database design is a complex topic, requiring careful planning, testing and revision to create an effective and user-friendly database. You are not expected to produce a perfect design first time: what is important is to illustrate what you have learnt. Therefore, the evaluation is crucial to obtaining a Distinction grade.

Glossary

Acronym   Words made from the initial letters of other words, e.g. RAM (random access memory), BIOS (basic input output system).

Agenda   A list of subjects for discussion at a meeting.

Applications software   Programs designed to help people perform particular types of work on the computer by manipulating text, numbers, graphics, etc.

Attribute   A characteristic of something. For example, a page attribute might be orientation or margins. An image attribute might be the colour or size.

Back-up   A copy of a data file made on a secondary storage medium such as floppy disk or tape drive, to provide a secure copy in case the original becomes unusable – e.g. because of system failure or virus.

Bit   The smallest unit of data that can be stored in a computer.

Bit map graphics   A picture/pattern made up of dots, known as pixels. Each dot is equivalent to one bit of computer memory.

Boot   Term used to describe the start-up or resetting procedure of a computer.

Browser (or Web browser)   A software program which enables you to read hypertext markup language (HTML).

Business letter   A formal written communication from one company/person to another.

Byte   A byte is approximately equal to one keyboard character and contains 8 bits. The size of data or storage capacity of a computer is measured in bytes.

CD-ROM   Compact Disk Read Only Memory. Used to store large amounts of information, e.g. encyclopaedias, which can be read from but not written to.

CD Writer   Enables data to be written onto CD.

Central Processing Unit (CPU)   The part of the computer that interprets and carries out the commands. Sometimes known as the 'brain' of the computer.

Configuration   The setting up of hardware devices and software applications to ensure the system operates in the most efficient and effective way for the user.

Copyright   Copyright protects the work of authors, artists, composers, as well as software, from being reproduced by anyone without permission.

Data   Data is entered (input) into the computer in the form of text, numbers, shapes, etc. The data is stored, processed and is output.

Data correctness   Data must be checked to make sure it is meaningful. Data might be spelt correctly, be valid but still not make sense.

Data process   Data is processed according to commands entered into the computer – e.g. it might be sorted, reformatted or calculated.

Data Protection Act 1984   The Data Protection Act was passed to protect the rights of individuals against misuse of personal data held on computer. The Act was updated in 1998.

Database   An organised store of data or information.

Default   The standard settings that you find each time you switch the computer on. For example, word processing software is always set to A4 portrait.

Directories/Folders   A method of organising data files so they can be found easily.

Disk drive   A storage device which transfers data to and from magnetic or optical disk.

DVD-ROM   Digital Video (or Versatile) Disk Read Only Memory. Similar in size to a CD but with much greater storage capacity – currently used for storing films.

E-mail   An informal, written electronic message sent from one person to another via the computer.

Field   One particular item of data within a record. For example, in a database this might be a person's date of birth or a product's reference number.

File   Data permanently stored on disk (or tape). For example, a word processed document, a spreadsheet or a database.

Filename   A set of letters, numbers or symbols that you assign to a data file to distinguish it from other files.

Folders/Directories   A method of organising data files so they can be found easily.

Foreign key   A unique field from a record in one table of a database, used in another table.

Formula   A set of instructions entered into a spreadsheet to perform a calculation.

Graph   Method of displaying numerical data in graphical form, usually as line graphs, bar charts, column charts, pie charts or pictograms.

GUI   Graphical User Interface. A method of showing information on screen graphically. A mouse is used to click on an icon/picture image to tell the computer what to do.

Handles   The name given to the 'boxes' that appear round an object or image when you click on it. They are used to resize the object.

Hardware   The parts of a computer system you can see and touch (e.g. keyboard, mouse, screen).

House style   A company adopts a house style to present a standard, easily recognisable look to their documentation.

HTML   Hypertext Markup Language. The computer code used to write web pages.

HTTP   Hypertext Transmission Transfer Protocol. The protocol (or rules) used by network servers to transmit and receive files on the World Wide Web.

Hypertext database   Pages of information with highlighted items creating links to other pages.

Icon   A small picture/graphic in a GUI which represents a program or a function that will run when the picture is clicked with the mouse. For example, clicking the printer symbol sends a file to be printed.

Input devices   Input devices enable you to enter data, commands and programs into a computer – e.g. mouse, keyboard, scanner.

Internet   The means by which different local networks are linked together to form an international network which has become known as the World Wide Web.

Intranet   An intranet is a network of computers, often in a company, which uses Internet technology but is only accessible to people within the company.

Invoice   A statement of how much money is owed for goods or services.

LAN   Local Area Network. A network located in a small area – probably a building.

Language style   Language style can be formal or informal and the choice of style is important to ensure the right message is conveyed.

Macro   A series of actions you regularly perform which are recorded and reactivated by a special key combination or icon.

Memo   A brief document used to communicate with colleagues in the same office or organisation.

MHz   Megahertz. The speed at which a computer can process information is measured in millions of cycles or pulses per second. The higher the number the faster the speed.

Minutes   A record of a meeting recording decisions and agreements which matches the points on the agenda.

Modem   A modem allows two computers to communicate through the telephone system. It translates the digital signals of a computer into analogue signals, which can be sent down the telephone line. The receiving computer converts the analogue signals back into digital signals.

Motherboard   The main printed circuit board of the computer. The other components are plugged into the motherboard – e.g. CPU, memory.

Network   A network allows linked computers to share resources and information.

Newsletter   A publication providing general information to staff.

Number Structured Database (or Spreadsheet)
Software designed for storing and manipulating numerical data, for example making calculations.

Operating system   The software programs through which all application programs run, e.g. Windows.

Orientation   Used to describe a page layout – portrait (usually used for text) or landscape (often used for tables, spreadsheets, charts and graphs).

Output device   An output device lets you see or hear the results of the computer's operations, e.g. VDU, printer.

PC   Personal computer.

Peripheral device   Devices plugged into the computer, e.g. keyboard, printer.

Pixel   Short for 'picture element'. Bitmapped graphics are comprised of rows and columns of dots or pixels.

Plug-in   A mini-program attached to your web browser which allows it to handle unusual file formats.

Port   A socket at the back of the main processing unit used to attach peripheral devices (e.g. keyboard, mouse).

Portfolio   File in which you store all your completed assessments.

Primary key   A unique field in a database that identifies each record as different from another, e.g. Student ID.

Program   A set of instructions that are written to enable a computer to perform a particular task.

Programming language   The language used to write programs (or instructions) for the computer.

Query   A search within a database to find particular information. For example, all students in a particular college who are working towards the GNVQ Intermediate Certificate in ICT.

RAM   Random Access Memory. The temporary, working memory where programs and data are stored when the computer is running.

Range check   A data validation technique that checks data entered into a number field falls within a specified range.

Record   A group of related data items. For example, in a database this might be all the information about one person or product.

Record Structured Database (or Database)   An organised collection of data or information.

Relational database   A database with two or more tables that relate to each other by means of a common field.

Report   A detailed description of an investigation and its results.

Resolution   The resolution determines the sharpness or clarity of an image on a VDU. The higher the number the clearer the picture.

ROM   Read Only Memory. The permanent memory that is available whether the computer is switched on or off.

RSI   Repetitive Strain Injury. A condition caused by making continuous movements. Symptoms include pain, numbness and swelling in hands, wrists and arms.

Software   A set of instructions written to make the computer work.

Spreadsheet   Software designed for storing and manipulating numerical data, for example making calculations.

Sub-directory   A directory within a directory for storing data files – similar to a drawer in a filing cabinet.

Template   A template is a standard layout for text, graphics and formatting in a document.

Thesaurus   A list organised to show words with the same or similar meanings.

Type check   A validation technique that checks data input into a computer matches the specified data type, e.g. text or number.

URL   Universal Resource Locator. The web address used to locate a particular web site.

User requirements   A specification detailing exactly what a user wants a computer system to be able to carry out.

Utilities   Small programs that carry out essential tasks such as virus checking.

Validation   A method of checking data to see that it is suitable for its purpose. Validation checks include type check and range check.

Vector graphics   A graphic made up of unconnected elements such as lines, curves, circles or squares. Resolution is maintained when the graphic is enlarged.

Verification   A method of checking the correctness of data. Verification checks include entering data twice to compare the accuracy, spell checks, grammar checks and, very important, proofreading.

Virus   A computer virus is a program, developed by someone intending to cause problems in your computer system such as clearing screens, deleting data or, at worst, making the whole system unusable.

WAN   Wide Area Network. A network connected over a wide area – e.g. different towns or continents.

Web browser   A dedicated software application that will enable you to browse the web and view your own web pages.

White space   Areas of the page deliberately left blank to aid presentation or the readability of a document.

Word processing   Word processing applications are used to process text-based documents.

WWW   World Wide Web. A user-friendly way of navigating data stored on computers connected to the Internet.

Index

Ready to move on?

This is exactly what you need for the Advanced Vocational Certificate of Education in ICT

- The Student Book contains all of the compulsory content for the award.

- The chapters in the book match the order of the VCE award units, so it's easy to find your way around the text.

- Lively case studies and tasks help you to carry out research on visits and work placements and demonstrate your ICT skills to the full.

There's an easy way to find out all the latest information about GNVQs. Just visit
www.heinemann.co.uk/gnvq

Heinemann Advanced VCE for ICT
ISBN: 0 435 45307 6

Order from your local bookshop or call
(01865) 888068.